SURVIVE! INSIDE THE HUMAN BODY

VOL. 1: THE DIGESTIVE SYSTEM

SURVIVE! INSIDE THE HUMAN BODY

VOL. 1: THE DIGESTIVE SYSTEM

GOMDORI CO. AND HYUN-DONG HAN

no starch
press

SAN FRANCISCO

SURVIVE! INSIDE THE HUMAN BODY, VOL. 1: THE DIGESTIVE SYSTEM.
English translation copyright © 2013 by No Starch Press.

Survive! Inside the Human Body, Vol. 1: The Digestive System is a translation of the Korean original, *Comic Survival Science Series 25 - Survival in the Human Body 1* (서바이벌 만화 과학상식 25 – 인체에서 살아남기 1), published by Mirae N Co., Ltd. of Seoul, South Korea, text copyright © 2009 by Gomdori co. and illustration copyright © 2009 by Hyun-dong Han. This English translation is arranged with Mirae N Co., Ltd. (I-seum).

Printed in China
First printing

17 16 15 14 13   1 2 3 4 5 6 7 8 9

ISBN-10: 1-59327-471-8
ISBN-13: 978-1-59327-471-9

Publisher: William Pollock
Author: Gomdori co.
Illustrator: Hyun-dong Han
Coloring: Jae-woong Lee
Technical Assistance: Byung-sup Lee (Assistant Professor at Seoul Asan Medical Center)
Images: Wikimedia Commons
Production Editor: Alison Law
Developmental Editor: Tyler Ortman
Technical Reviewers: Wei Cheng Chen and Dan-Vinh Nguyen
Copyeditor: Pam Schroeder
Compositors: Riley Hoffman and Lynn L'Heureux
Proofreader: Kate Blackham
Indexer: BIM Indexing and Proofreading Services

For information on bulk sales, please contact No Starch Press, Inc. directly:

No Starch Press, Inc.
38 Ringold Street, San Francisco, CA 94103
phone: 415.863.9900; fax: 415.863.9950; info@nostarch.com; www.nostarch.com

Library of Congress Cataloging-in-Publication Data

Inside the human body / by Gomdori Co. and Hyun-dong Han.
    p. cm. -- (Survive!)
  ISBN 978-1-59327-471-9 (v. 1) -- ISBN 978-1-59327-472-6 (v. 2) -- ISBN 978-1-59327-473-3 (v. 3)
 1. Human physiology--Juvenile literature. 2. Human physiology--Comic books, strips, etc. 3. Graphic novels. I. Han, Hyun-dong, ill. II. Gomdori Co.
  QP37.I563 2013
  612--dc23
                         2013002904

Production Date: 5/24/2013
Plant & Location: Printed by Everbest Printing (Guangzhou, China), Co. Ltd
Job / Batch #: 110474.2

PREFACE

Every morning, we open our eyes and get out of bed to start the day. We eat breakfast, wash our faces, and pack our bags to go to school. But what's really happening inside our bodies all this time? It's quite easy to take our amazing bodies for granted.

Even when we are not conscious of it, our bodies are doing a *lot* of work. Each and every day, you blink 10,000 times and your heart beats *100,000 times*. And you never even think about it! Our bodies also digest food, fight germs and bacteria, and do all sorts of incredible things.

Aren't you curious about the body and all the work it does to keep you alive? Knowing more about your body can help keep you happy and healthy.

And the more you learn, the more you'll discover that our bodies have many wonderful surprises. I hope that Geo's exciting adventures inside the human body will show you just how complex our bodies are, how each part cooperates with the others, and what really gets our bodies moving.

Our adventure features Geo, a troublemaker with endless curiosity; the eccentric Dr. Brain, who claims to have invented the world's first human-piloted, artificial virus; his assistant, the high-strung Kay; and their friend, the kind-hearted Phoebe. What kind of adventure awaits them? Let's take a journey into the human body!

Hyun-dong Han

CONTENTS

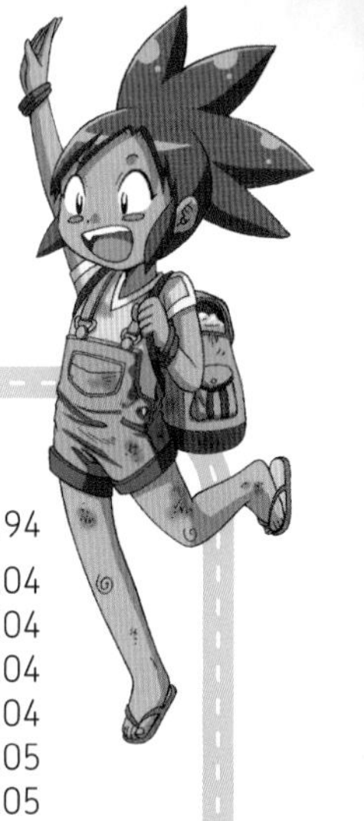

MEET THE CAST!

I WON'T LET ANYTHING HURT PHOEBE! I'M THE KING OF SURVIVAL!

GEO

Our fearless hero. He says that he can withstand any hardship for Phoebe—a true and loyal friend! Although he often seems at the brink of disaster, he's quick-witted in times of crisis. Dr. Brain is lucky to have him around on their trip inside the human body. Geo is a true master of survival!

DID YOU THINK THE AMAZING DR. BRAIN WOULDN'T BE PREPARED FOR THAT?!

DR. BRAIN

A self-proclaimed genius. He's the eccentric inventor of the SS *Hippocrates*, a probe that can shrink down to the size of a nanometer. But he can't resist boasting about his incredible invention and gets swept into a dangerous adventure. He always gets an earful of nagging from his assistant Kay.

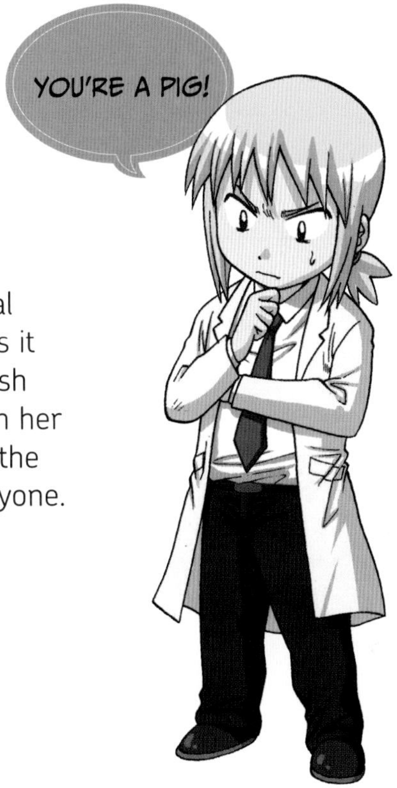
YOU'RE A PIG!

KAY

A high-strung but good-hearted medical student. What is bothering Kay today? Is it Dr. Brain's crazy experiments, Geo's brash antics, or just Phoebe forgetting to wash her hands? The voice of caution, Kay is like the fairy godmother who takes care of everyone.

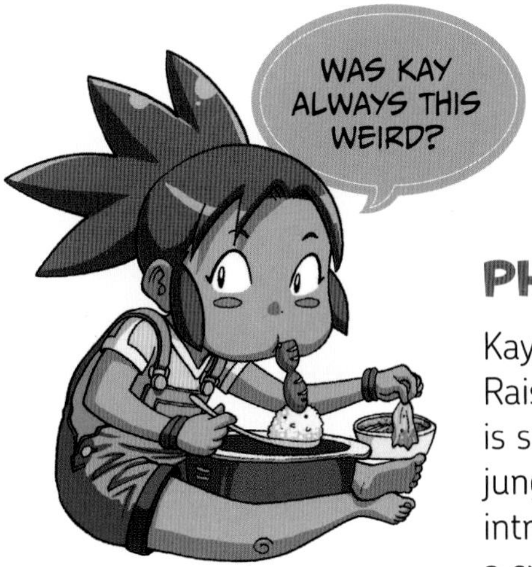
WAS KAY ALWAYS THIS WEIRD?

PHOEBE

Kay and Geo's friend from past adventures. Raised in the wilds of a faraway land, Phoebe is spunky and full of life, but she's still got her jungle instincts. She's a faithful friend and an intrepid adventurer. And she never says no to a snack!

PHOEBE'S VISIT

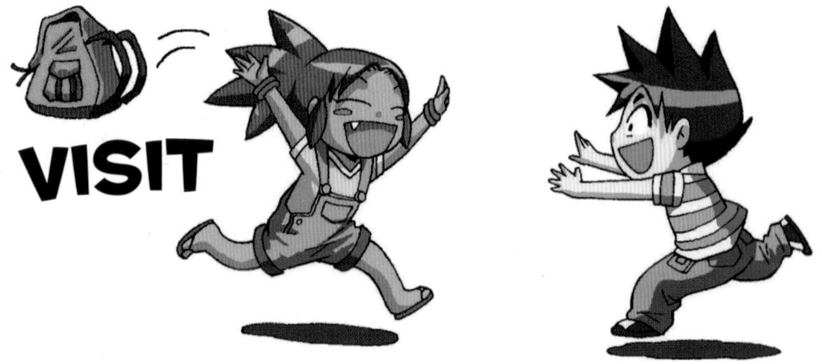

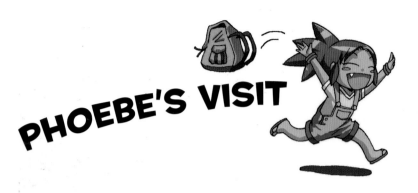

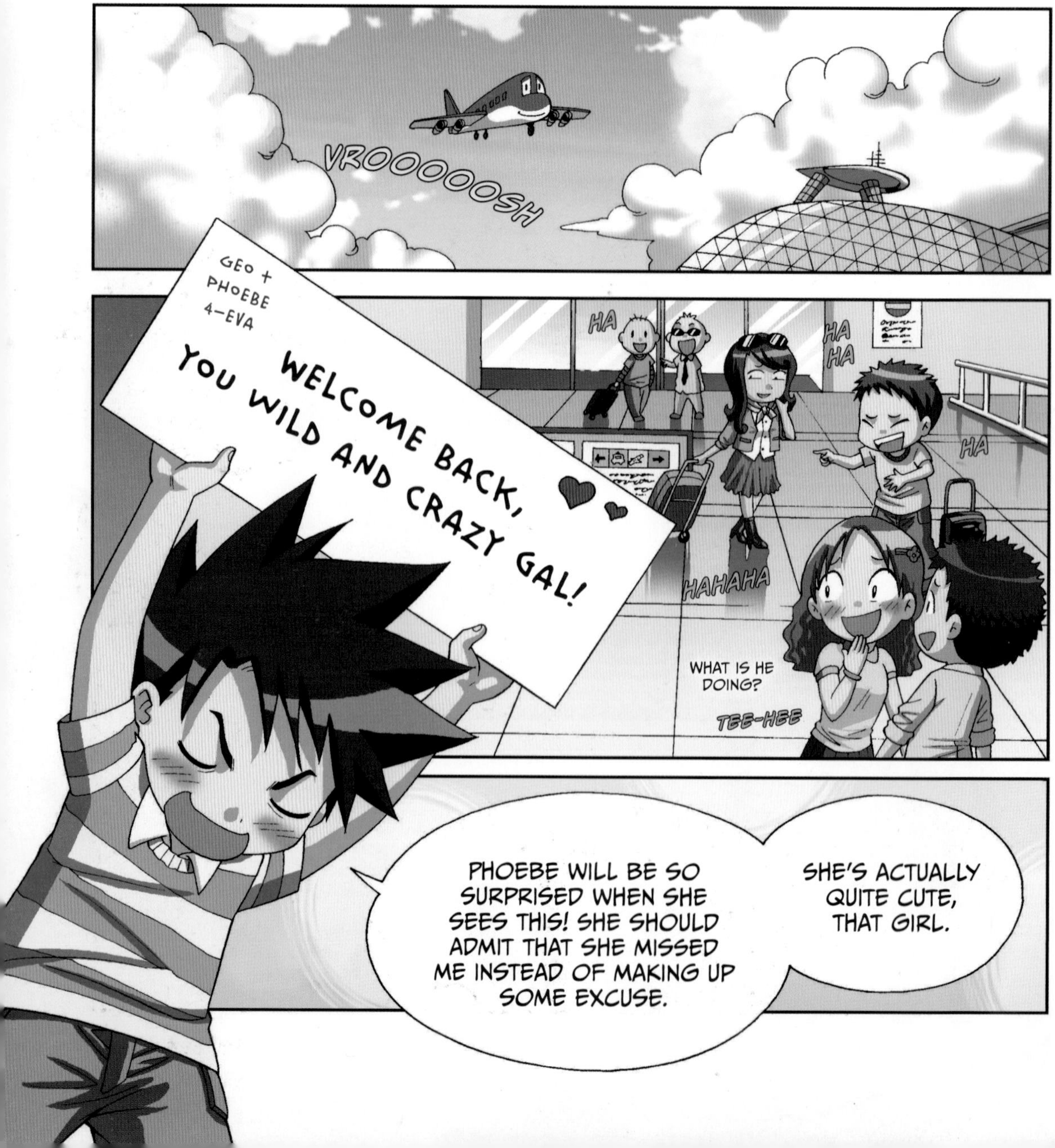
VROOOOOOSH
GEO + PHOEBE 4-EVA
WELCOME BACK, YOU WILD AND CRAZY GAL!
HA
HA HA
HA
HAHAHA
WHAT IS HE DOING?
TEE-HEE
PHOEBE WILL BE SO SURPRISED WHEN SHE SEES THIS! SHE SHOULD ADMIT THAT SHE MISSED ME INSTEAD OF MAKING UP SOME EXCUSE.
SHE'S ACTUALLY QUITE CUTE, THAT GIRL.

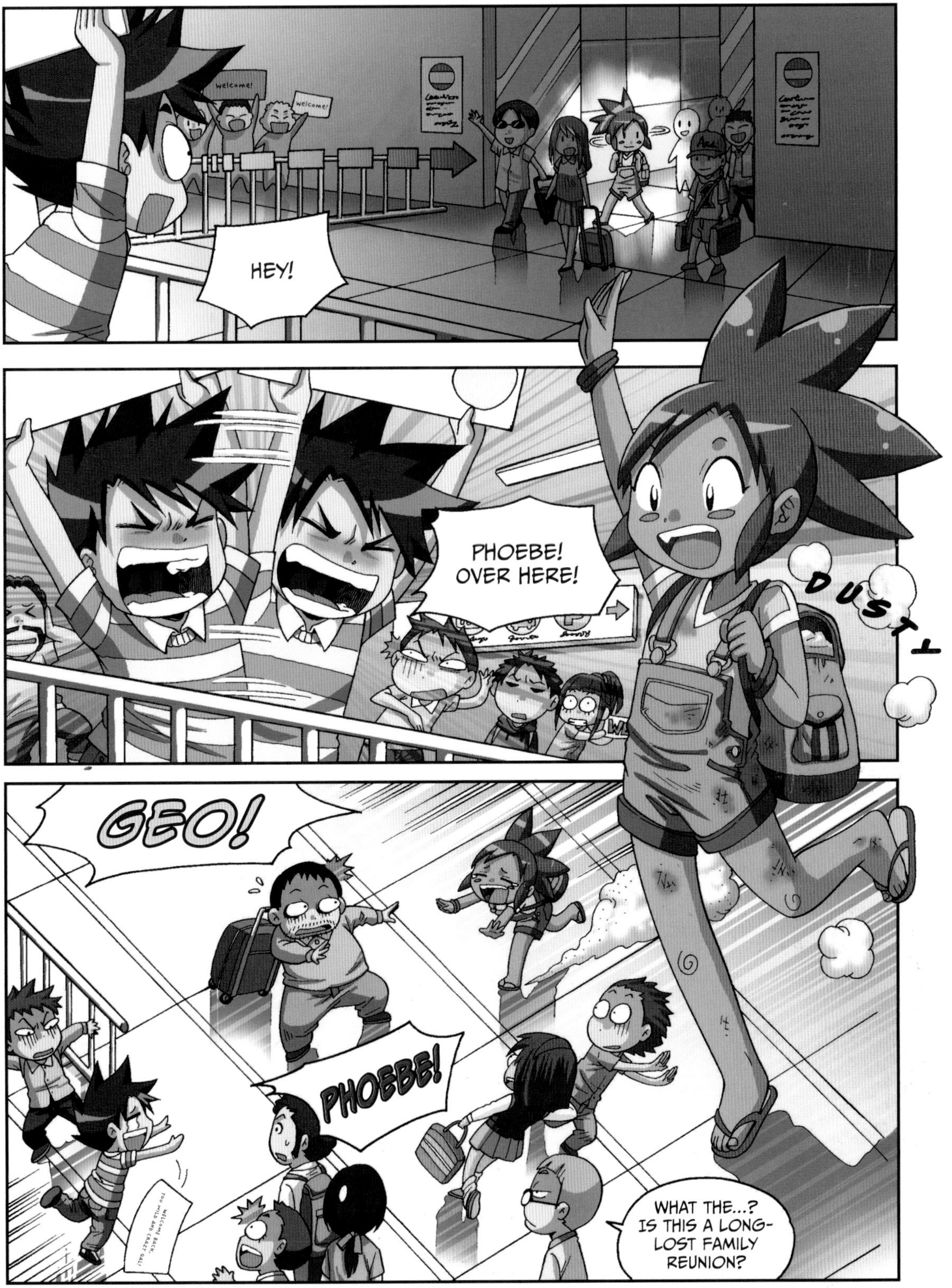
welcome!
welcome!
HEY!
PHOEBE! OVER HERE!
DUSTY
GEO!
PHOEBE!
WELCOME BACK, YOU WILD AND CRAZY GAL!
WHAT THE...? IS THIS A LONG-LOST FAMILY REUNION?

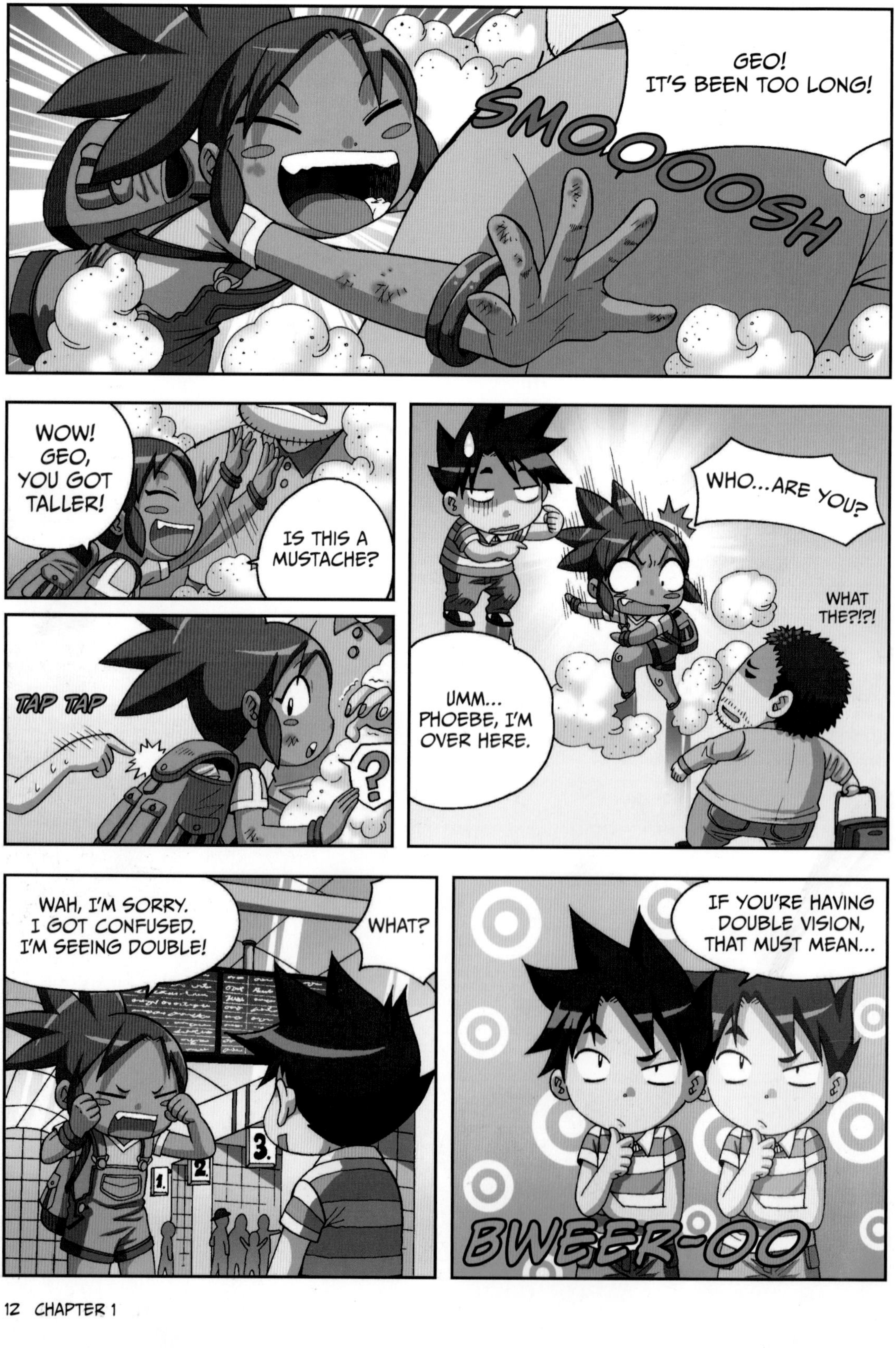

GEO! IT'S BEEN TOO LONG!
SMOOOOOSH
WOW! GEO, YOU GOT TALLER!
IS THIS A MUSTACHE?
TAP TAP
?
WHO...ARE YOU?
WHAT THE?!?!
UMM... PHOEBE, I'M OVER HERE.
WAH, I'M SORRY. I GOT CONFUSED. I'M SEEING DOUBLE!
WHAT?
IF YOU'RE HAVING DOUBLE VISION, THAT MUST MEAN...
BWEER-OO

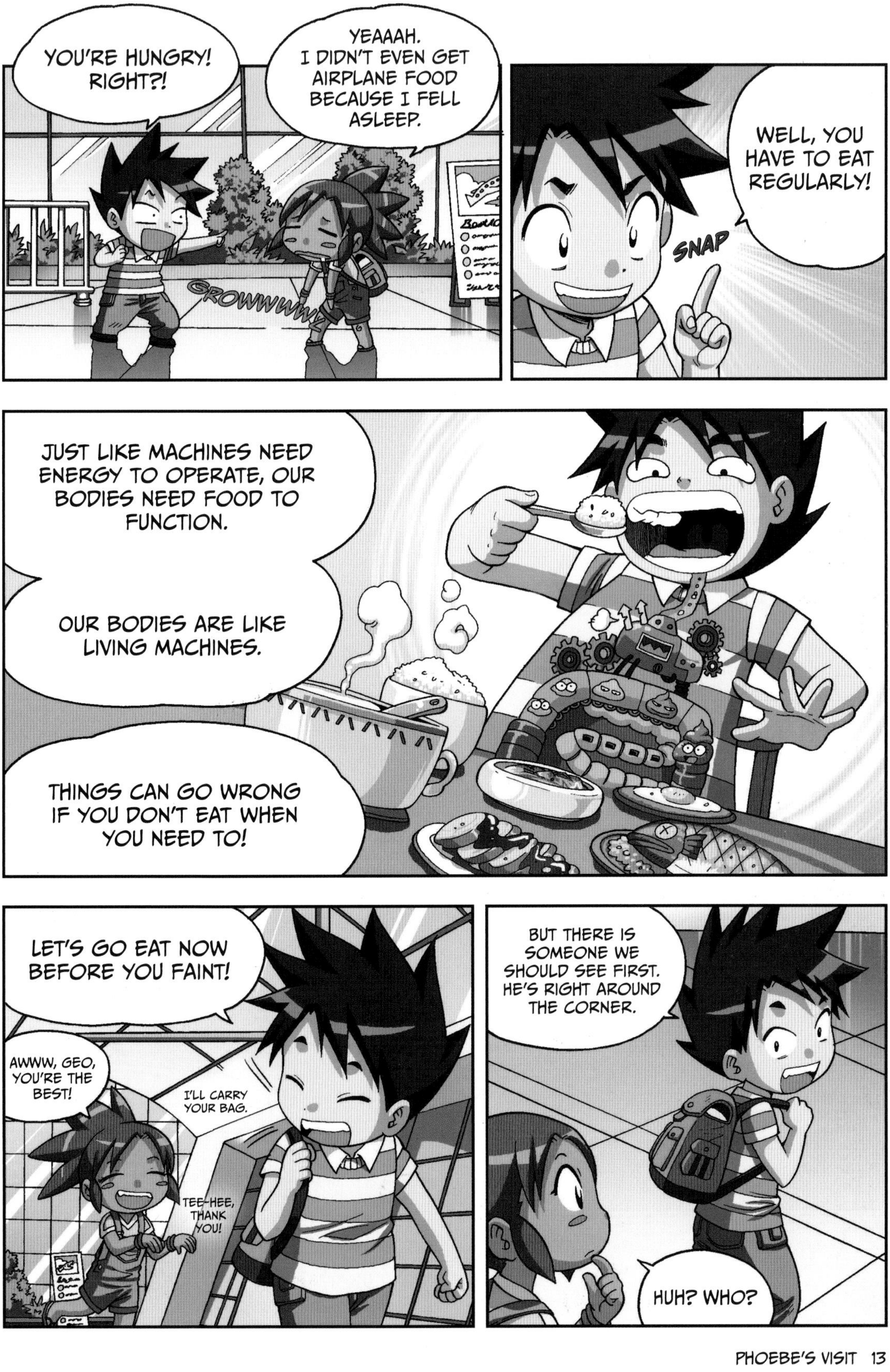
YOU'RE HUNGRY! RIGHT?!
YEAAAH. I DIDN'T EVEN GET AIRPLANE FOOD BECAUSE I FELL ASLEEP.
GROWWWWWL
WELL, YOU HAVE TO EAT REGULARLY!
SNAP
JUST LIKE MACHINES NEED ENERGY TO OPERATE, OUR BODIES NEED FOOD TO FUNCTION.
OUR BODIES ARE LIKE LIVING MACHINES.
THINGS CAN GO WRONG IF YOU DON'T EAT WHEN YOU NEED TO!
LET'S GO EAT NOW BEFORE YOU FAINT!
AWWW, GEO, YOU'RE THE BEST!
I'LL CARRY YOUR BAG.
TEE-HEE, THANK YOU!
BUT THERE IS SOMEONE WE SHOULD SEE FIRST. HE'S RIGHT AROUND THE CORNER.
HUH? WHO?

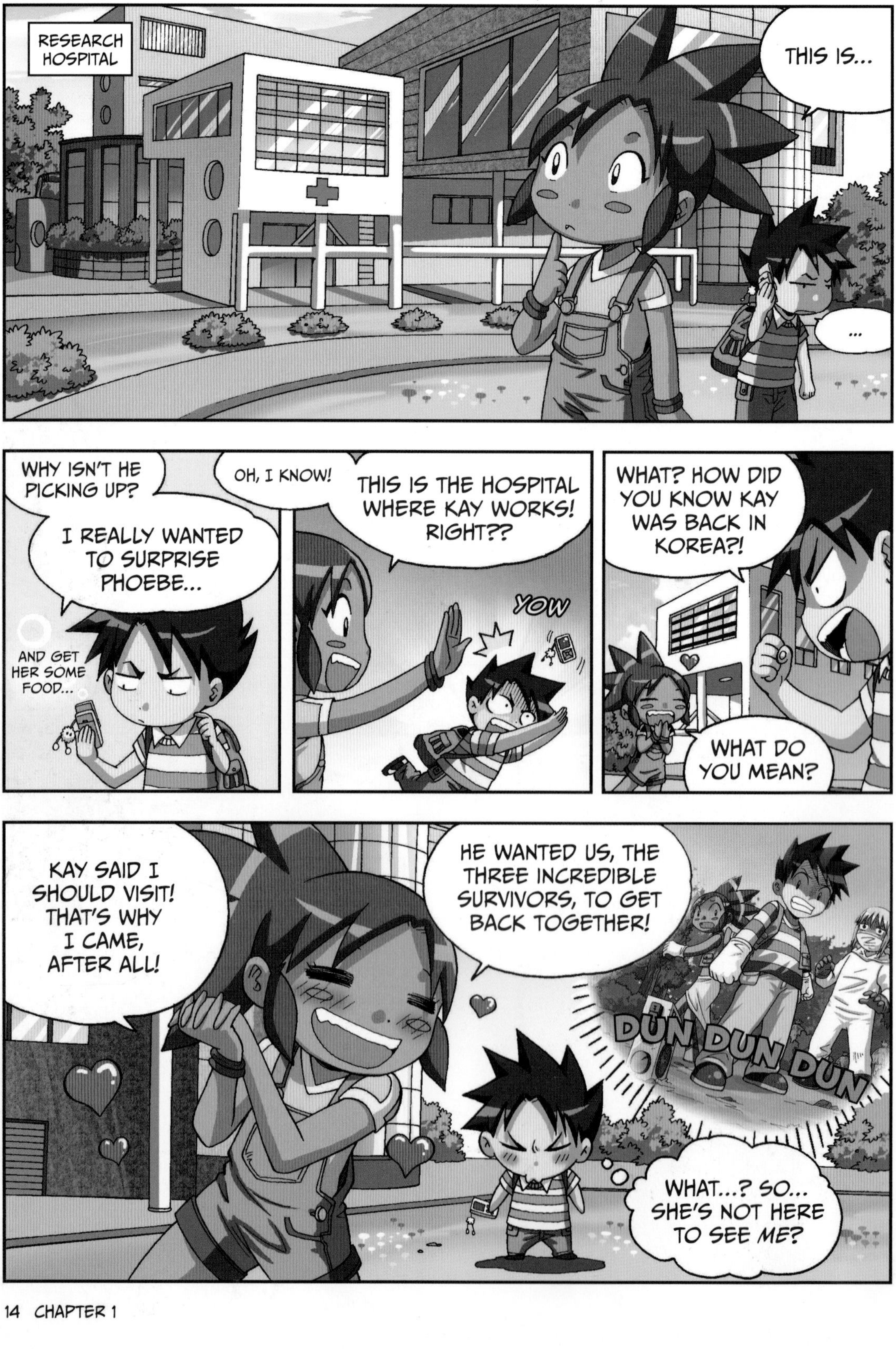
RESEARCH HOSPITAL
THIS IS...
...
WHY ISN'T HE PICKING UP?
I REALLY WANTED TO SURPRISE PHOEBE...
AND GET HER SOME FOOD...
OH, I KNOW!
THIS IS THE HOSPITAL WHERE KAY WORKS! RIGHT??
YOW
WHAT? HOW DID YOU KNOW KAY WAS BACK IN KOREA?!
WHAT DO YOU MEAN?
KAY SAID I SHOULD VISIT! THAT'S WHY I CAME, AFTER ALL!
HE WANTED US, THE THREE INCREDIBLE SURVIVORS, TO GET BACK TOGETHER!
DUN DUN DUN
WHAT...? SO... SHE'S NOT HERE TO SEE *ME*?

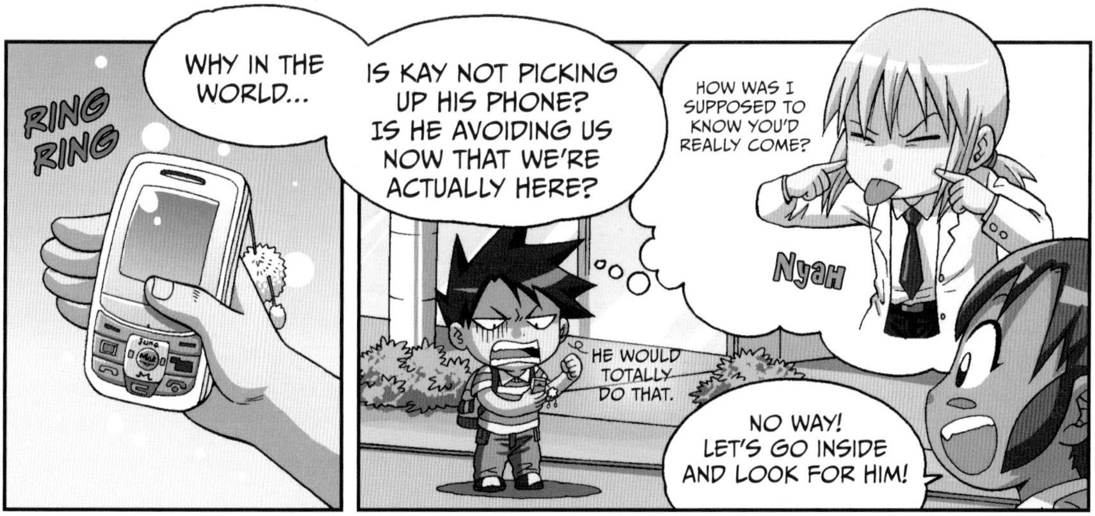
RING RING
WHY IN THE WORLD...
IS KAY NOT PICKING UP HIS PHONE? IS HE AVOIDING US NOW THAT WE'RE ACTUALLY HERE?
HOW WAS I SUPPOSED TO KNOW YOU'D REALLY COME?
Nyah
HE WOULD TOTALLY DO THAT.
NO WAY! LET'S GO INSIDE AND LOOK FOR HIM!

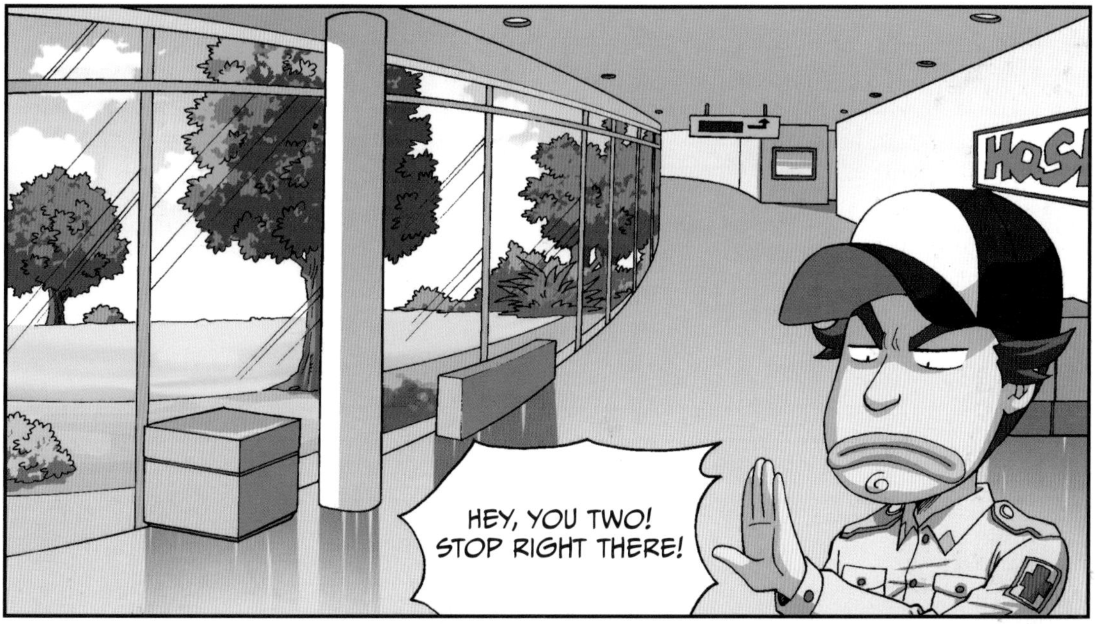
HEY, YOU TWO! STOP RIGHT THERE!

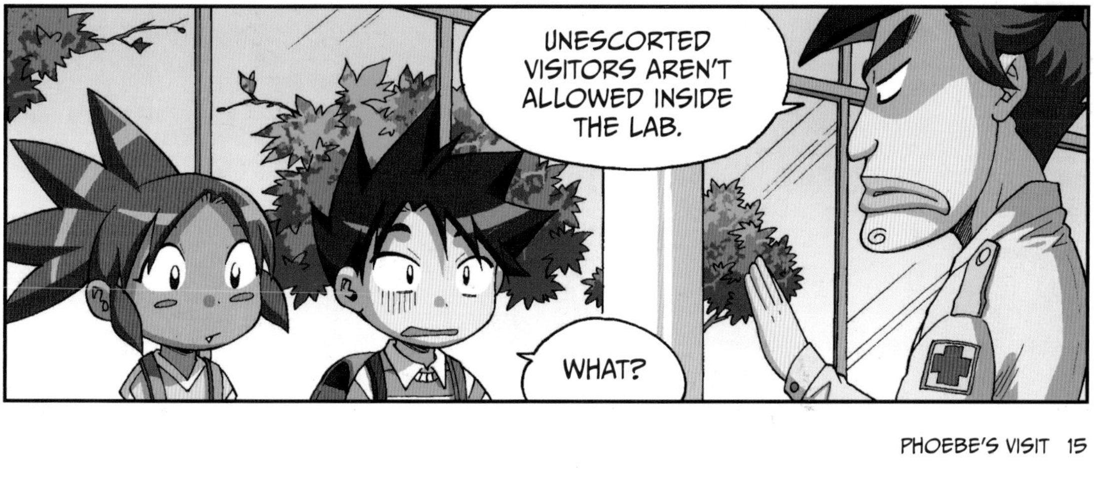
UNESCORTED VISITORS AREN'T ALLOWED INSIDE THE LAB.
WHAT?

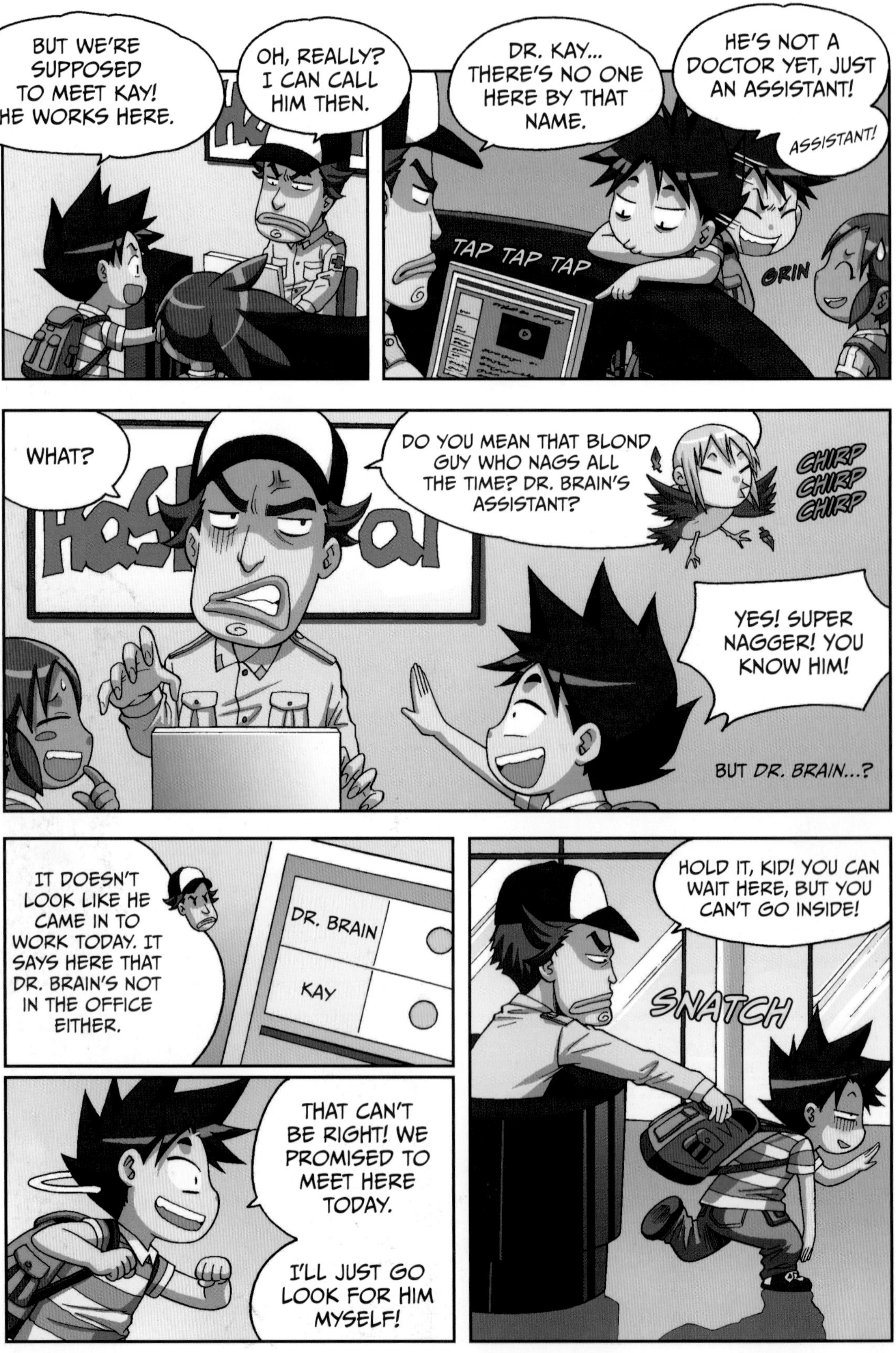
BUT WE'RE SUPPOSED TO MEET KAY! HE WORKS HERE.
OH, REALLY? I CAN CALL HIM THEN.
DR. KAY... THERE'S NO ONE HERE BY THAT NAME.
TAP TAP TAP
HE'S NOT A DOCTOR YET, JUST AN ASSISTANT!
ASSISTANT!
GRIN
WHAT?
DO YOU MEAN THAT BLOND GUY WHO NAGS ALL THE TIME? DR. BRAIN'S ASSISTANT?
CHIRP CHIRP CHIRP
YES! SUPER NAGGER! YOU KNOW HIM!
BUT DR. BRAIN...?
IT DOESN'T LOOK LIKE HE CAME IN TO WORK TODAY. IT SAYS HERE THAT DR. BRAIN'S NOT IN THE OFFICE EITHER.
DR. BRAIN
KAY
THAT CAN'T BE RIGHT! WE PROMISED TO MEET HERE TODAY.
I'LL JUST GO LOOK FOR HIM MYSELF!
HOLD IT, KID! YOU CAN WAIT HERE, BUT YOU CAN'T GO INSIDE!
SNATCH

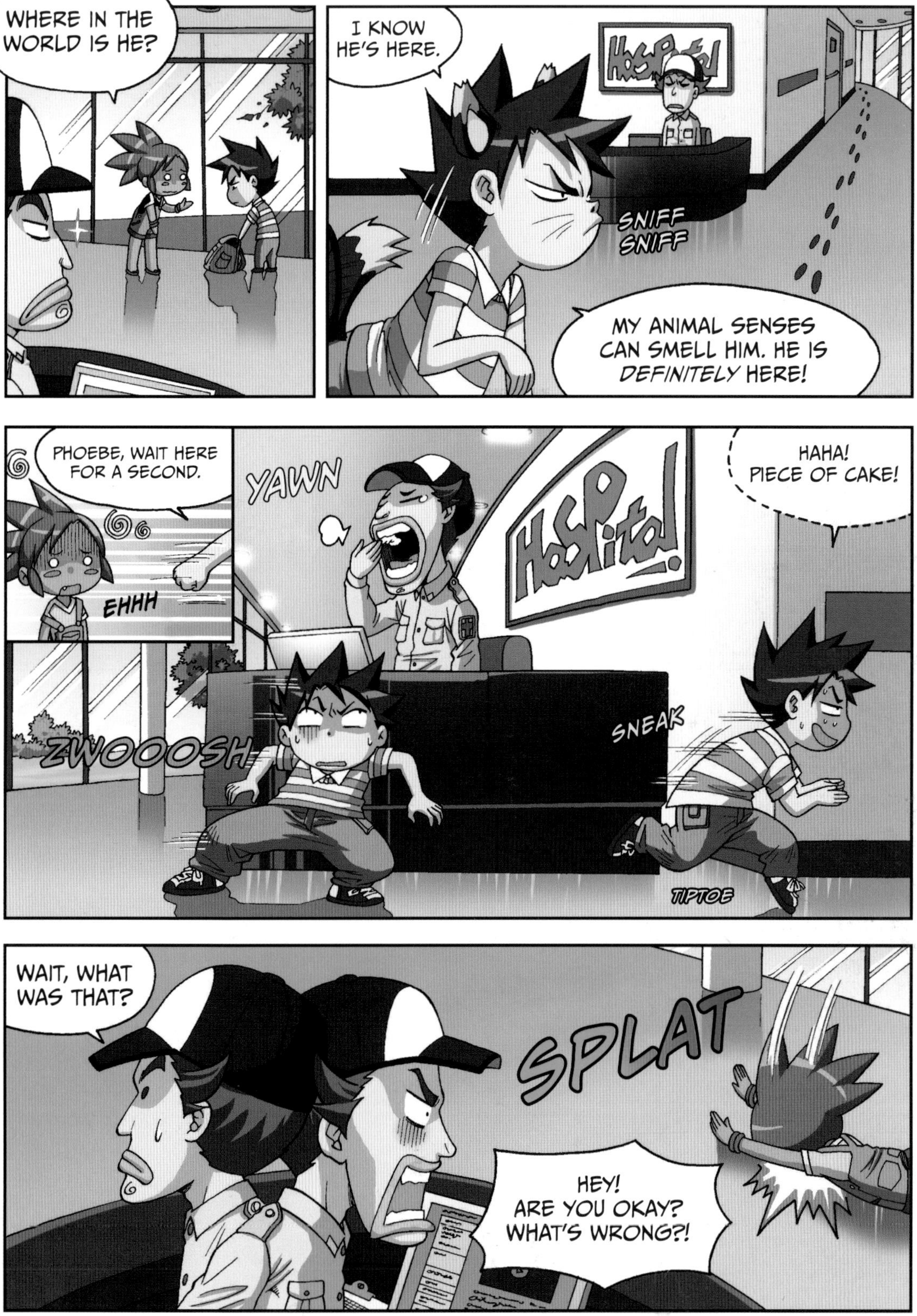

WHERE IN THE WORLD IS HE?
I KNOW HE'S HERE.
HosPital
SNIFF SNIFF
MY ANIMAL SENSES CAN SMELL HIM. HE IS *DEFINITELY* HERE!
PHOEBE, WAIT HERE FOR A SECOND.
EHHH
YAWN
HosPital
HAHA! PIECE OF CAKE!
ZWOOOOSH
SNEAK
TIPTOE
WAIT, WHAT WAS THAT?
SPLAT
HEY! ARE YOU OKAY? WHAT'S WRONG?!

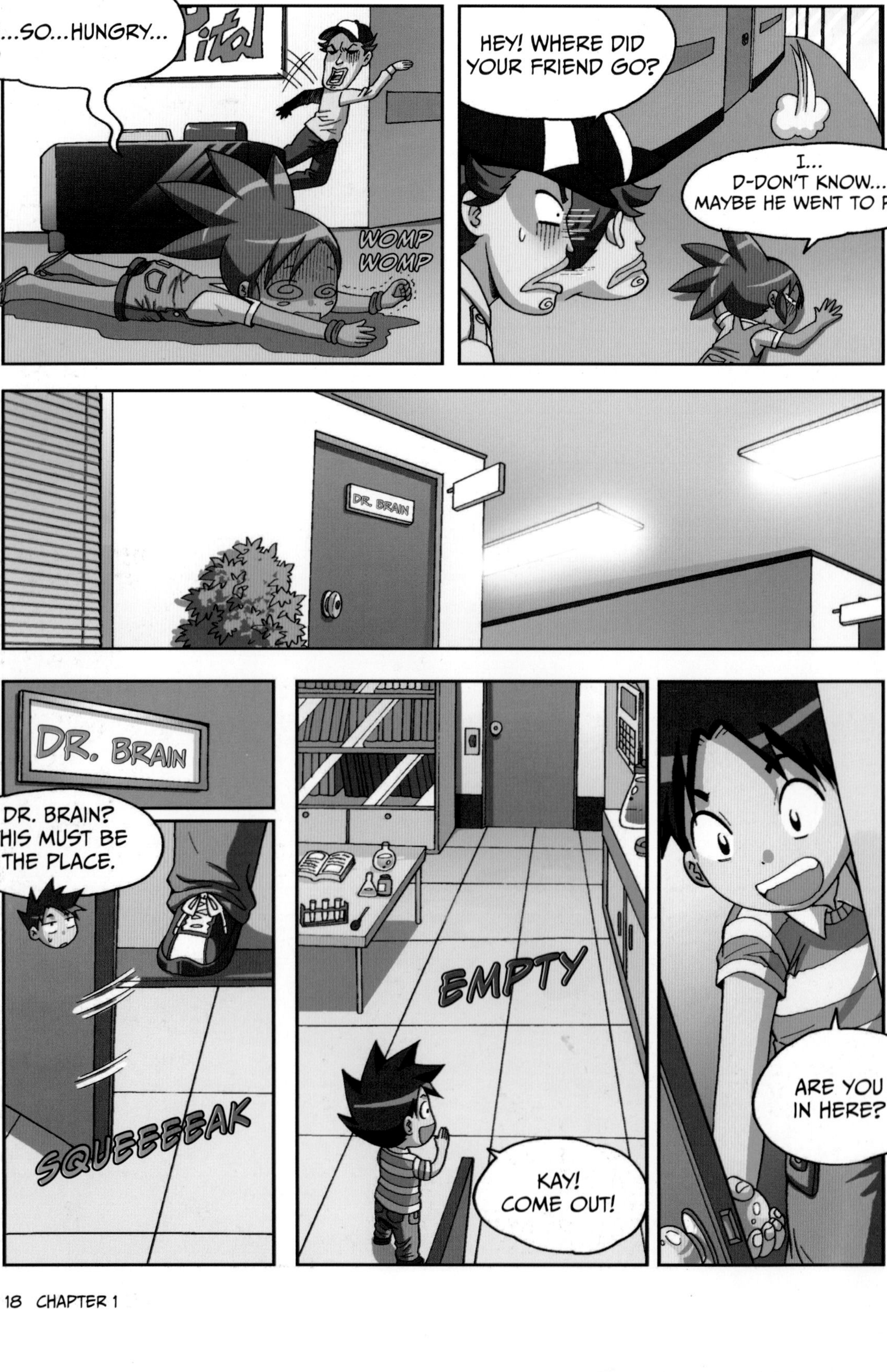
I'M...SO...HUNGRY...
WOMP WOMP
HEY! WHERE DID YOUR FRIEND GO?
I... D-DON'T KNOW... MAYBE HE WENT TO PEE?
DR. BRAIN
DR. BRAIN
DR. BRAIN? THIS MUST BE THE PLACE.
SQUEEEEEAK
EMPTY
KAY! COME OUT!
ARE YOU IN HERE?

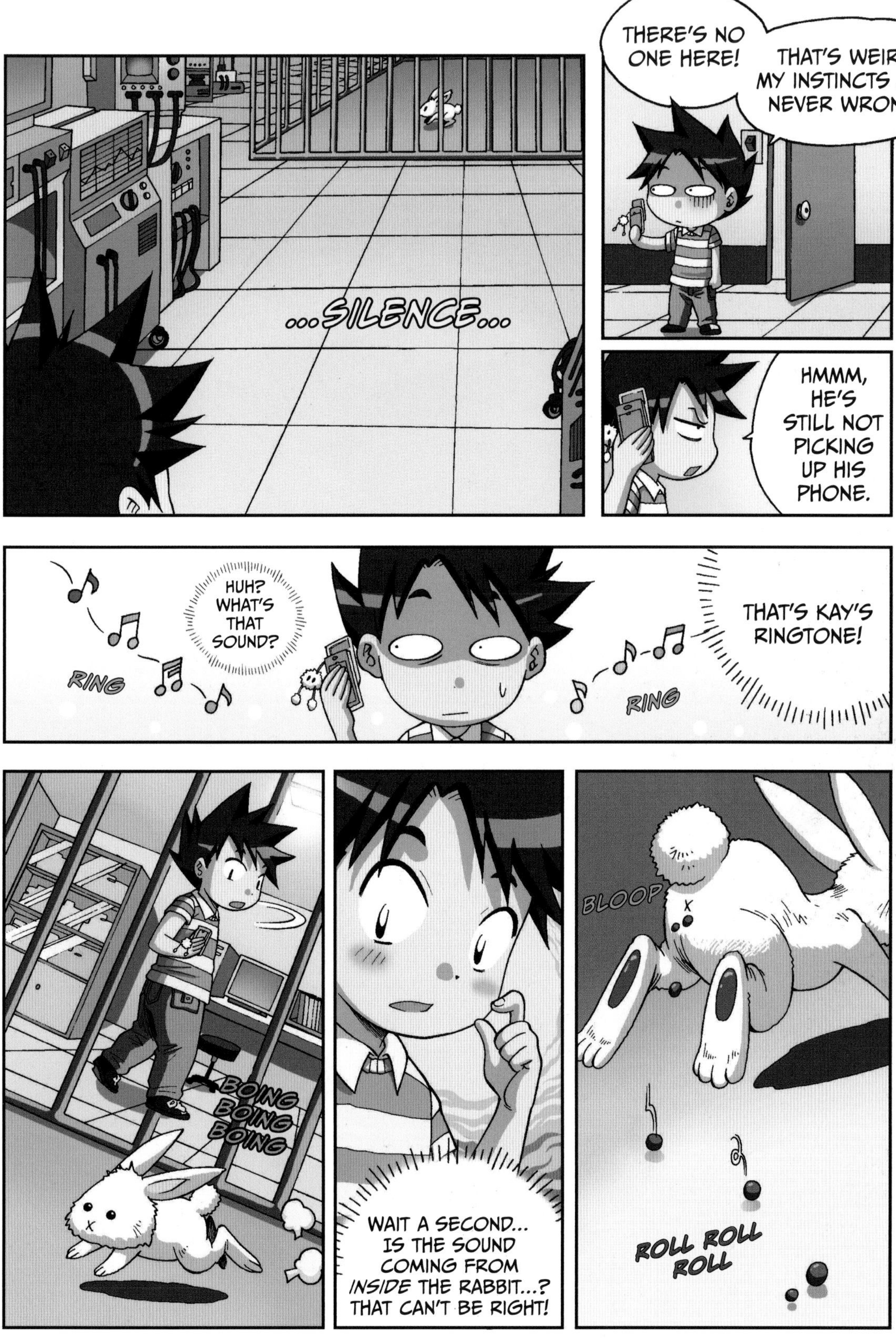
THERE'S NO ONE HERE!
THAT'S WEIRD. MY INSTINCTS ARE NEVER WRONG!
...SILENCE...
HMMM, HE'S STILL NOT PICKING UP HIS PHONE.
HUH? WHAT'S THAT SOUND?
RING
RING
THAT'S KAY'S RINGTONE!
BOING BOING BOING
WAIT A SECOND... IS THE SOUND COMING FROM *INSIDE* THE RABBIT...? THAT CAN'T BE RIGHT!
BLOOP
ROLL ROLL ROLL

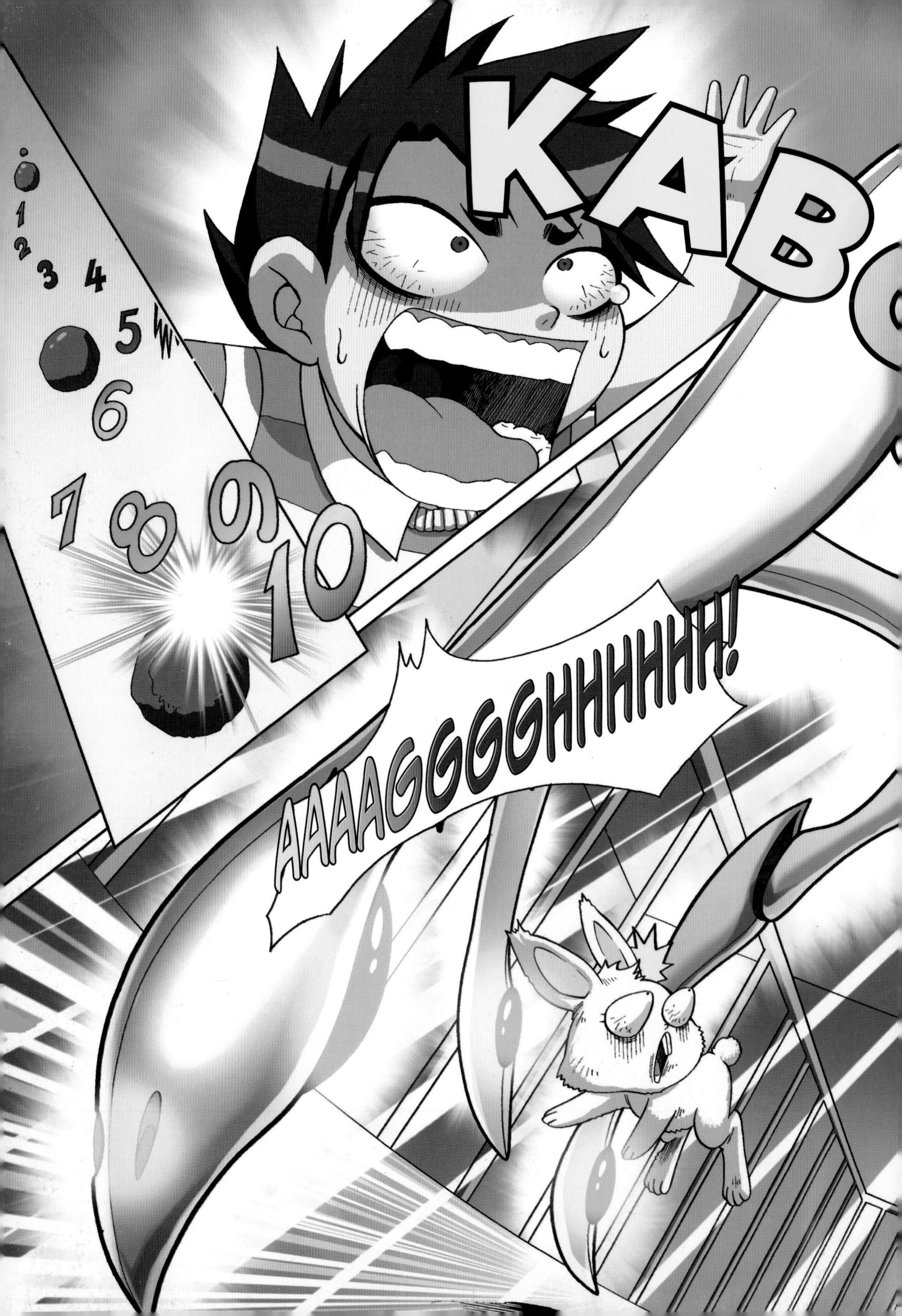
1
2 3 4
5
W
6
7 8 9 10
KABO
AAAAGGGGHHHHHH!

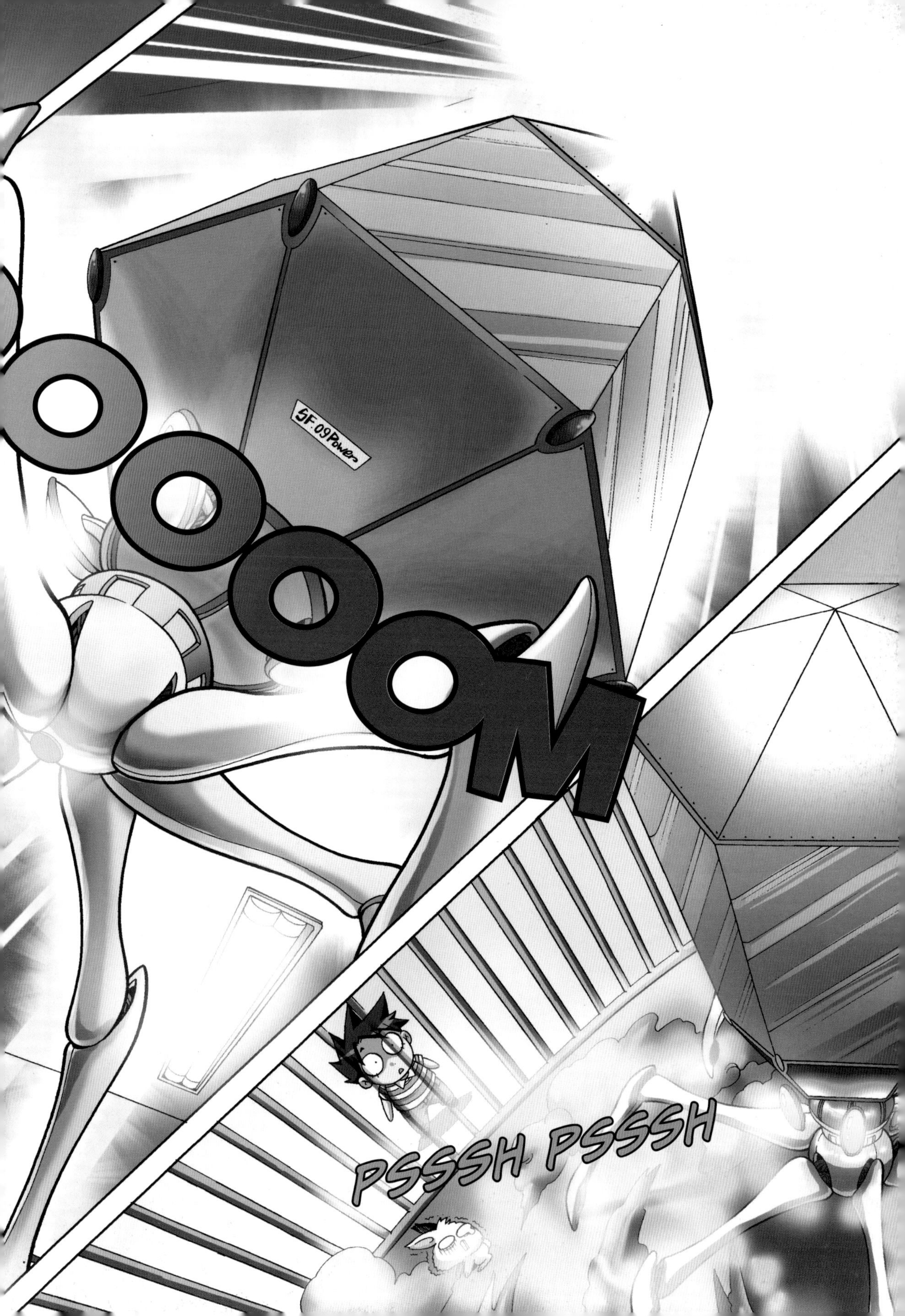
OOOOOM
SF-09 Power
PSSSH PSSSH

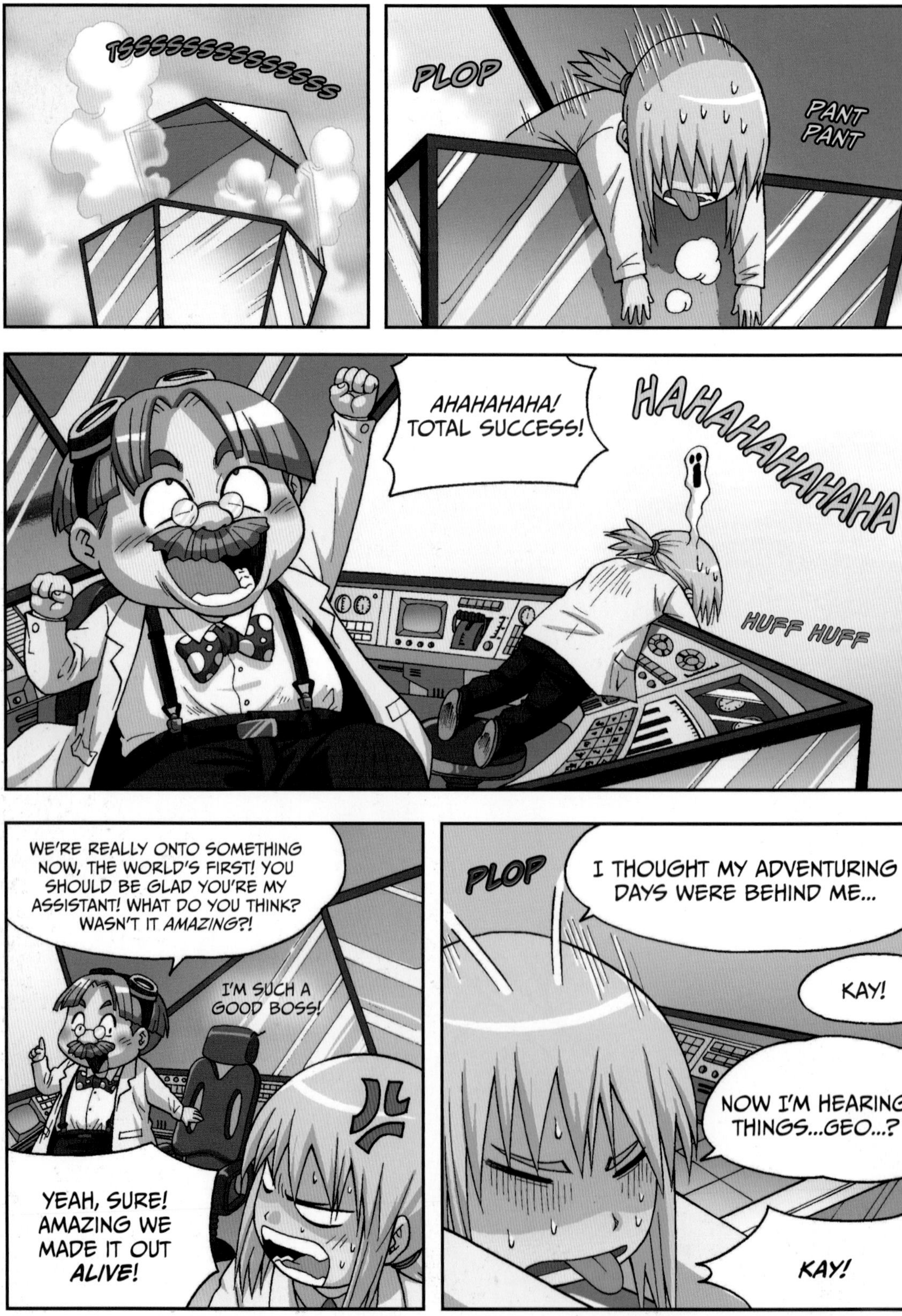

TSSSSSSSSSSSSSSS
PLOP
PANT PANT
AHAHAHAHA! TOTAL SUCCESS!
HAHAHAHAHAHAHA
HUFF HUFF
WE'RE REALLY ONTO SOMETHING NOW, THE WORLD'S FIRST! YOU SHOULD BE GLAD YOU'RE MY ASSISTANT! WHAT DO YOU THINK? WASN'T IT *AMAZING*?!
I'M SUCH A GOOD BOSS!
YEAH, SURE! AMAZING WE MADE IT OUT *ALIVE*!
PLOP
I THOUGHT MY ADVENTURING DAYS WERE BEHIND ME...
KAY!
NOW I'M HEARING THINGS...GEO...?
KAY!

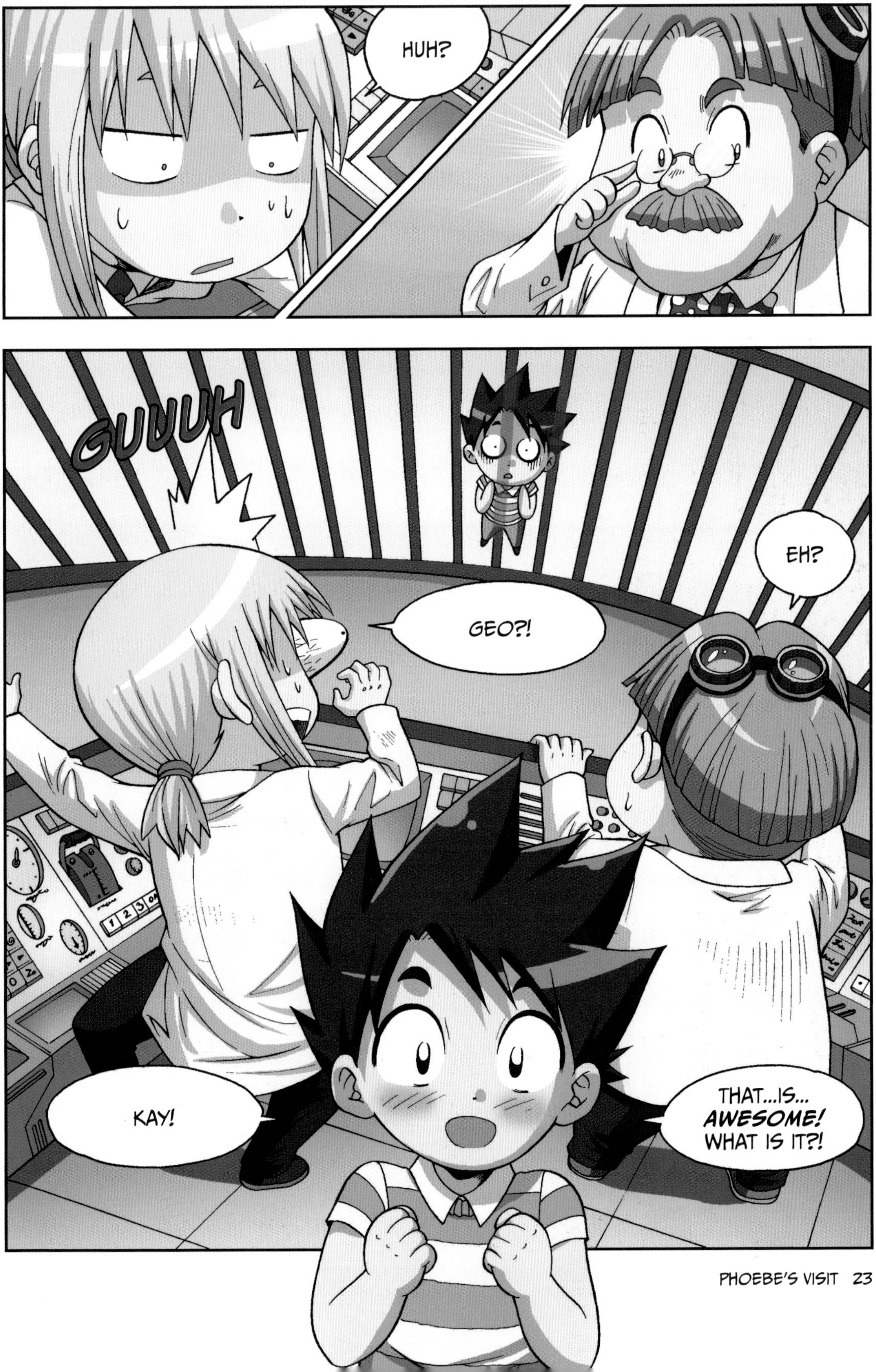
HUH?
GUUUH
EH?
GEO?!
KAY!
THAT...IS...
AWESOME!
WHAT IS IT?!

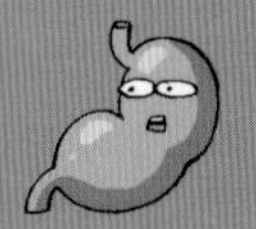

OUR INCREDIBLE BODIES

Our bodies are like sophisticated machinery. Just like how dozens of tiny gears work together to move a clock's hands, your body's organs must work together to keep you healthy. By working together, your organs form systems that make your heart beat, help you digest the food you eat, and allow you to move and think—without you even realizing it!

THE AUTOMATED SYSTEM: AUTONOMIC NERVOUS SYSTEM

Your body's autonomic nervous system automatically responds to your surroundings, just like an automatic door that opens when you come near it. This system detects changes inside *and* outside your body and adjusts your breathing, digestion, body temperature, and heart rate in response. The autonomic nervous system controls these basic functions that keep you alive, and the best part is that you don't even have to think about them! Imagine if you had to remember to keep your heart beating!

THE POWER PLANT: DIGESTIVE SYSTEM

Just as cars need gasoline or electricity to move, our bodies need food in order to stay alive. The food we eat must be broken down and converted into energy. The many organs in this process are part of the digestive system.

You can think of this system as a very long tube—it includes the mouth, esophagus, stomach, small intestine, and large intestine. These organs chew, churn, and dissolve food into tiny nutrient pieces like glucose, amino acids, and fatty acids. The energy that we need comes from absorbing these nutrients—they power the entire body! Then, anything left over is passed out of the body when you go to the bathroom.

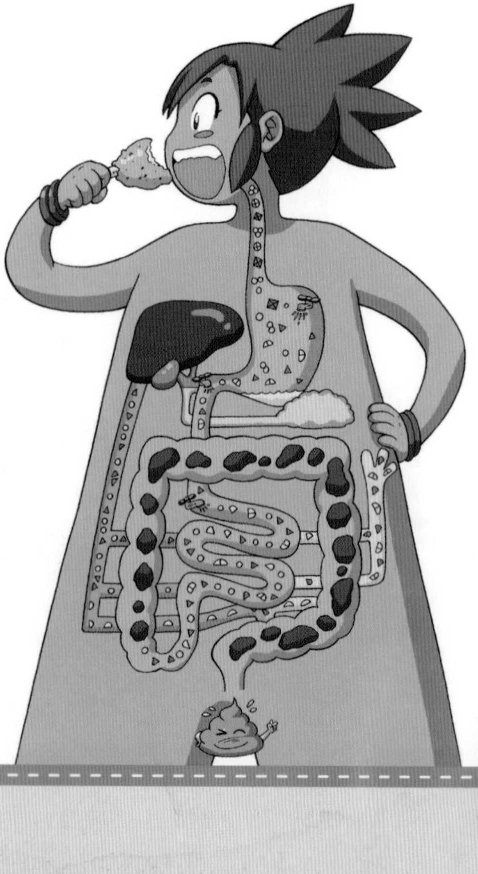

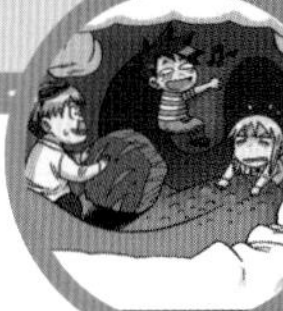

THE PUMP AND THE PIPES: CIRCULATORY SYSTEM

Our bodies use blood to transport the nutrients we get from food and the oxygen we get from breathing. The heart pushes blood to every nook and cranny of our bodies in tubes called *blood vessels*. This is a lot like how pumps and pipes send water through a big apartment building, from the penthouse down to the basement. The heart and blood vessels make up the circulatory system.

The heart beats about 40 million times a year without rest and pumps more than 2.5 million liters of blood in that time. That's one strong organ. And with the help of the autonomic nervous system, it beats slow and steady while you sleep and speeds up when you're exercising hard—all without a single thought.

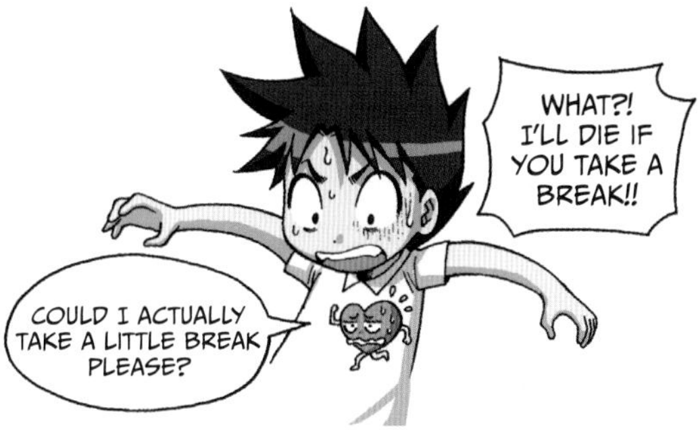
WHAT?! I'LL DIE IF YOU TAKE A BREAK!!
COULD I ACTUALLY TAKE A LITTLE BREAK PLEASE?

THE COMPUTER NETWORK: BRAIN AND NERVOUS SYSTEM

Each organ has its own job, but we need a boss to gather all the information from the body, make decisions, and take action. That is what your brain and nervous system do. Everything we see and feel is sent to the brain through chemical and electrical signals in the nerves. These signals can move at 120 meters per second (about 250 miles per hour)—very fast, indeed!

The brain, spinal cord, and nerves are made up of very special cells called *neurons*. Your brain alone has billions of neurons that collect information to make decisions, manage your organs, and keep you alive.

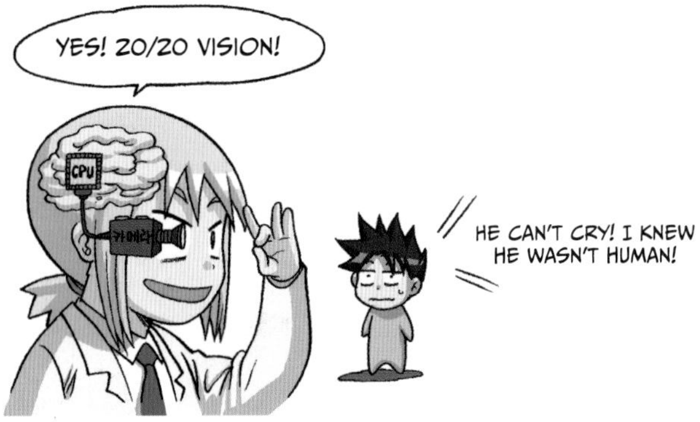
YES! 20/20 VISION!
CPU
HE CAN'T CRY! I KNEW HE WASN'T HUMAN!

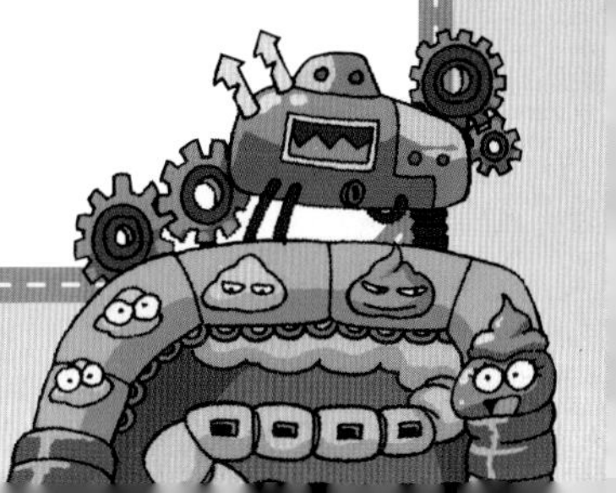

THE GOOD SHIP SS HIPPOCRATES

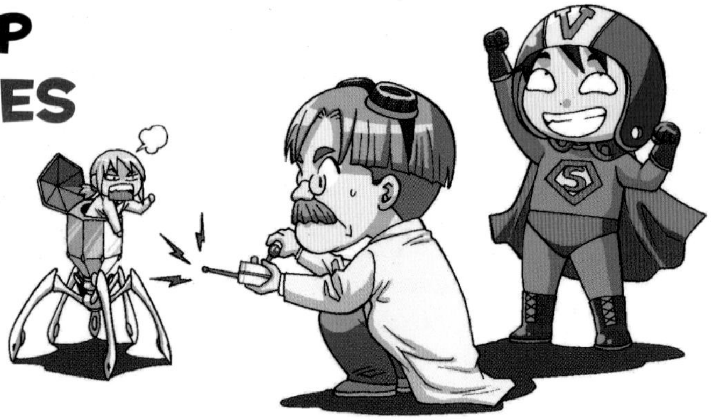

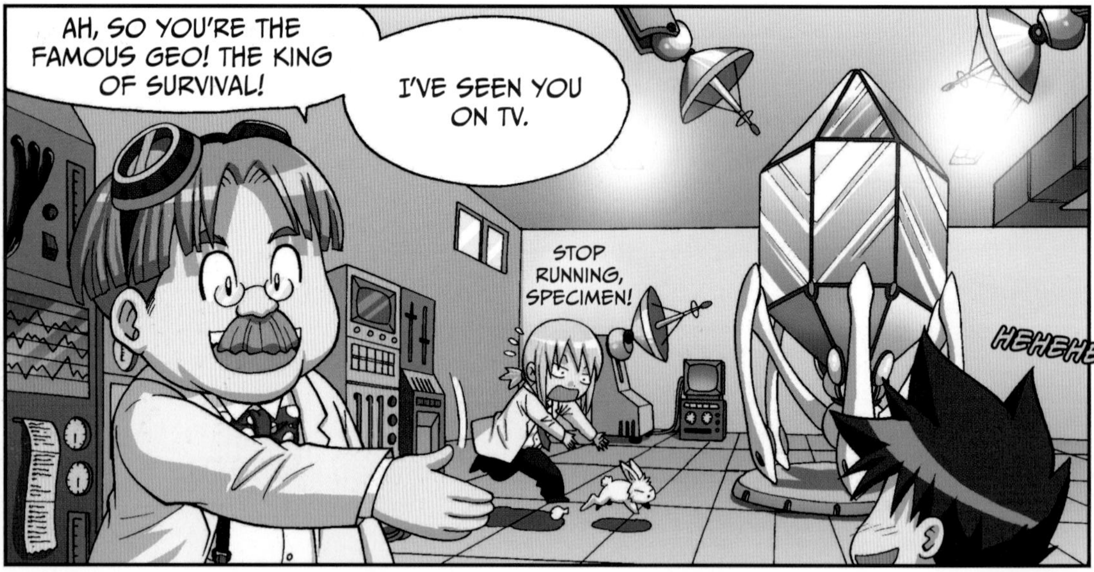
AH, SO YOU'RE THE FAMOUS GEO! THE KING OF SURVIVAL!
I'VE SEEN YOU ON TV.
STOP RUNNING, SPECIMEN!
HEHEHE

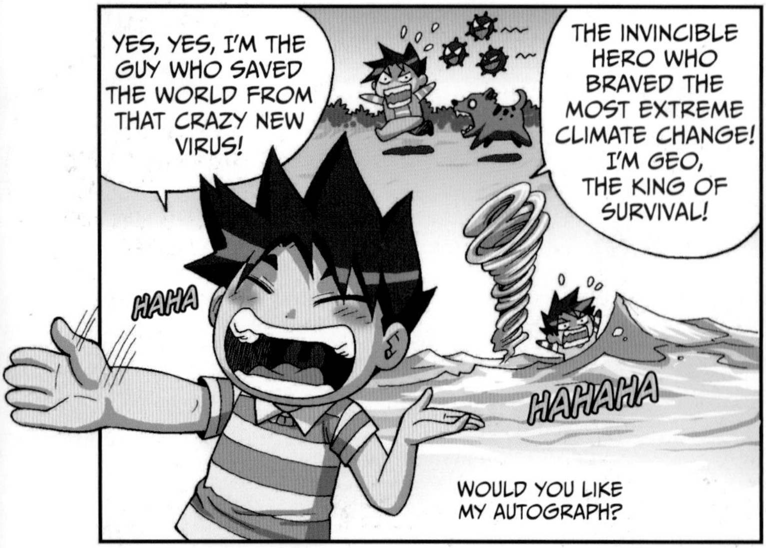
YES, YES, I'M THE GUY WHO SAVED THE WORLD FROM THAT CRAZY NEW VIRUS!
THE INVINCIBLE HERO WHO BRAVED THE MOST EXTREME CLIMATE CHANGE! I'M GEO, THE KING OF SURVIVAL!
HAHA
HAHAHA
WOULD YOU LIKE MY AUTOGRAPH?

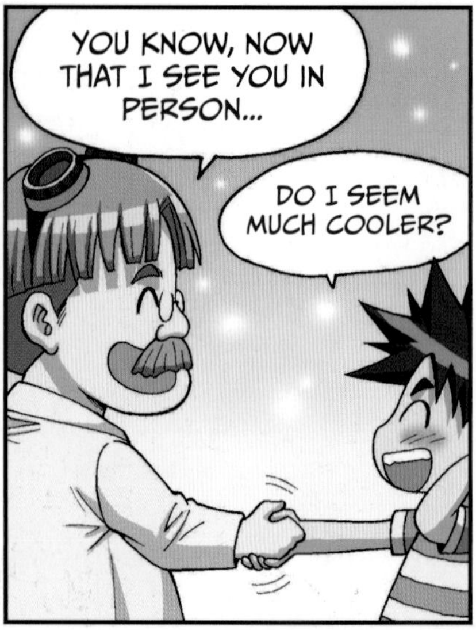
YOU KNOW, NOW THAT I SEE YOU IN PERSON...
DO I SEEM MUCH COOLER?

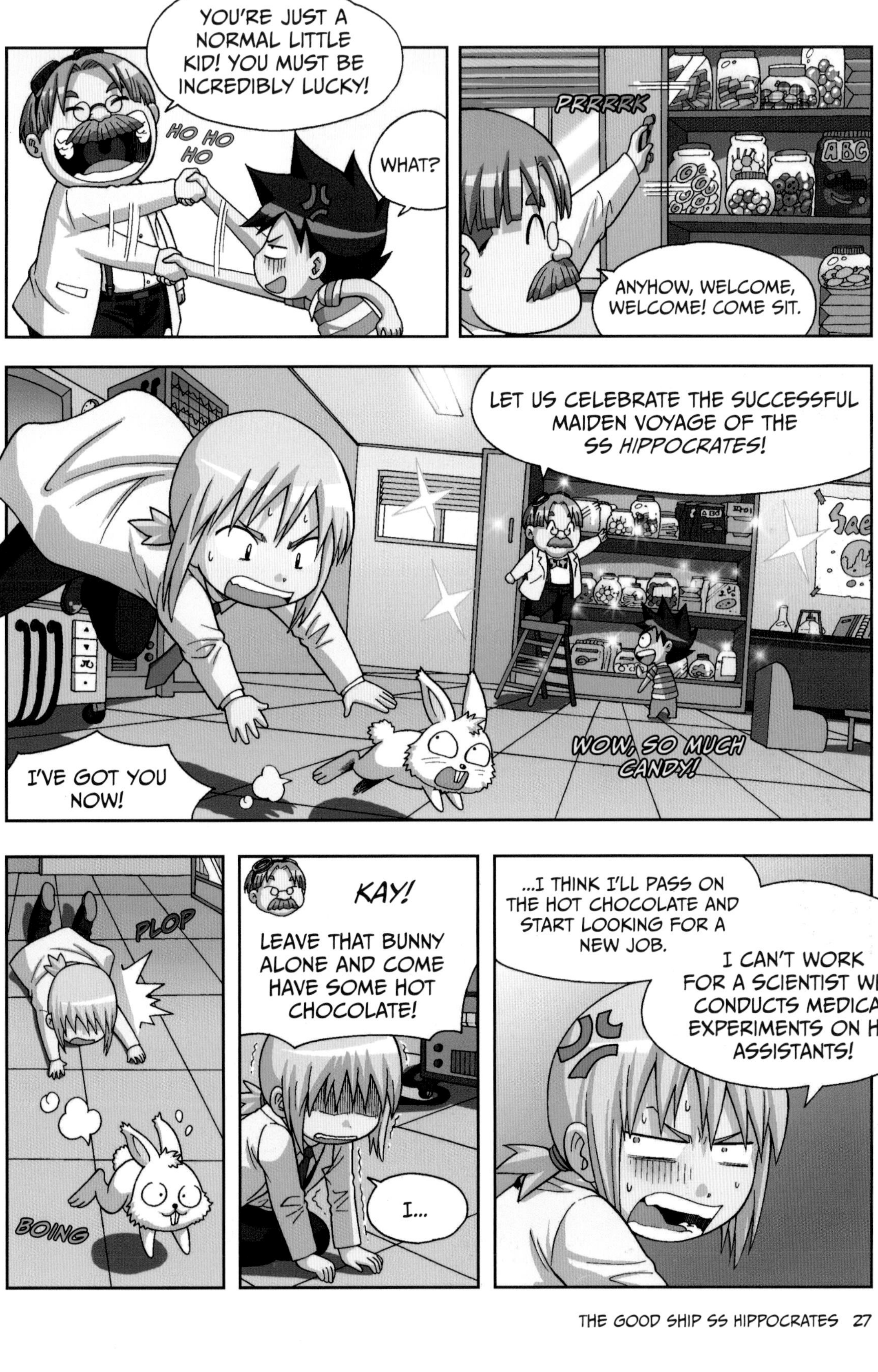
YOU'RE JUST A NORMAL LITTLE KID! YOU MUST BE INCREDIBLY LUCKY!
HO HO HO
WHAT?
PRRRRK
ANYHOW, WELCOME, WELCOME! COME SIT.
LET US CELEBRATE THE SUCCESSFUL MAIDEN VOYAGE OF THE SS *HIPPOCRATES!*
WOW, SO MUCH CANDY!
I'VE GOT YOU NOW!
PLOP
BOING
KAY!
LEAVE THAT BUNNY ALONE AND COME HAVE SOME HOT CHOCOLATE!
I...
...I THINK I'LL PASS ON THE HOT CHOCOLATE AND START LOOKING FOR A NEW JOB.
I CAN'T WORK FOR A SCIENTIST WHO CONDUCTS MEDICAL EXPERIMENTS ON HIS ASSISTANTS!

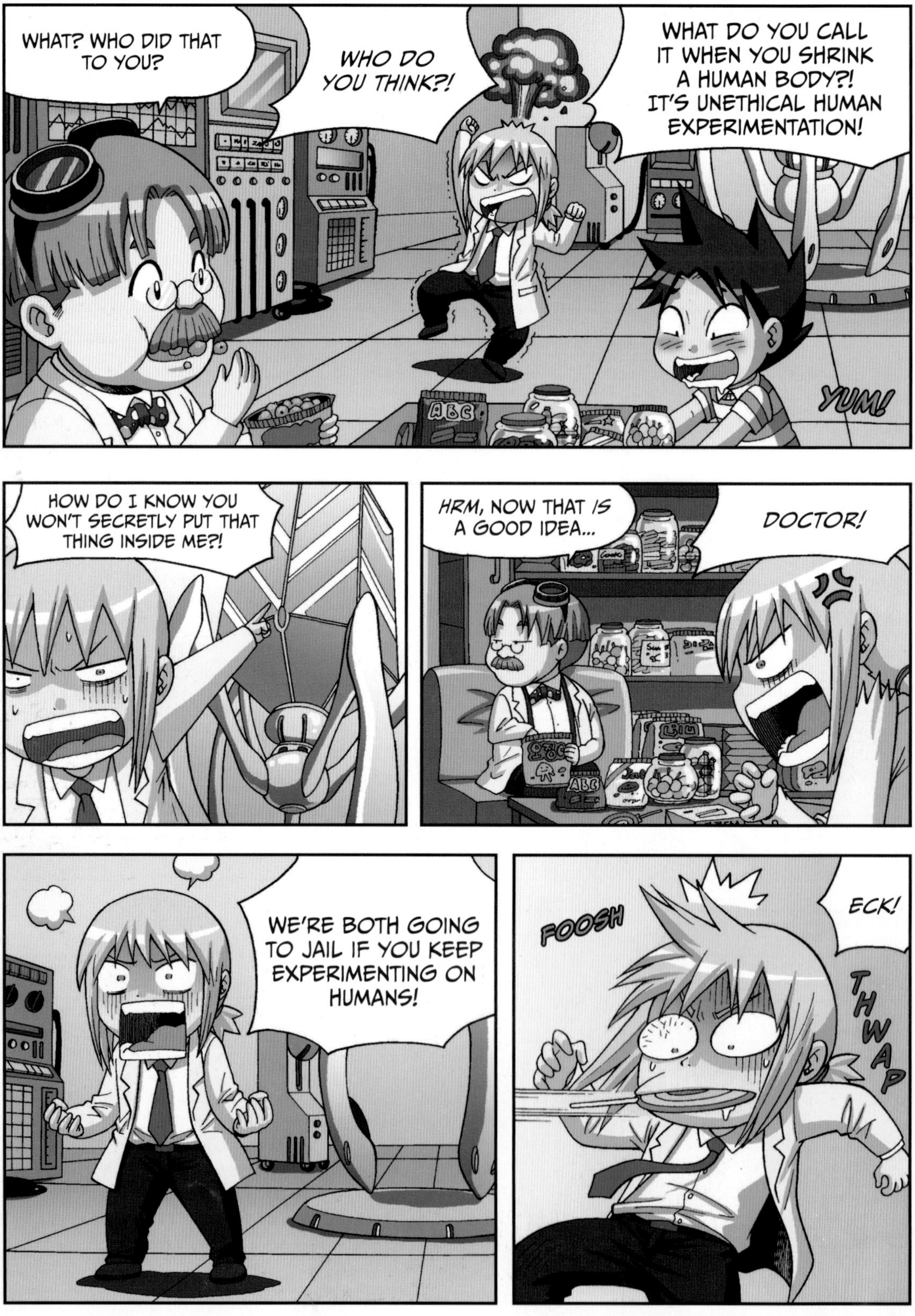
WHAT? WHO DID THAT TO YOU?
WHO DO YOU THINK?!
WHAT DO YOU CALL IT WHEN YOU SHRINK A HUMAN BODY?! IT'S UNETHICAL HUMAN EXPERIMENTATION!
YUM!
HOW DO I KNOW YOU WON'T SECRETLY PUT THAT THING INSIDE ME?!
HRM, NOW THAT IS A GOOD IDEA...
DOCTOR!
WE'RE BOTH GOING TO JAIL IF YOU KEEP EXPERIMENTING ON HUMANS!
FOOSH
ECK!
THWAP

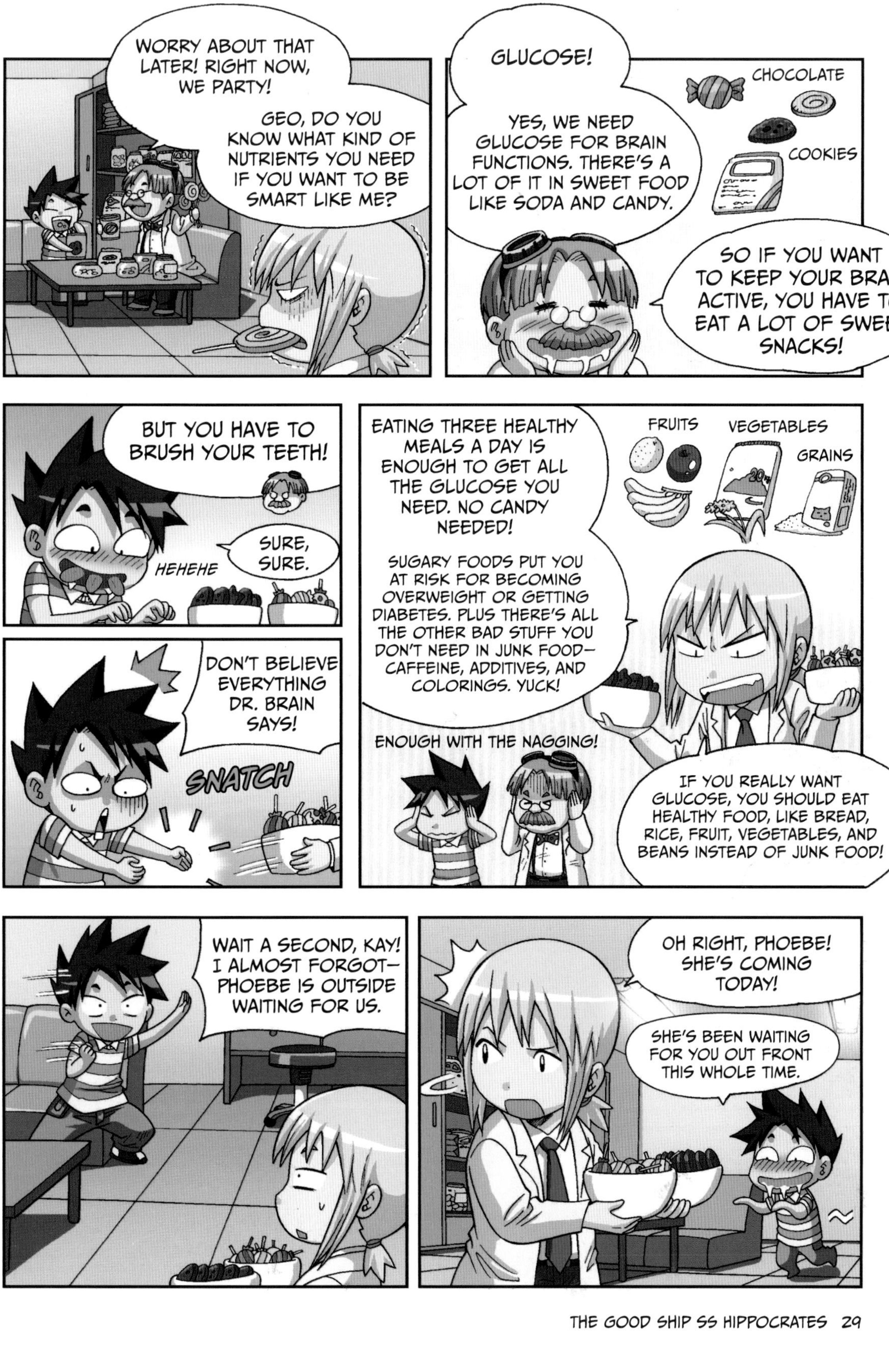
WORRY ABOUT THAT LATER! RIGHT NOW, WE PARTY!
GEO, DO YOU KNOW WHAT KIND OF NUTRIENTS YOU NEED IF YOU WANT TO BE SMART LIKE ME?
GLUCOSE!
YES, WE NEED GLUCOSE FOR BRAIN FUNCTIONS. THERE'S A LOT OF IT IN SWEET FOOD LIKE SODA AND CANDY.
CHOCOLATE
COOKIES
SO IF YOU WANT TO KEEP YOUR BRAIN ACTIVE, YOU HAVE TO EAT A LOT OF SWEET SNACKS!
BUT YOU HAVE TO BRUSH YOUR TEETH!
HEHEHE
SURE, SURE.
DON'T BELIEVE EVERYTHING DR. BRAIN SAYS!
SNATCH
EATING THREE HEALTHY MEALS A DAY IS ENOUGH TO GET ALL THE GLUCOSE YOU NEED. NO CANDY NEEDED!
FRUITS
VEGETABLES
GRAINS
SUGARY FOODS PUT YOU AT RISK FOR BECOMING OVERWEIGHT OR GETTING DIABETES. PLUS THERE'S ALL THE OTHER BAD STUFF YOU DON'T NEED IN JUNK FOOD—CAFFEINE, ADDITIVES, AND COLORINGS. YUCK!
ENOUGH WITH THE NAGGING!
IF YOU REALLY WANT GLUCOSE, YOU SHOULD EAT HEALTHY FOOD, LIKE BREAD, RICE, FRUIT, VEGETABLES, AND BEANS INSTEAD OF JUNK FOOD!
WAIT A SECOND, KAY! I ALMOST FORGOT—PHOEBE IS OUTSIDE WAITING FOR US.
OH RIGHT, PHOEBE! SHE'S COMING TODAY!
SHE'S BEEN WAITING FOR YOU OUT FRONT THIS WHOLE TIME.

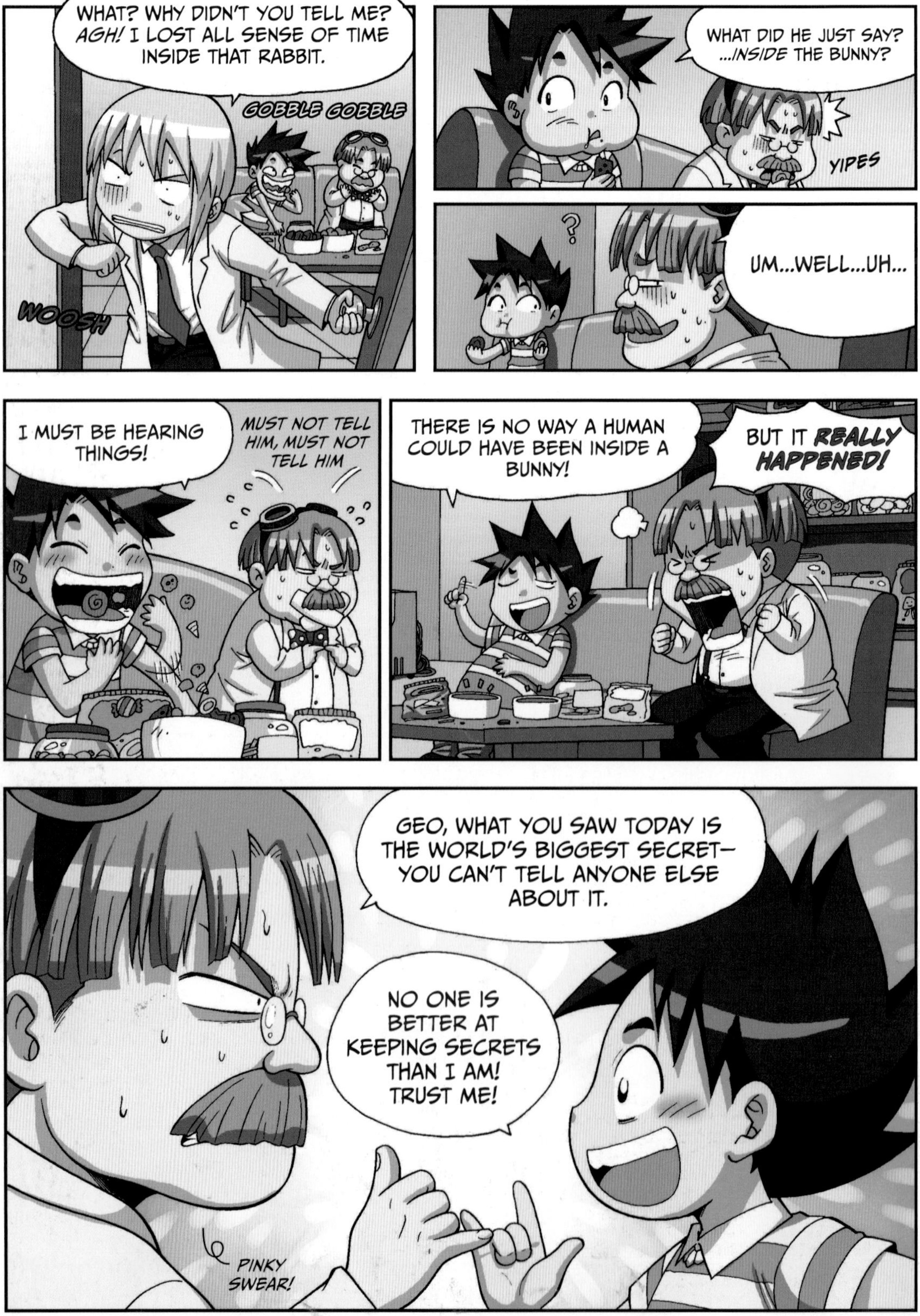
WHAT? WHY DIDN'T YOU TELL ME? *AGH!* I LOST ALL SENSE OF TIME INSIDE THAT RABBIT.
GOBBLE GOBBLE
WOOSH
WHAT DID HE JUST SAY? ...*INSIDE* THE BUNNY?
YIPES
?
UM...WELL...UH...
I MUST BE HEARING THINGS!
MUST NOT TELL HIM, MUST NOT TELL HIM
THERE IS NO WAY A HUMAN COULD HAVE BEEN INSIDE A BUNNY!
BUT IT **REALLY HAPPENED!**
GEO, WHAT YOU SAW TODAY IS THE WORLD'S BIGGEST SECRET—YOU CAN'T TELL ANYONE ELSE ABOUT IT.
NO ONE IS BETTER AT KEEPING SECRETS THAN I AM! TRUST ME!
PINKY SWEAR!

HAVE YOU HEARD OF THE NAME *HIPPOCRATES*?

OH, SURE! LIKE THE HIPPOCRATIC OATH THAT DOCTORS TAKE...

I SWEAR, BY APOLLO THE HEALER...

THAT'S RIGHT! HIPPOCRATES IS A DOCTOR FROM ANCIENT GREECE— 2,500 YEARS AGO.

IN THOSE DAYS, PEOPLE BELIEVED THAT DISEASES CAME FROM THE GODS, AS PUNISHMENT. BUT HIPPOCRATES TOOK A MORE SCIENTIFIC APPROACH AND TRIED TO CURE DISEASES BY FINDING THEIR REAL CAUSES. THAT IS WHY HE IS STILL KNOWN AS THE "FATHER OF MEDICINE."

MY INVENTION IS CALLED THE SS *HIPPOCRATES* BECAUSE...

JUST LIKE HIPPOCRATES, THIS SHIP WILL BEGIN A WHOLE NEW ERA OF MEDICINE.

A NEW ERA OF MEDICINE?

FOR MANY YEARS, I HAVE BEEN RESEARCHING HOW TO MAKE THINGS SMALLER TO HELP DOCTORS TREAT THE HUMAN BODY. IF I'M SUCCESSFUL, SURGERIES THAT ARE IMPOSSIBLE TODAY WILL BE POSSIBLE TOMORROW!

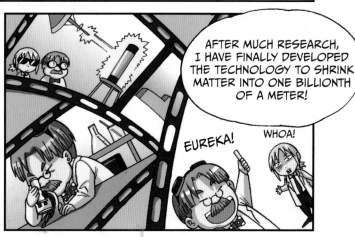

AFTER MUCH RESEARCH, I HAVE FINALLY DEVELOPED THE TECHNOLOGY TO SHRINK MATTER INTO ONE BILLIONTH OF A METER!

EUREKA!

WHOA!

THE GOOD SHIP SS HIPPOCRATES 31

WHAT YOU JUST SAW IS THE RESULT OF MY INVENTION! FOR THE FIRST TIME EVER, WE TOOK THE *HIPPOCRATES* AND WENT ON AN ADVENTURE INSIDE THE BUNNY!

SOON, MY *HIPPOCRATES* WILL CONQUER ALL HUMAN DISEASES!

...CHIRP...CHIRP...

SNICKER

YEAH, RIGHT!

YOU... MOCK ME?

DR. BRAIN, I THINK YOU'VE SEEN TOO MANY SCI-FI MOVIES!

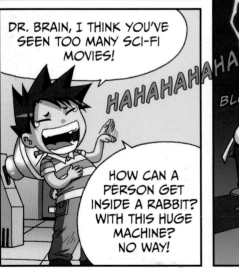

HAHAHAHAHA

HOW CAN A PERSON GET INSIDE A RABBIT? WITH THIS HUGE MACHINE? NO WAY!

AND BESIDES, IF YOU HAVE THIS TECHNOLOGY, WHY DIDN'T YOU SHRINK YOUR OWN BELLY FIRST?

BLOB

FINE! IF YOU WON'T BELIEVE ME, I'LL JUST HAVE TO *SHOW* YOU.

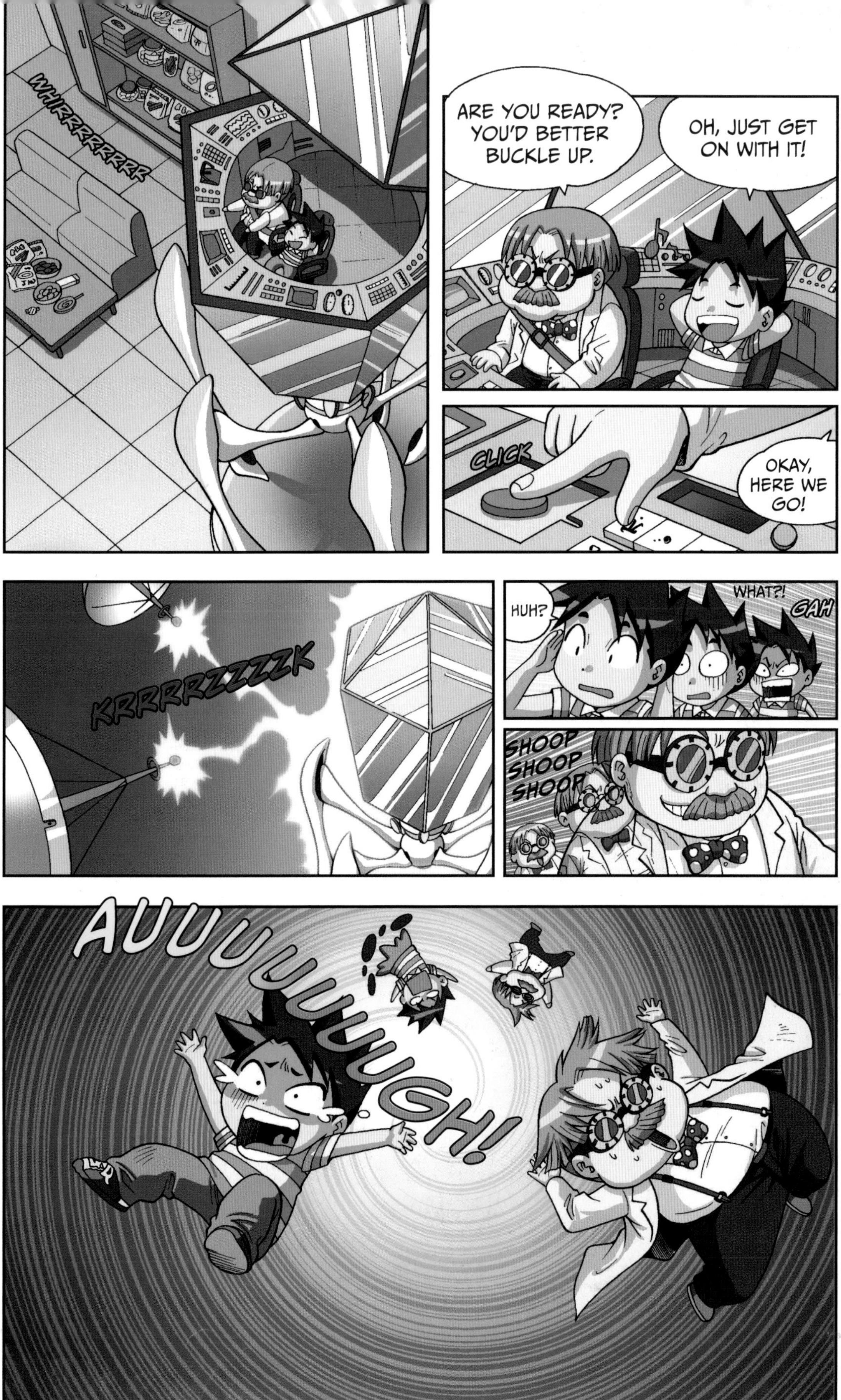
WHIRRRRRRRRR
ARE YOU READY? YOU'D BETTER BUCKLE UP.
OH, JUST GET ON WITH IT!
CLICK
OKAY, HERE WE GO!
KRRRRZZZZZK
HUH?
WHAT?!
GAH
SHOOP
SHOOP
SHOOP
AUUUUUUUUGH!

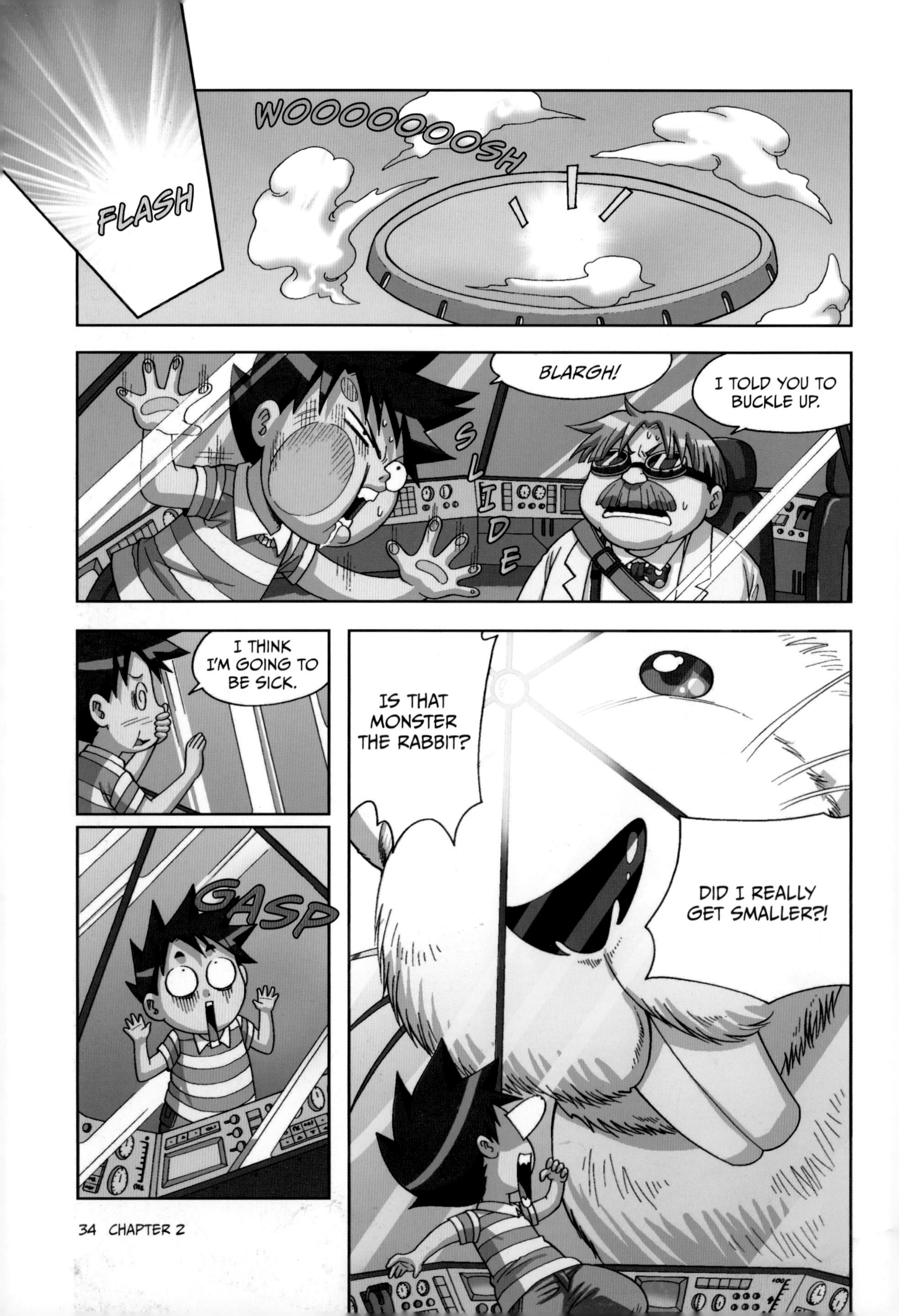
FLASH
WOOOOOOOOSH
BLARGH!
I TOLD YOU TO BUCKLE UP.
SLIDE
I THINK I'M GOING TO BE SICK.
GASP
IS THAT MONSTER THE RABBIT?
DID I REALLY GET SMALLER?!

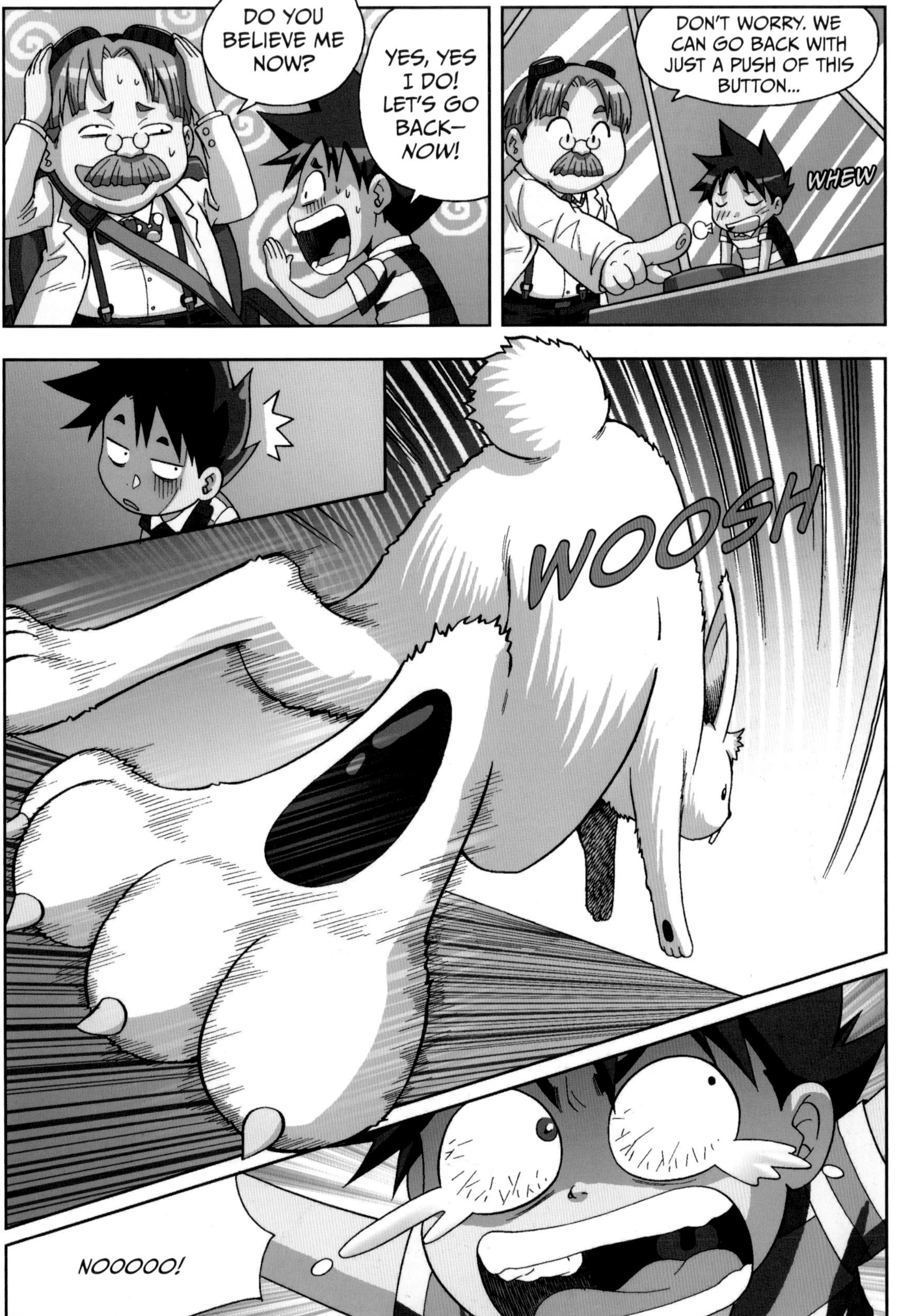
DO YOU BELIEVE ME NOW?
YES, YES I DO! LET'S GO BACK—NOW!
DON'T WORRY. WE CAN GO BACK WITH JUST A PUSH OF THIS BUTTON...
WHEW
WOOSH
NOOOOO!

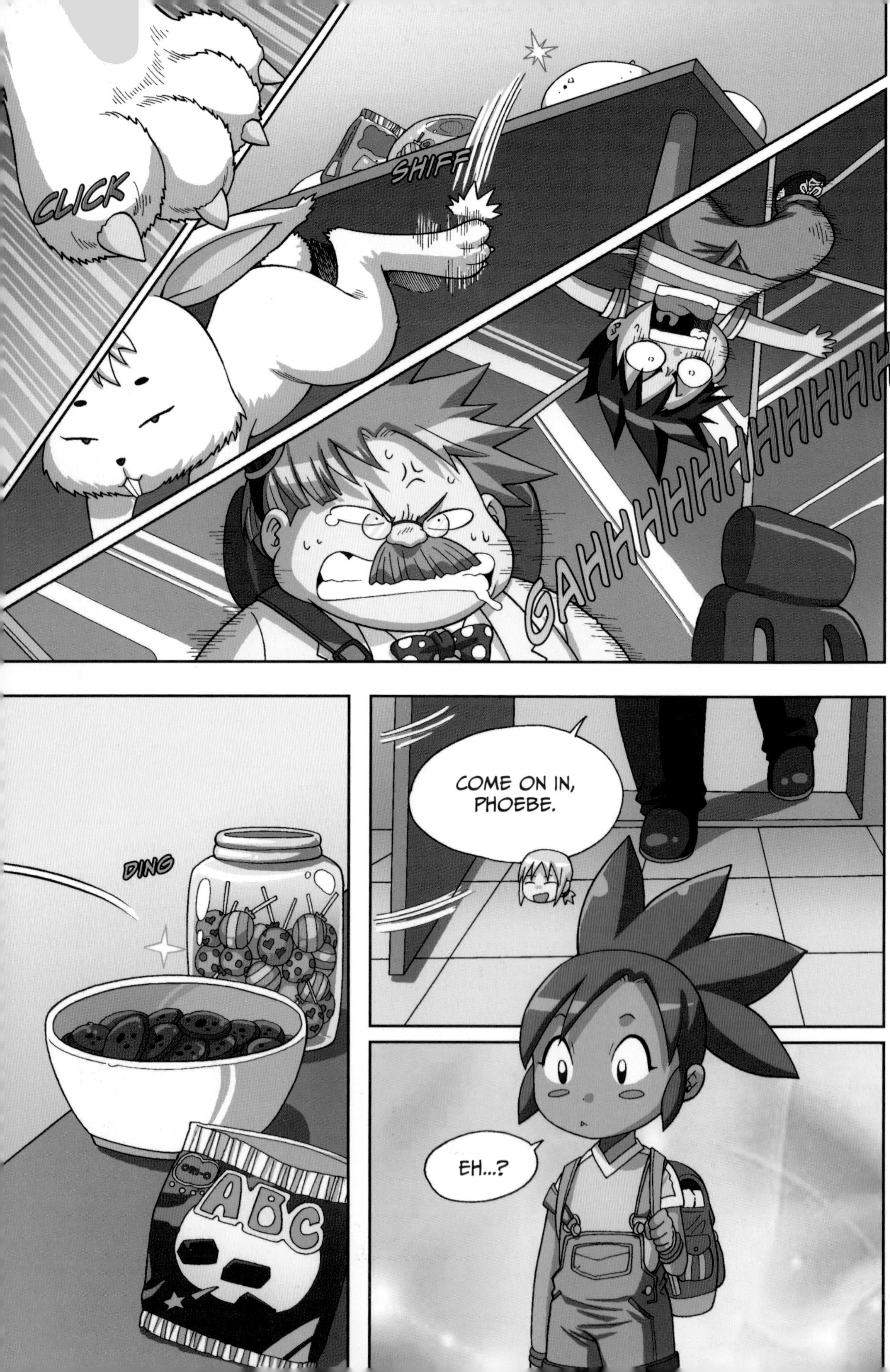
CLICK
SHIFF
GAHHHHHHHHHHHHHH!
DING
COME ON IN, PHOEBE.
EH...?
ABC

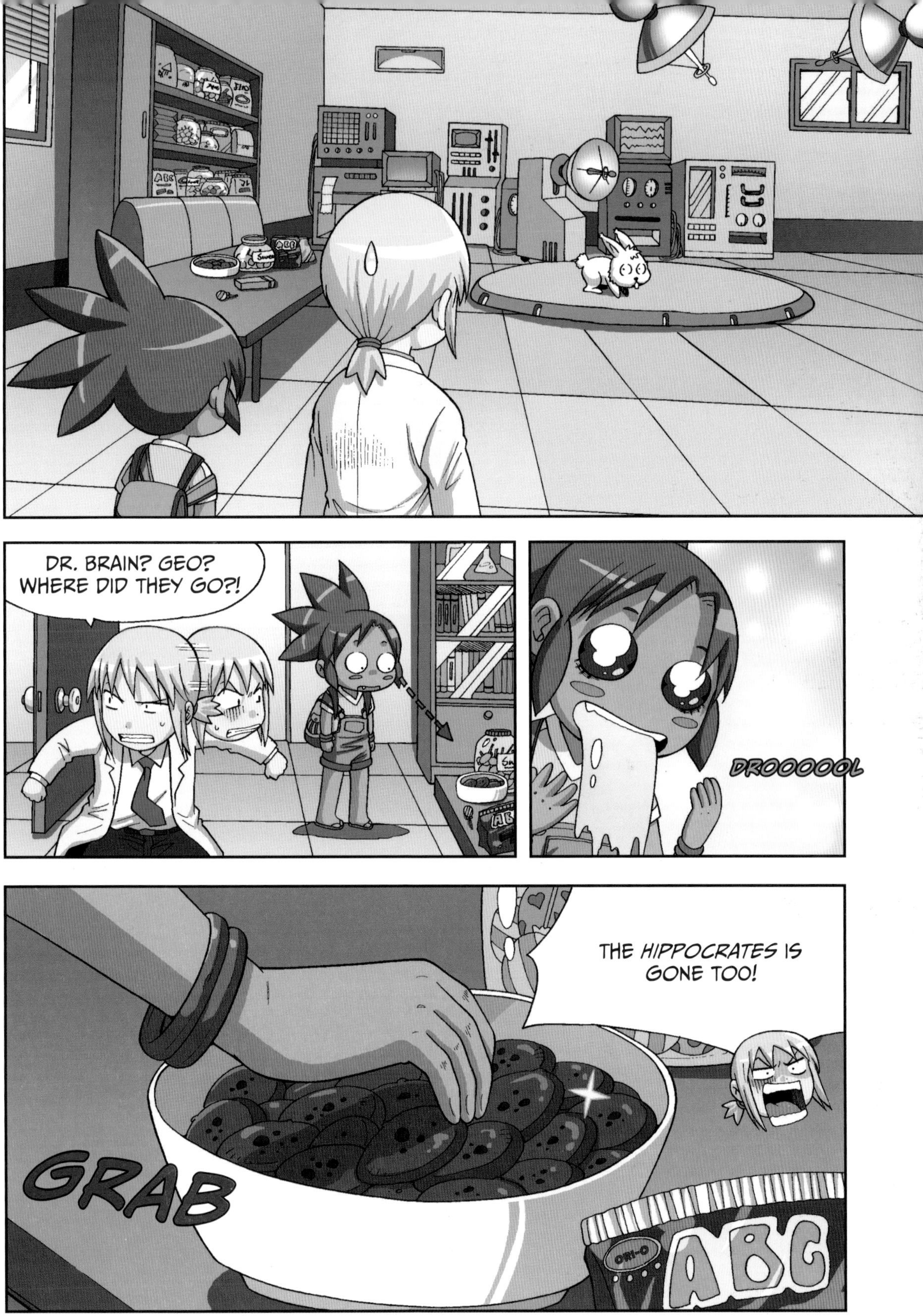
DR. BRAIN? GEO? WHERE DID THEY GO?!
DROOOOOOL
THE HIPPOCRATES IS GONE TOO!
GRAB
ABC
ORI-O

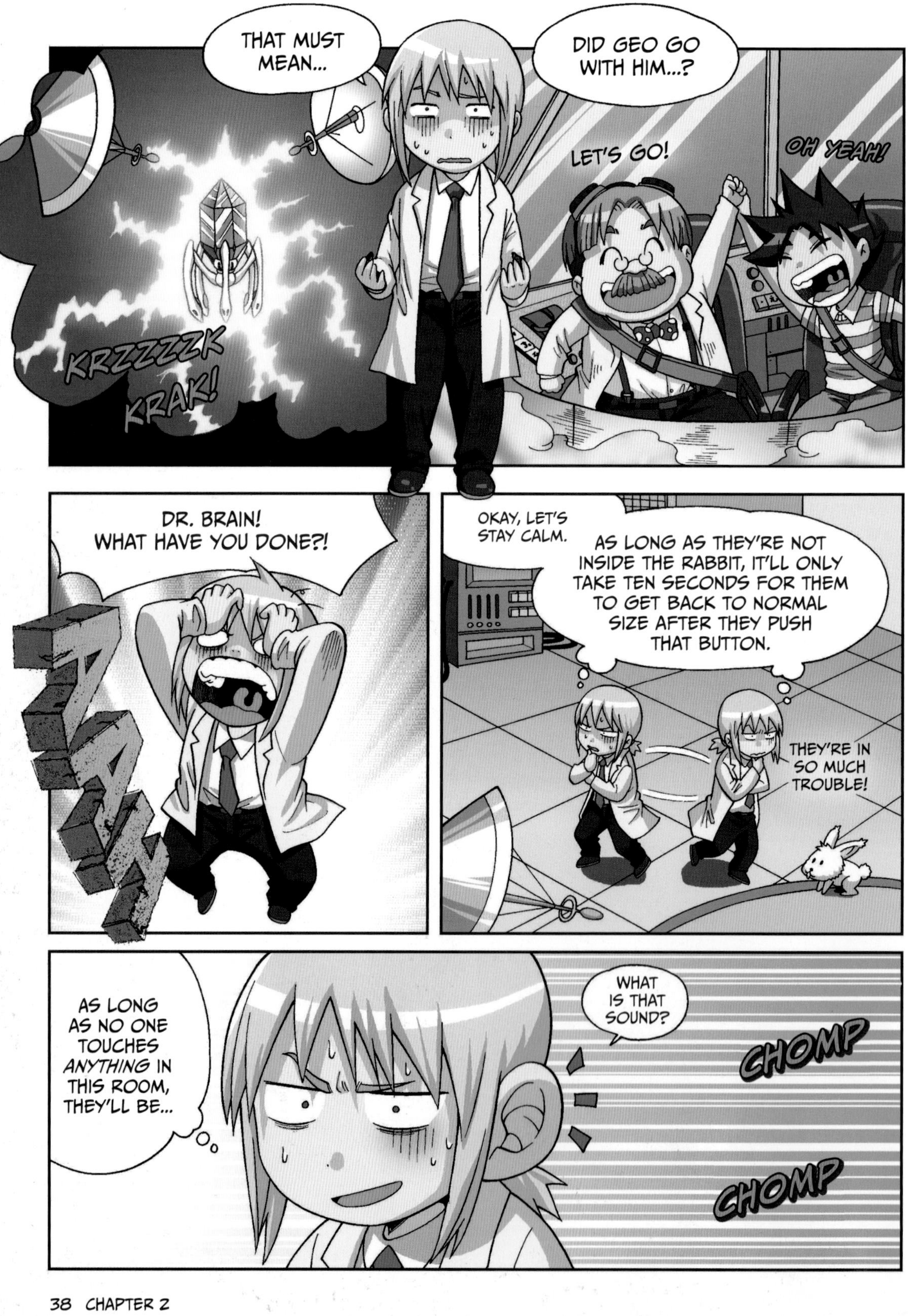
THAT MUST MEAN...
DID GEO GO WITH HIM...?
KRZZZZK
KRAK!
LET'S GO!
OH YEAH!
DR. BRAIN! WHAT HAVE YOU DONE?!
OKAY, LET'S STAY CALM.
AS LONG AS THEY'RE NOT INSIDE THE RABBIT, IT'LL ONLY TAKE TEN SECONDS FOR THEM TO GET BACK TO NORMAL SIZE AFTER THEY PUSH THAT BUTTON.
THEY'RE IN SO MUCH TROUBLE!
AS LONG AS NO ONE TOUCHES *ANYTHING* IN THIS ROOM, THEY'LL BE...
WHAT IS THAT SOUND?
CHOMP
CHOMP

CHOMP
MUNCH
MUNCH
AIIIIIEEEE!
AGHHH!
SHWOOOOOP
AHHHHHHHH!
NOOOOO!

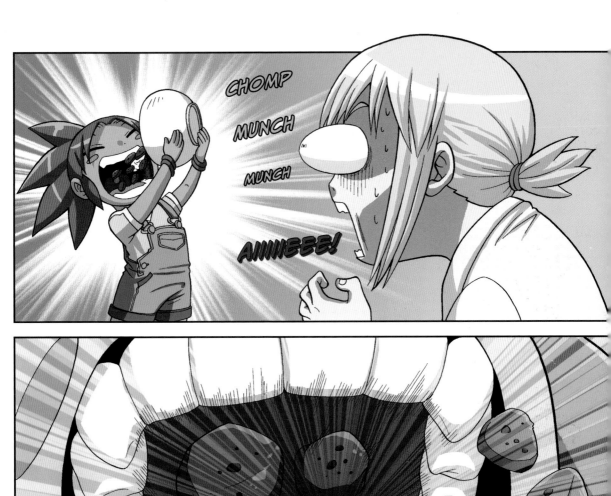

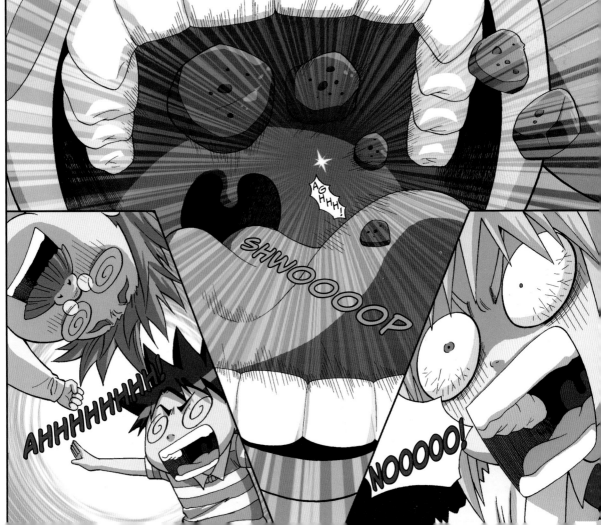

DIGESTIVE SYSTEM

NUTRIENTS AND OUR BODIES

Our bodies need three major kinds of nutrients to survive: carbohydrates, fat, and protein. These nutrients provide the energy we need to live, but we also need vitamins and minerals to help us grow and keep our bodies working. That's why it's important to have a balanced and nutritious diet with plenty of vegetables, fruits, and whole grains. Although everyone deserves a nice treat every once in a while, eating too much candy, soda, and fast food can lead to problems like heart disease, diabetes, and obesity.

CARBOHYDRATES

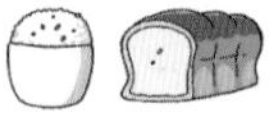

Foods made from rice, flour, and sugar have a lot of carbohydrates. Carbohydrates are important because our bodies break them down into glucose, our main source of energy. Because of glucose, we can maintain our body temperature and keep our muscles moving. But our bodies turn leftover carbohydrates into body fat, so eating too many carbohydrates can cause health problems. Eating foods with whole grains (like whole wheat bread, oatmeal, or brown rice) is much healthier than eating processed grains (like white bread and white rice) and candy.

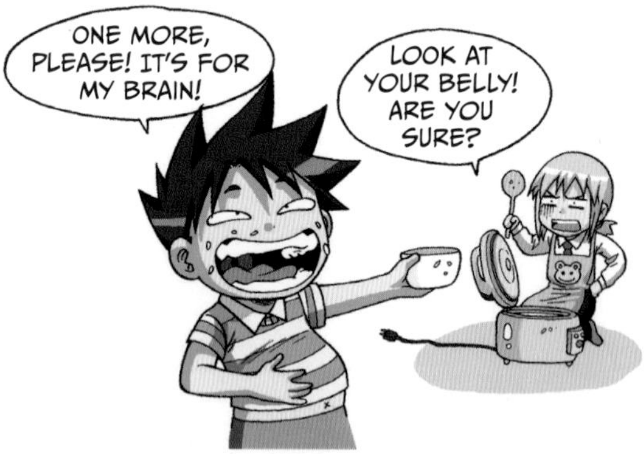
ONE MORE, PLEASE! IT'S FOR MY BRAIN!
LOOK AT YOUR BELLY! ARE YOU SURE?

FAT

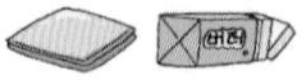

Fat is one of the three main nutrients that give energy to our bodies. All of our bodies naturally have some fat in them too, and that's a good thing. Fat is really useful. It helps us stay warm, protects our organs, and can be used as energy. But too much fat (like too much of any nutrient) can cause health problems, like diabetes. Sometimes when there's too much fat in the body, there's too much cholesterol as well. That can slow blood flow, and it may cause arteriosclerosis (hardening of the blood vessels) or high blood pressure.

PROTEIN

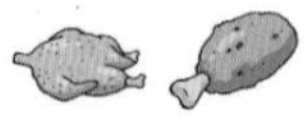

Protein is the building block of our bodies. It makes up most of our muscles, cells, skin, fingernails, and toenails, and without it, these parts of our bodies would be very weak. A well-balanced diet with protein-rich foods is important for staying healthy. There is a lot of protein in meat, fish, nuts like walnuts and almonds, and dairy products like milk.

VITAMINS AND MINERALS

Vitamins and minerals affect your body's ability to fight off disease, digest food, and grow up big and strong. Dietary minerals are elements like iron and calcium. Vitamins are more complex compounds that our bodies cannot produce on their own. You need only a small amount of vitamins and minerals compared to other nutrients.

But a shortage of vitamins may cause problems, such as night blindness (vitamin A), weak bones (vitamin D), or poor healing of scratches and cuts (vitamin C). An extreme shortage of vitamin C is called *scurvy*. It makes the body weak and is very dangerous. Scurvy used to be common among sailors and pirates who couldn't eat fruit and vegetables on their long voyages, but people today can still get scurvy if they eat only junk food. This is one reason why you should eat plenty of fruits and vegetables—to get your share of vitamins and minerals.

Your body can make vitamin D when your skin is exposed to sunlight. Being in sunlight three times a week for 10 minutes at a time is enough for the body to create all the vitamin D it needs.

I HAVE TO MAKE MORE VITAMIN D FOR MY BONES!
PHOEBE!
PANT PANT

WATER

Water makes up two-thirds of the body. It's the main "ingredient" in blood, saliva, and other lesser known bodily fluids (like lymphatic fluid, tissue fluid, and even the fluid *inside* our cells). Water has many important jobs to do, like maintaining body temperature and transporting nutrients, oxygen, and waste. But we lose water through sweat and urine, so we must always drink enough water. Dehydration (too little water) can be very dangerous. When you're thirsty, drink some water! You also get water from the foods you eat.

The body can survive without food for a few weeks, but it can't go without water for more than four days. Water is one of the most important things our bodies need.

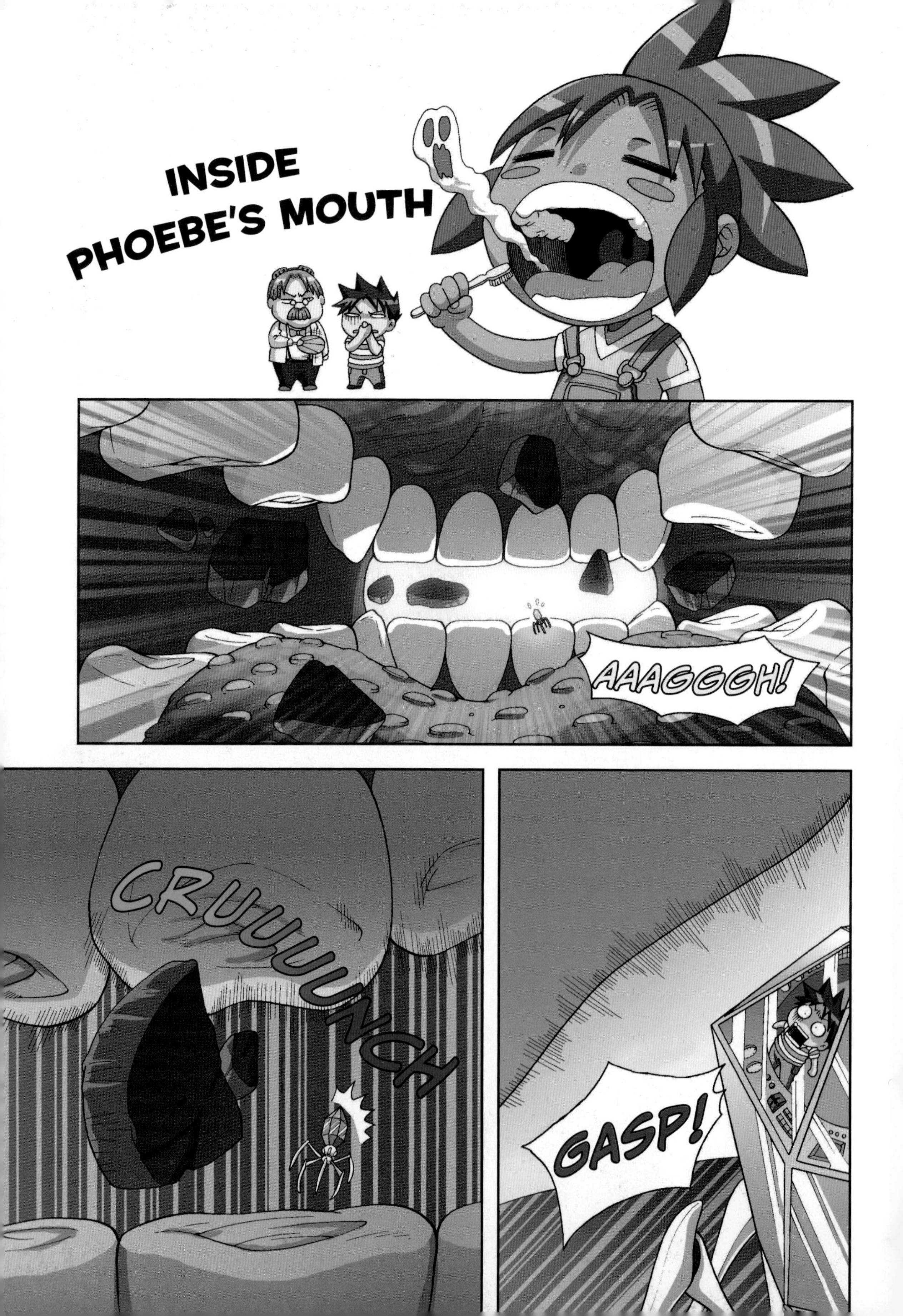
INSIDE PHOEBE'S MOUTH
AAAGGGH!
CRUUUUNCH
GASP!

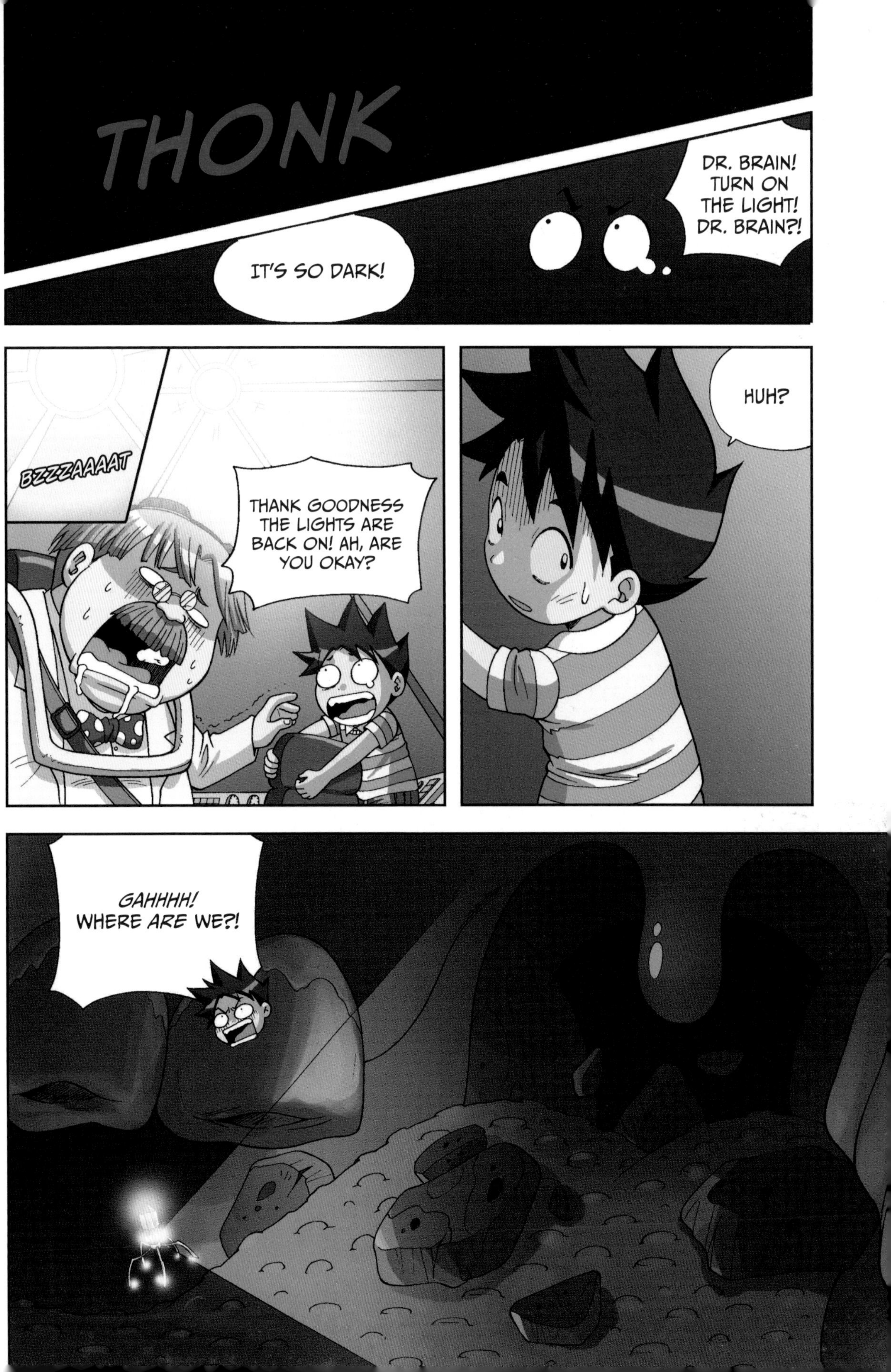
THONK
IT'S SO DARK!
DR. BRAIN! TURN ON THE LIGHT! DR. BRAIN?!
BZZZAAAAT
THANK GOODNESS THE LIGHTS ARE BACK ON! AH, ARE YOU OKAY?
HUH?
GAHHHH! WHERE ARE WE?!

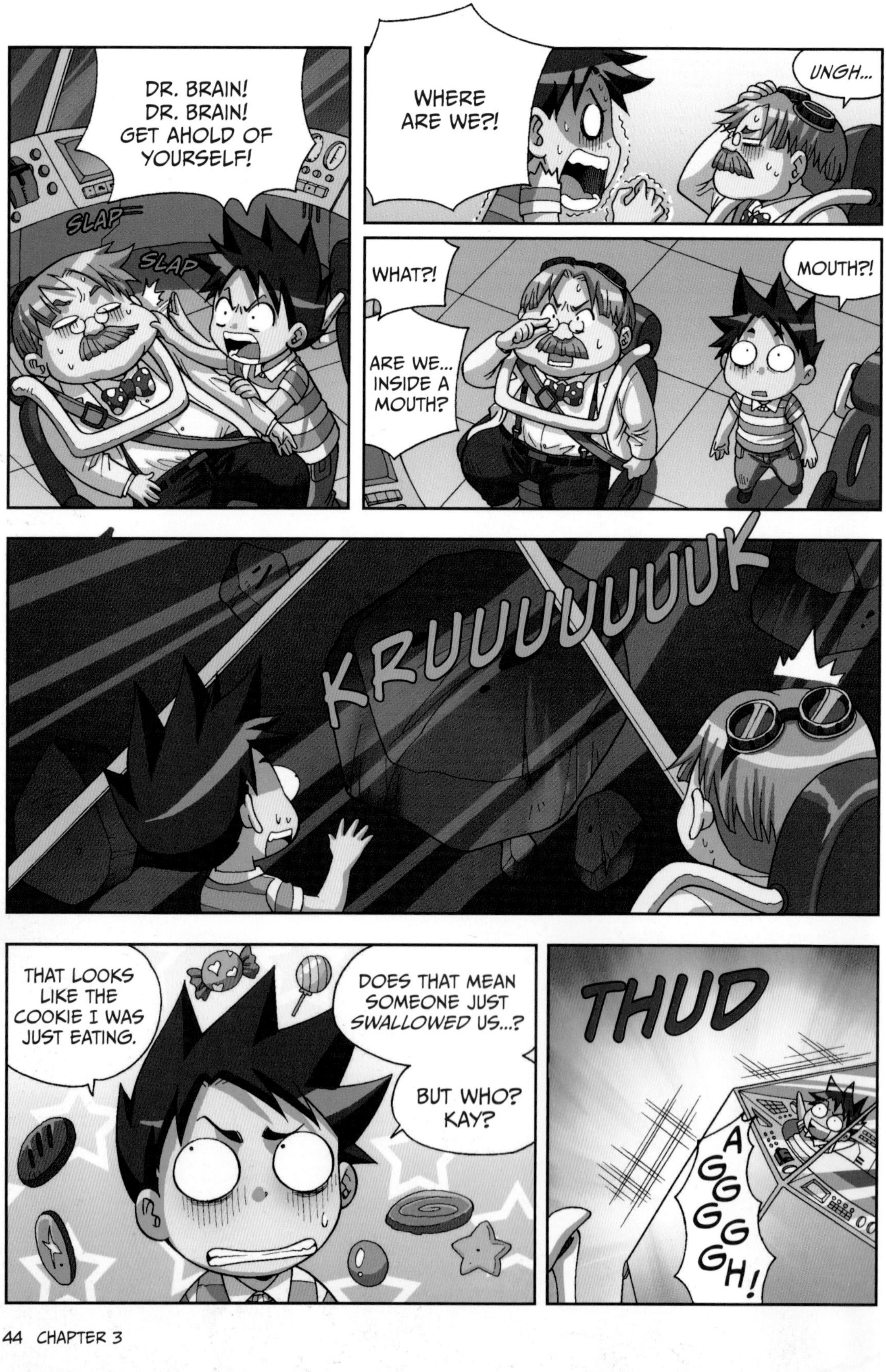
DR. BRAIN! DR. BRAIN! GET AHOLD OF YOURSELF!
SLAP
SLAP
WHERE ARE WE?!
UNGH...
WHAT?!
ARE WE... INSIDE A MOUTH?
MOUTH?!
KRUUUUUUUUK
THAT LOOKS LIKE THE COOKIE I WAS JUST EATING.
DOES THAT MEAN SOMEONE JUST SWALLOWED US...?
BUT WHO? KAY?
THUD
AGGGGH!

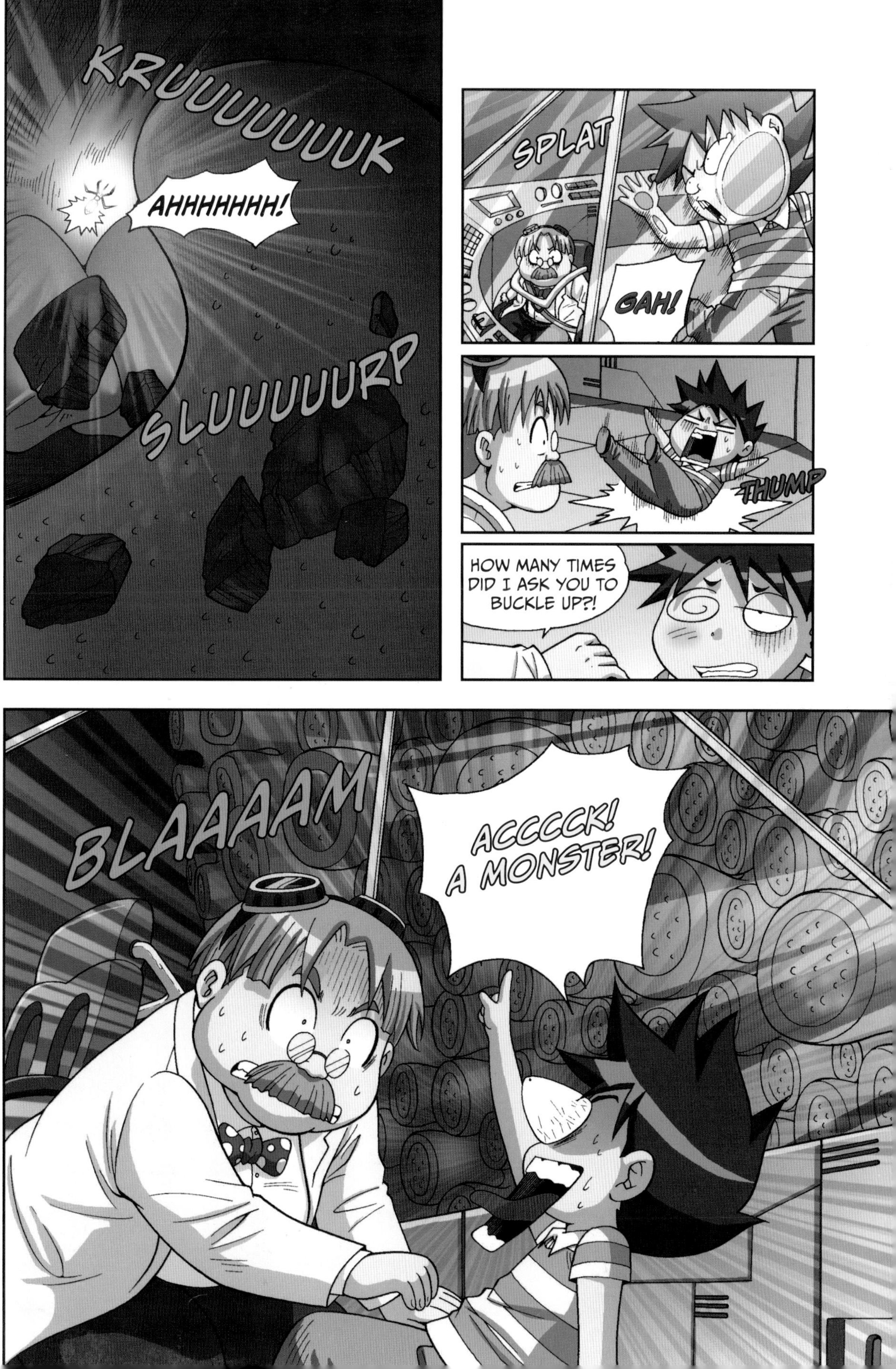
KRUUUUUUUUK
AHHHHHHH!
SLUUUUUURP
SPLAT
GAH!
THUMP
HOW MANY TIMES DID I ASK YOU TO BUCKLE UP?!
BLAAAAM
ACCCCK! A MONSTER!

PLEASE STOP SCREAMING. THAT'S NOT A MONSTER. YOU HAVE THE SAME THING INSIDE YOUR BODY TOO.

WIGGLE

WIGGLE

YOU'RE GOING TO MAKE ME GO DEAF.

THERE'S SOMETHING MONSTROUS LIKE THAT INSIDE MY BODY?

MONSTROUS? THAT'S A TONGUE! THE PART THAT'S STICKING OUT IS A TASTE BUD.

TH-THIS IS REALLY A TONGUE?

A HUMAN TONGUE HAS UP TO 10,000 TASTE BUDS, AND EACH TASTE BUD HAS ABOUT 60 TASTE CELLS. THESE TASTE CELLS LET US SENSE FLAVORS OF FOOD.

TASTE CELLS ARE ABLE TO TASTE MANY DIFFERENT FLAVORS!

TASTE BUD

CROSS SECTION OF THE TONGUE

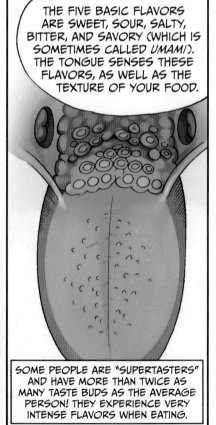

THE FIVE BASIC FLAVORS ARE SWEET, SOUR, SALTY, BITTER, AND SAVORY (WHICH IS SOMETIMES CALLED UMAMI). THE TONGUE SENSES THESE FLAVORS, AS WELL AS THE TEXTURE OF YOUR FOOD.

SOME PEOPLE ARE "SUPERTASTERS" AND HAVE MORE THAN TWICE AS MANY TASTE BUDS AS THE AVERAGE PERSON! THEY EXPERIENCE VERY INTENSE FLAVORS WHEN EATING.

I DIDN'T KNOW MY TONGUE LOOKED SO DISGUSTING...

WHAT DO YOU MEAN, DISGUSTING?

NYAH

IF YOU DIDN'T HAVE A TONGUE, YOU WOULD NEVER KNOW WHAT ANYTHING TASTES LIKE!

YOU ALSO USE YOUR TONGUE TO SPEAK.

AFTER YOUR TEETH GRIND DOWN THE FOOD IN YOUR MOUTH, THE TONGUE MIXES THE FOOD WITH SALIVA AND SENDS IT DOWN THE ESOPHAGUS.

YOUR MOUTH IS THE FIRST STEP IN THE DIGESTIVE SYSTEM. IT STARTS EVERYTHING!

W-WAIT! DID YOU JUST SAY...*DIGESTIVE* SYSTEM?

DOES THAT MEAN...

WE'RE BEING EATEN?!

YOU'RE *JUST* GETTING THAT?

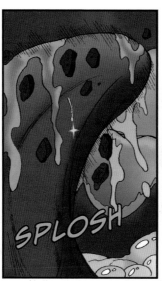

SPLOSH

AHHHHHHHH!

SHOOP

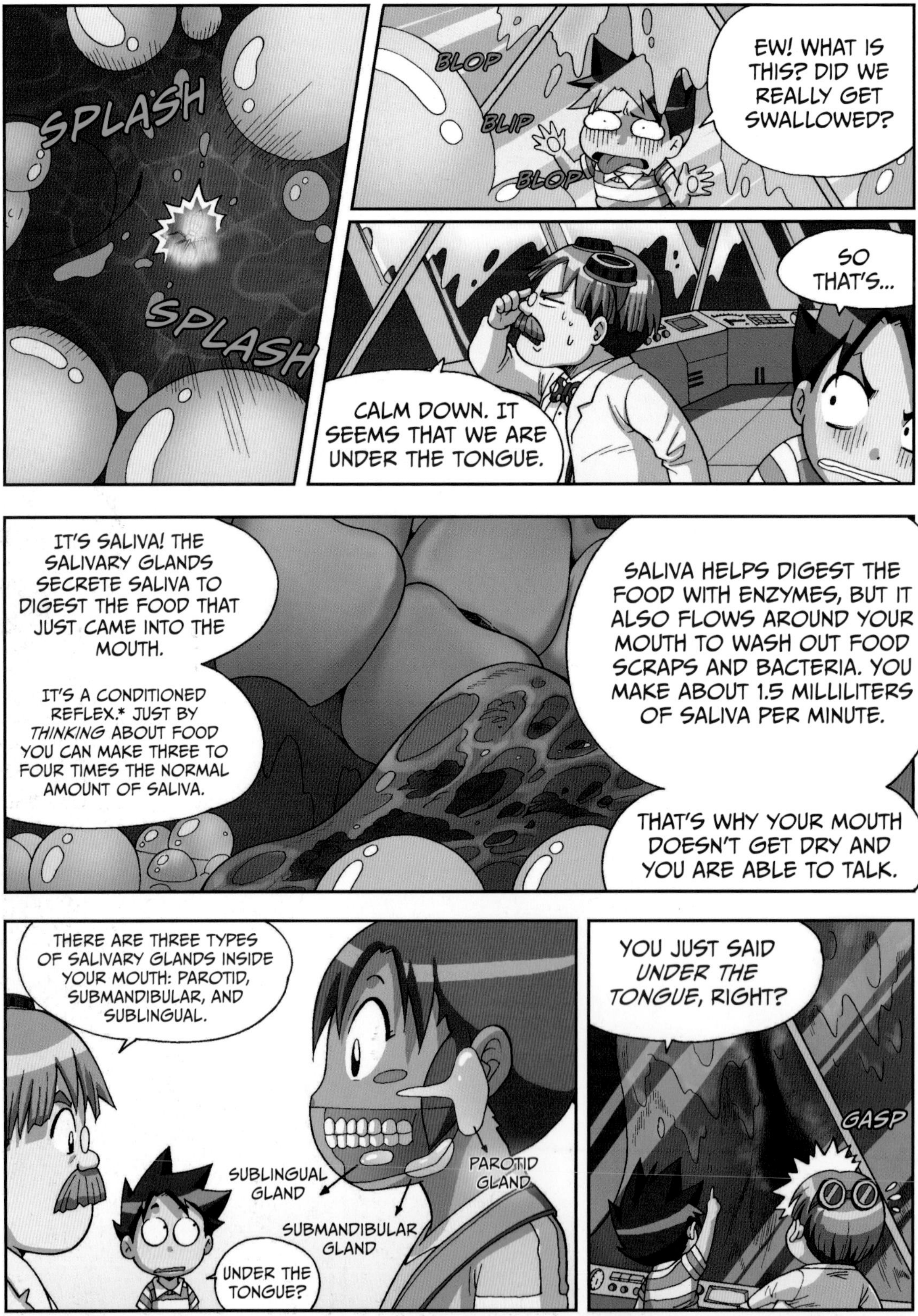
SPLASH
SPLASH
BLOP
BLIP
BLOP
EW! WHAT IS THIS? DID WE REALLY GET SWALLOWED?
SO THAT'S...
CALM DOWN. IT SEEMS THAT WE ARE UNDER THE TONGUE.
IT'S SALIVA! THE SALIVARY GLANDS SECRETE SALIVA TO DIGEST THE FOOD THAT JUST CAME INTO THE MOUTH.
IT'S A CONDITIONED REFLEX.* JUST BY *THINKING* ABOUT FOOD YOU CAN MAKE THREE TO FOUR TIMES THE NORMAL AMOUNT OF SALIVA.
SALIVA HELPS DIGEST THE FOOD WITH ENZYMES, BUT IT ALSO FLOWS AROUND YOUR MOUTH TO WASH OUT FOOD SCRAPS AND BACTERIA. YOU MAKE ABOUT 1.5 MILLILITERS OF SALIVA PER MINUTE.
THAT'S WHY YOUR MOUTH DOESN'T GET DRY AND YOU ARE ABLE TO TALK.
THERE ARE THREE TYPES OF SALIVARY GLANDS INSIDE YOUR MOUTH: PAROTID, SUBMANDIBULAR, AND SUBLINGUAL.
SUBLINGUAL GLAND
PAROTID GLAND
SUBMANDIBULAR GLAND
UNDER THE TONGUE?
YOU JUST SAID *UNDER THE TONGUE*, RIGHT?
GASP

* A CONDITIONED REFLEX IS YOUR BODY'S AUTOMATIC RESPONSE TO SOMETHING THAT HAPPENS (A STIMULUS). YOU DON'T EVEN THINK ABOUT IT.

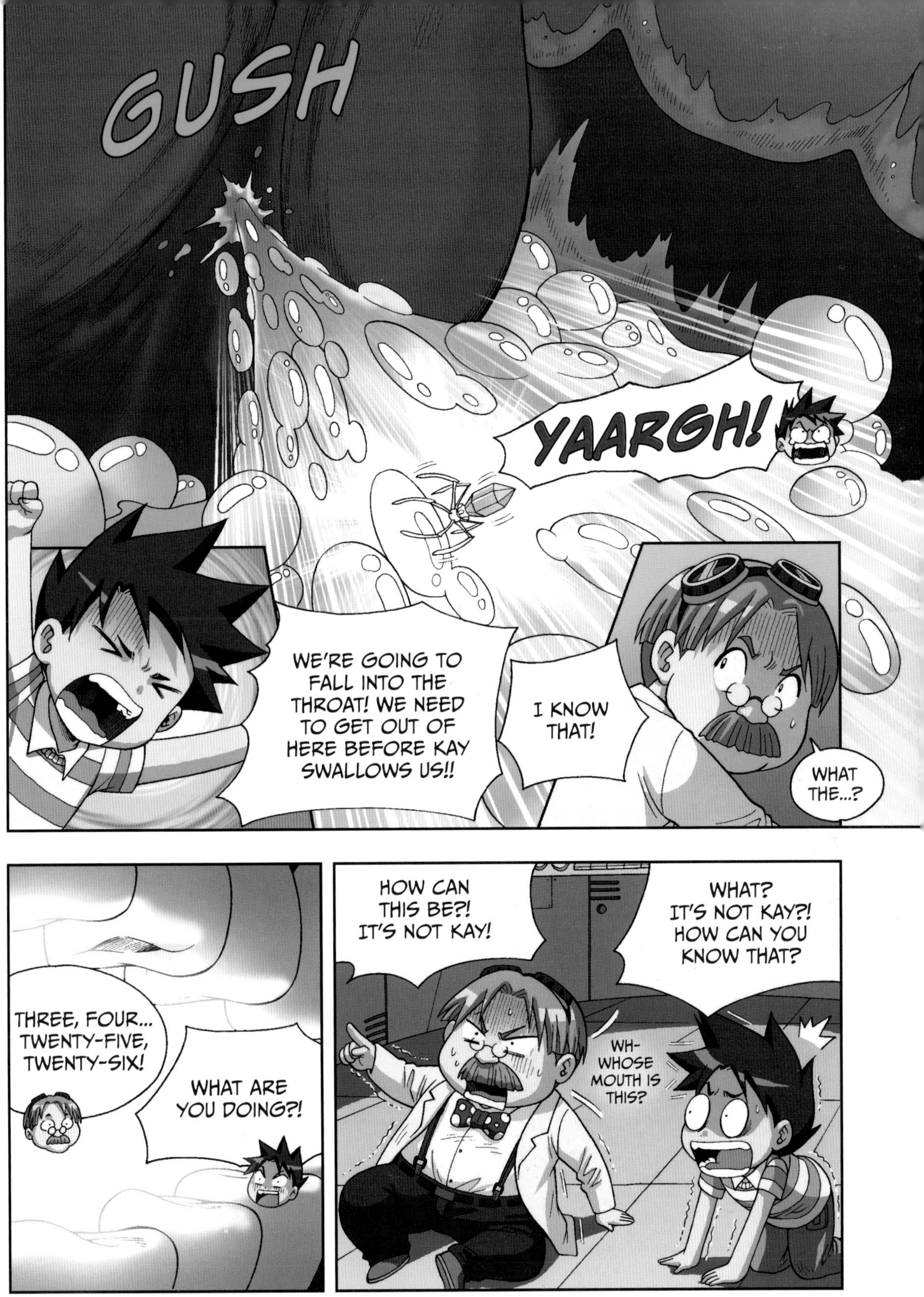
GUSH
YAARGH!
WE'RE GOING TO FALL INTO THE THROAT! WE NEED TO GET OUT OF HERE BEFORE KAY SWALLOWS US!!
I KNOW THAT!
WHAT THE...?
THREE, FOUR... TWENTY-FIVE, TWENTY-SIX!
WHAT ARE YOU DOING?!
HOW CAN THIS BE?! IT'S NOT KAY!
WHAT? IT'S NOT KAY?! HOW CAN YOU KNOW THAT?
WH-WHOSE MOUTH IS THIS?

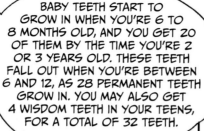

YOU GROW TWO SETS OF TEETH IN YOUR LIFE.

BABY TEETH START TO GROW IN WHEN YOU'RE 6 TO 8 MONTHS OLD, AND YOU GET 20 OF THEM BY THE TIME YOU'RE 2 OR 3 YEARS OLD. THESE TEETH FALL OUT WHEN YOU'RE BETWEEN 6 AND 12, AS 28 PERMANENT TEETH GROW IN. YOU MAY ALSO GET 4 WISDOM TEETH IN YOUR TEENS, FOR A TOTAL OF 32 TEETH.

BUT THERE ARE 26 TEETH IN THIS PERSON'S MOUTH, INCLUDING SOME SMALL PERMANENT TEETH JUST GROWING OUT OF THE GUMS.

MEANING THIS PERSON IS ONLY 6 TO 12 YEARS OLD!

6 months to 2–3 years old: 20 baby teeth

6–12 years old: 28 permanent teeth

Adult: 32 teeth including wisdom teeth

GASP

AND ANOTHER THING...

THESE TEETH ARE JUST TOO DIRTY TO BE KAY'S!

CAVITIES!

TARTAR!

THIS IS WHAT HAPPENS WHEN YOU DON'T BRUSH YOUR TEETH FOR MANY DAYS!

CHOMP CHOMP SCARF

PHOEBE!

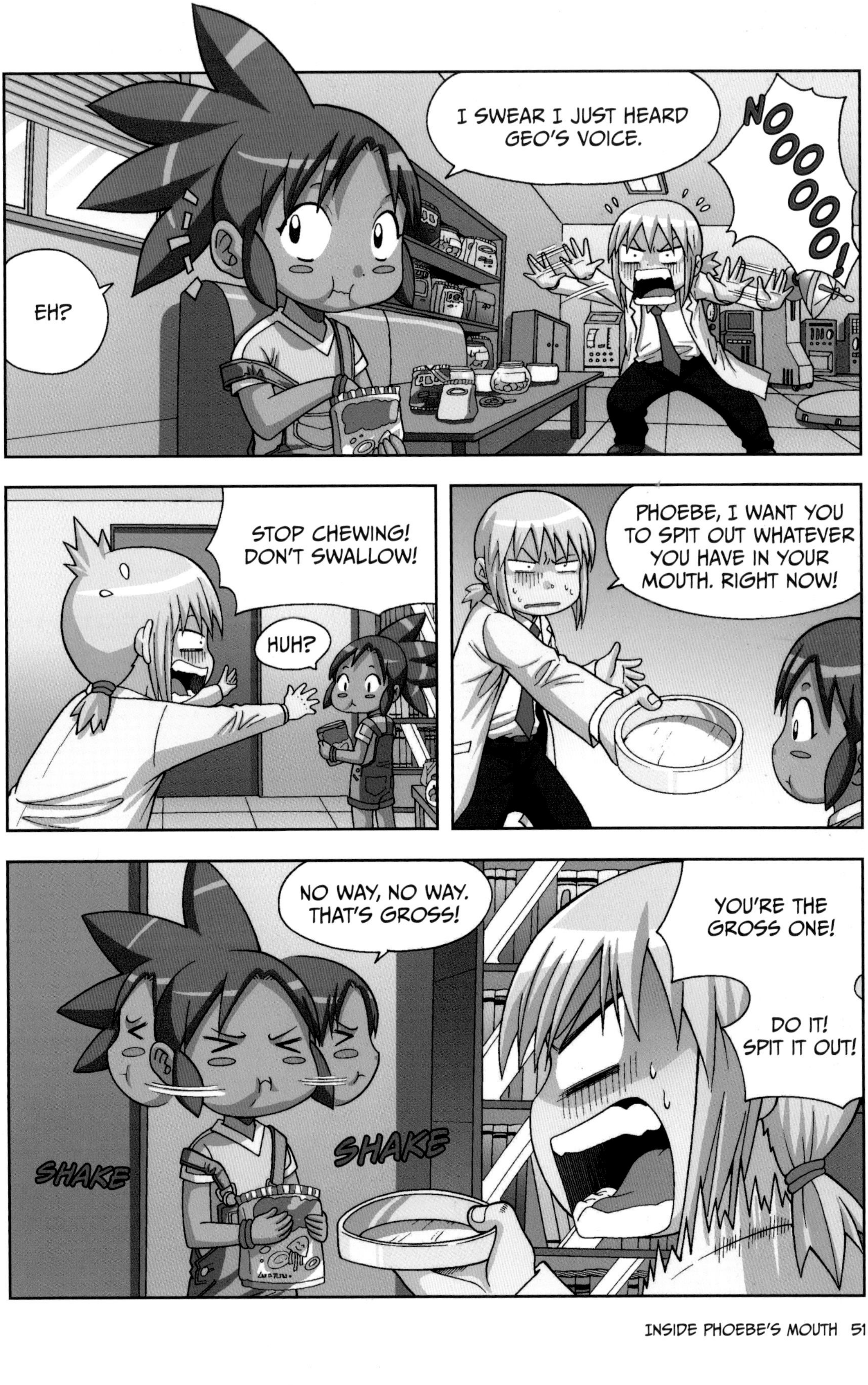
I SWEAR I JUST HEARD GEO'S VOICE.
NOOOOOO!
EH?
STOP CHEWING! DON'T SWALLOW!
HUH?
PHOEBE, I WANT YOU TO SPIT OUT WHATEVER YOU HAVE IN YOUR MOUTH. RIGHT NOW!
NO WAY, NO WAY. THAT'S GROSS!
YOU'RE THE GROSS ONE!
DO IT! SPIT IT OUT!
SHAKE
SHAKE

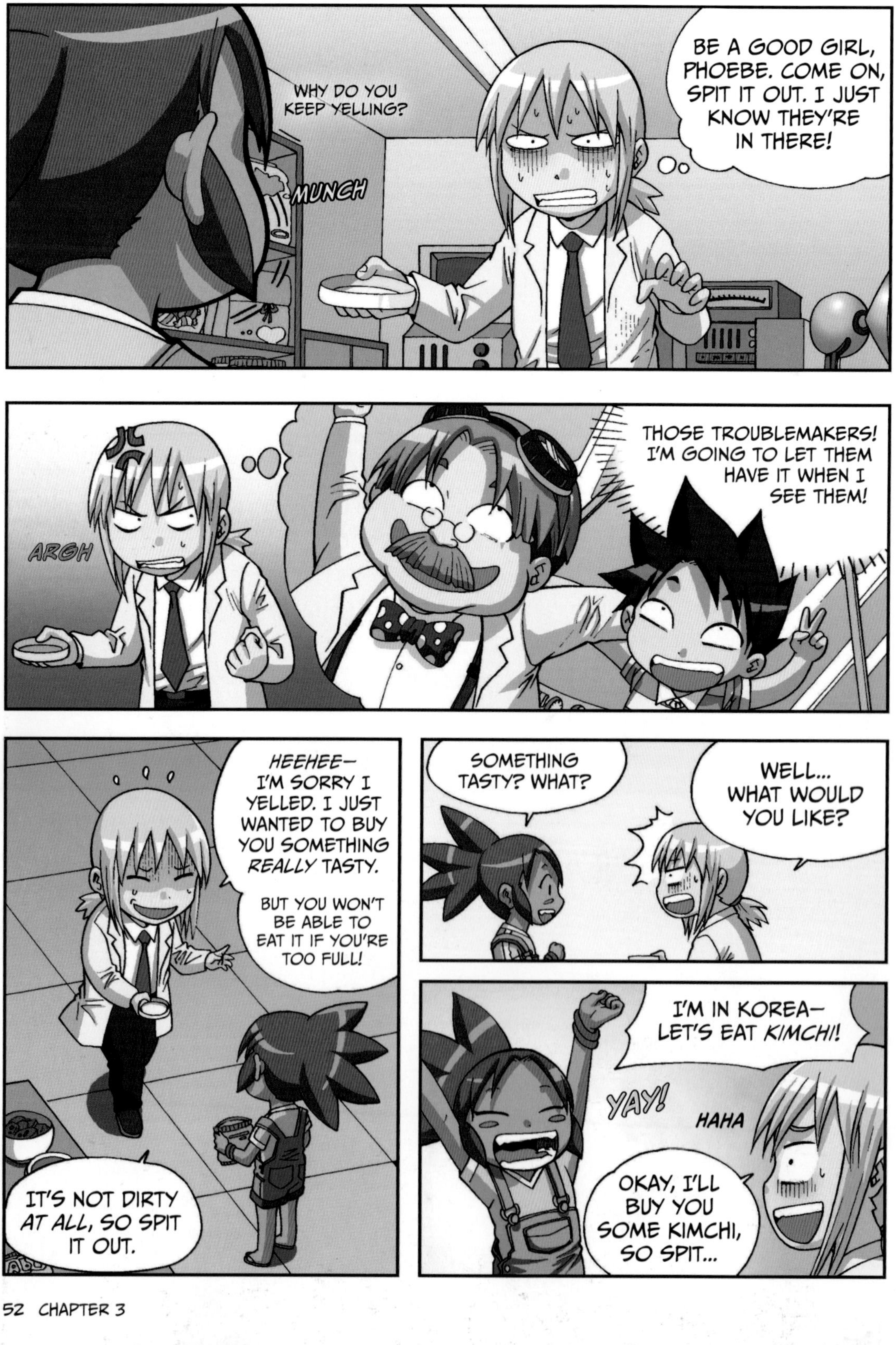
BE A GOOD GIRL, PHOEBE. COME ON, SPIT IT OUT. I JUST KNOW THEY'RE IN THERE!
WHY DO YOU KEEP YELLING?
MUNCH
THOSE TROUBLEMAKERS! I'M GOING TO LET THEM HAVE IT WHEN I SEE THEM!
ARGH
HEEHEE— I'M SORRY I YELLED. I JUST WANTED TO BUY YOU SOMETHING REALLY TASTY.
BUT YOU WON'T BE ABLE TO EAT IT IF YOU'RE TOO FULL!
IT'S NOT DIRTY AT ALL, SO SPIT IT OUT.
SOMETHING TASTY? WHAT?
WELL... WHAT WOULD YOU LIKE?
I'M IN KOREA— LET'S EAT KIMCHI!
YAY!
HAHA
OKAY, I'LL BUY YOU SOME KIMCHI, SO SPIT...

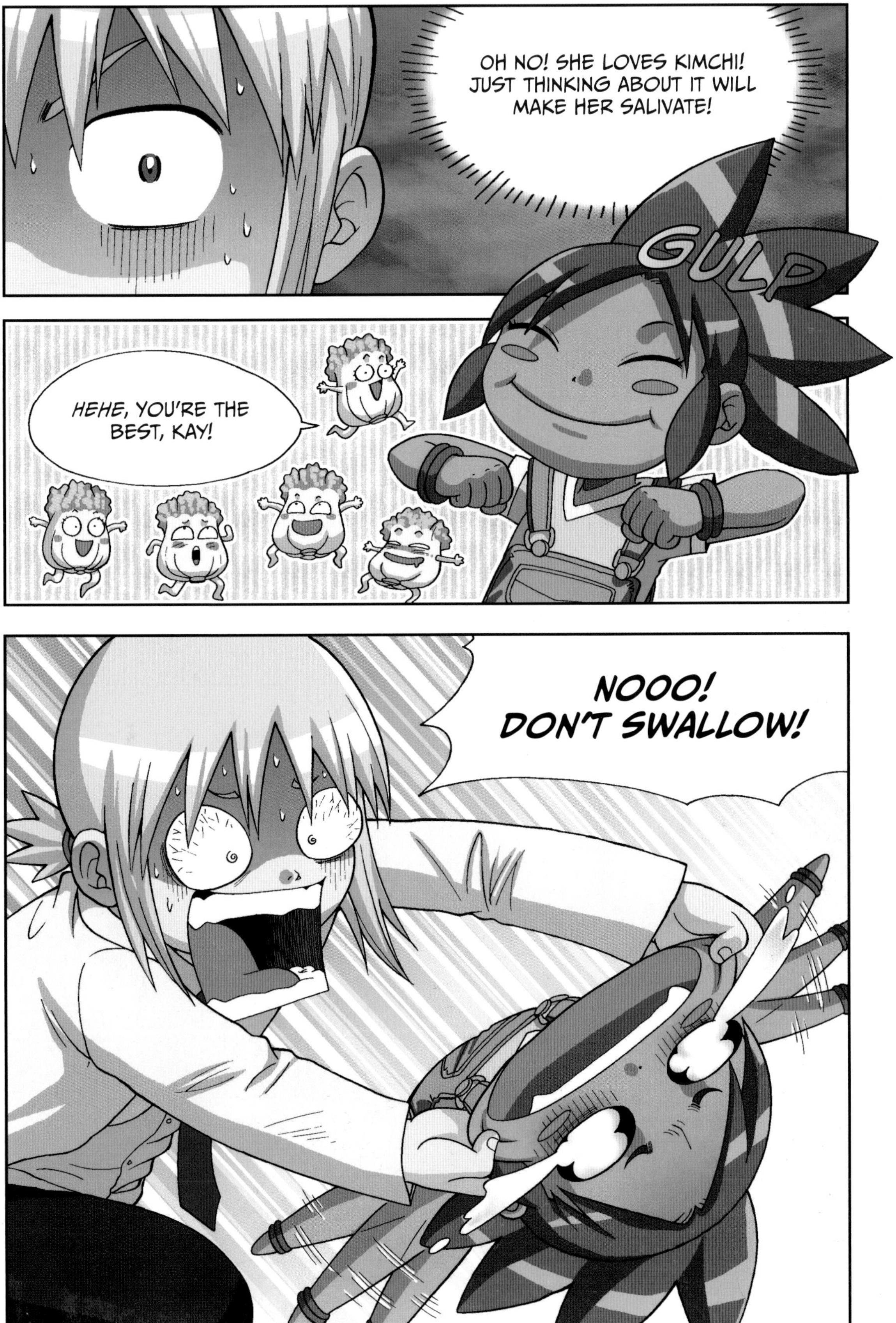
OH NO! SHE LOVES KIMCHI! JUST THINKING ABOUT IT WILL MAKE HER SALIVATE!
GULP
HEHE, YOU'RE THE BEST, KAY!
NOOO! DON'T SWALLOW!

FIRST STOP, THE MOUTH

The mouth is where digestion begins. You probably know this is where you chew your food, but your mouth has a few special tricks, too. For example, did you know that the wrinkled part of the roof your mouth—called the *palatine rugae*—stops food that hasn't been chewed from going down the throat? Let's see what else is inside your mouth.

TEETH

Made from the hardest substance in your body, your teeth chew food and grind it down. If you don't brush your teeth after you eat, food scraps and bacteria will build up and become tartar. The bacteria inside tartar make lactic acid, which can melt tooth enamel. Without this protective enamel covering, bacteria can get inside your teeth and cause cavities. Once destroyed, enamel can't be fixed. That's a good reason to brush your teeth regularly!

ENAMEL
DENTIN
GUM
DENTAL PULP (BLOOD VESSELS AND NERVES)

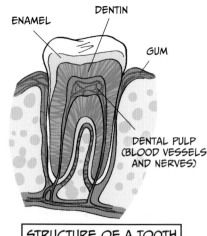

STRUCTURE OF A TOOTH

SALIVA

Located on the sides of your mouth and under your tongue, salivary glands release about 1–2 liters of saliva a day. More than 99 percent of saliva is water, and the rest is made of mucus and enzymes. Two of these enzymes, amylase and lipase, help break down starches and fats in food. Saliva keeps the inside of your mouth clean and moist, too—it washes away food scraps, bacteria, and dead cells.

PAROTID GLAND
SUBLINGUAL GLAND
SUBMANDIBULAR GLAND

SALIVARY GLAND LOCATIONS

TONGUE

Gently press the front part of your tongue with your finger, and try to swallow. You won't be able to! This is because you need your tongue to swallow—it pushes the food

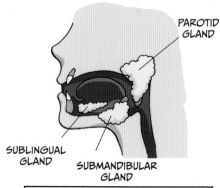

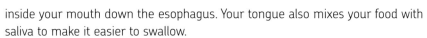

inside your mouth down the esophagus. Your tongue also mixes your food with saliva to make it easier to swallow.

The 10,000 taste buds on the top of your tongue help you to taste sweet, sour, bitter, salty, and savory flavors. You "taste" spicy foods through pain-transmitting cells in the skin of your mouth. Your tongue also senses if food is hot or cold and soft or rough.

AIIEEE! THAT'S SPICY! MY WHOLE TONGUE HURTS!!

THAT'S BECAUSE YOU TASTE SPICY FLAVORS THROUGH PAIN-TRANSMITTING CELLS.

THE RIGHT WAY TO BRUSH YOUR TEETH

❶ Start by putting your toothbrush at an angle (45 degrees) to your gums.

❸ Brush the surfaces of your teeth using short, gentle strokes.

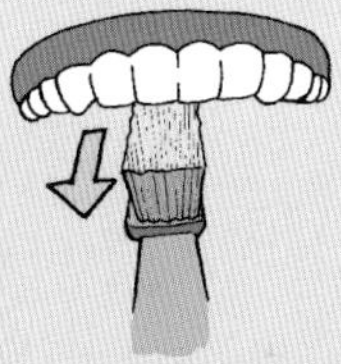

❷ Make sure you clean the inner and outer surfaces of all your teeth.

❹ Don't forget the backs of your front teeth! You can also brush the surface of your tongue from back to front. And remember to floss!

A 32-HOUR VOYAGE

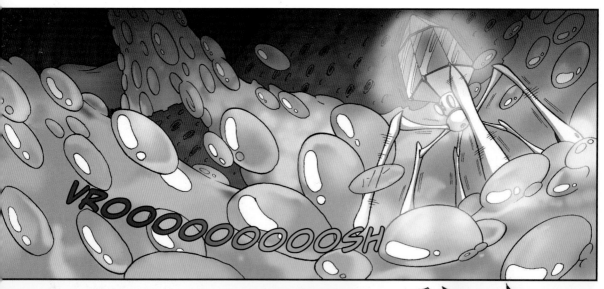

VROOOOOOOOOSH

SHOOOOOOOP

AGGGGHHH!

ACK! THE SALIVA IS RUSHING THIS WAY!

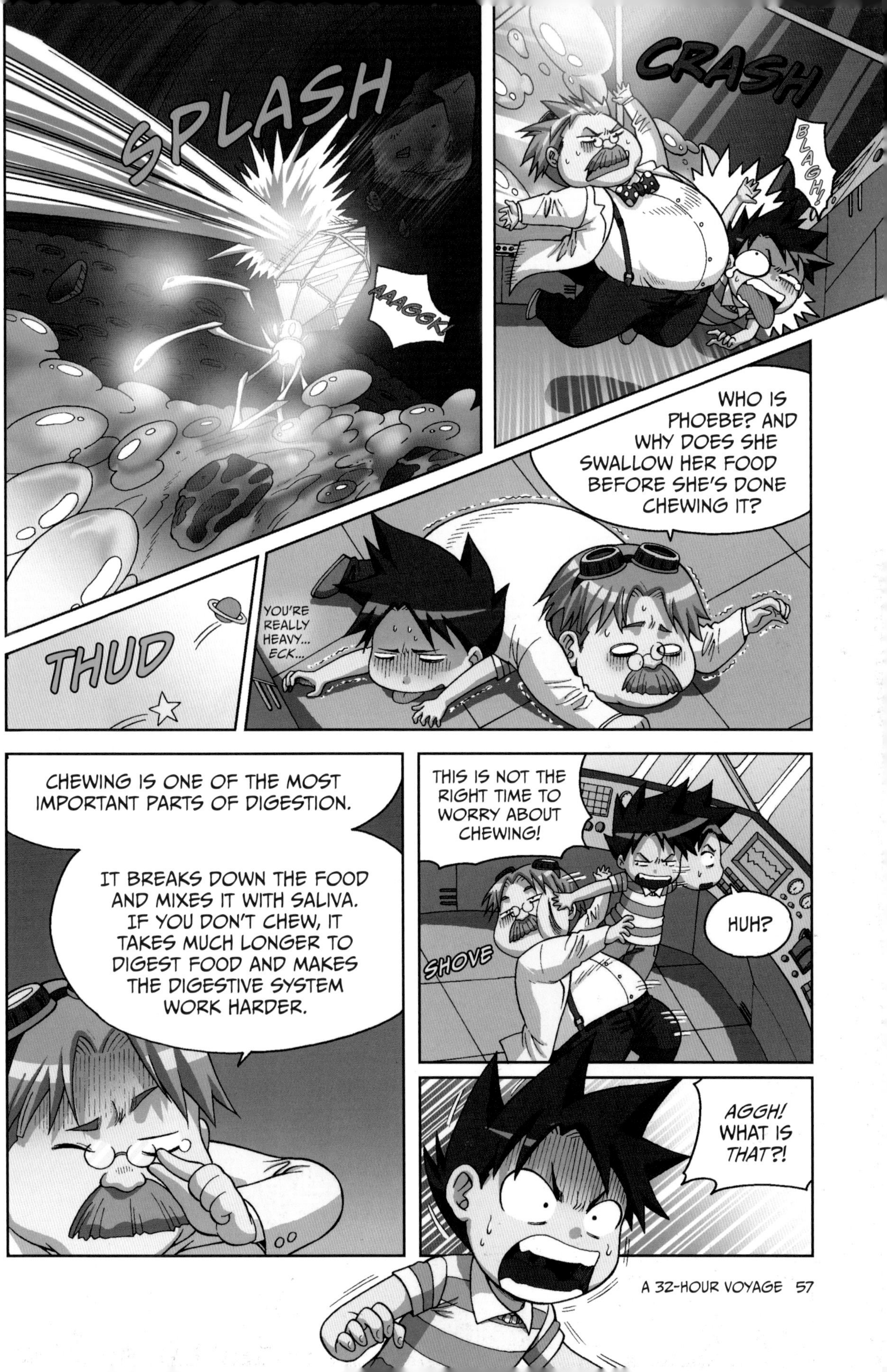
SPLASH
AAAGGK!
CRASH
BLAGH!
WHO IS PHOEBE? AND WHY DOES SHE SWALLOW HER FOOD BEFORE SHE'S DONE CHEWING IT?
THUD
YOU'RE REALLY HEAVY... ECK...
CHEWING IS ONE OF THE MOST IMPORTANT PARTS OF DIGESTION.
IT BREAKS DOWN THE FOOD AND MIXES IT WITH SALIVA. IF YOU DON'T CHEW, IT TAKES MUCH LONGER TO DIGEST FOOD AND MAKES THE DIGESTIVE SYSTEM WORK HARDER.
THIS IS NOT THE RIGHT TIME TO WORRY ABOUT CHEWING!
HUH?
SHOVE
AGGH! WHAT IS THAT?!

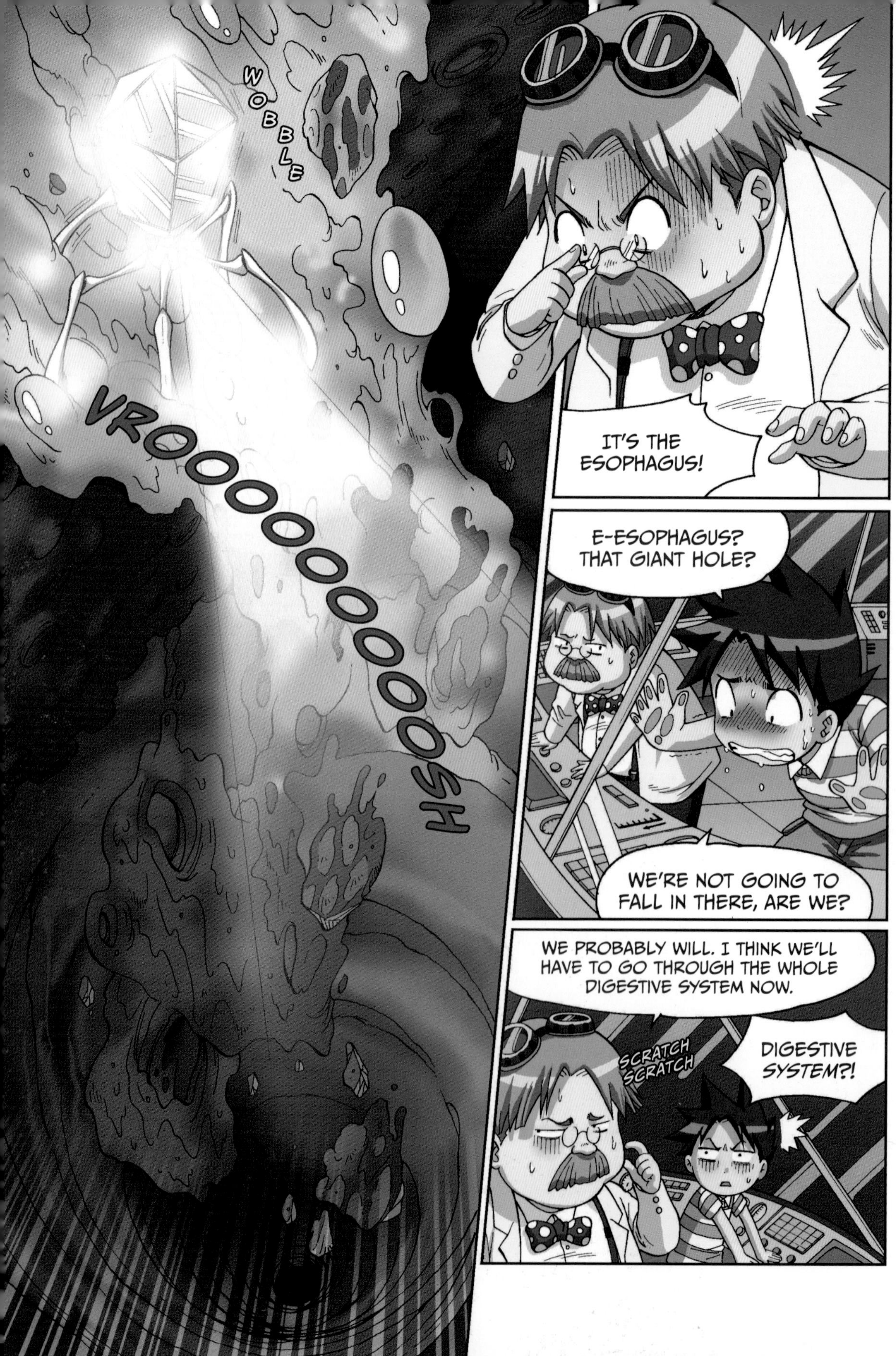
WOBBLE
VROOOOOOOOOOOOOSH
IT'S THE ESOPHAGUS!
E-ESOPHAGUS? THAT GIANT HOLE?
WE'RE NOT GOING TO FALL IN THERE, ARE WE?
WE PROBABLY WILL. I THINK WE'LL HAVE TO GO THROUGH THE WHOLE DIGESTIVE SYSTEM NOW.
SCRATCH SCRATCH
DIGESTIVE SYSTEM?!

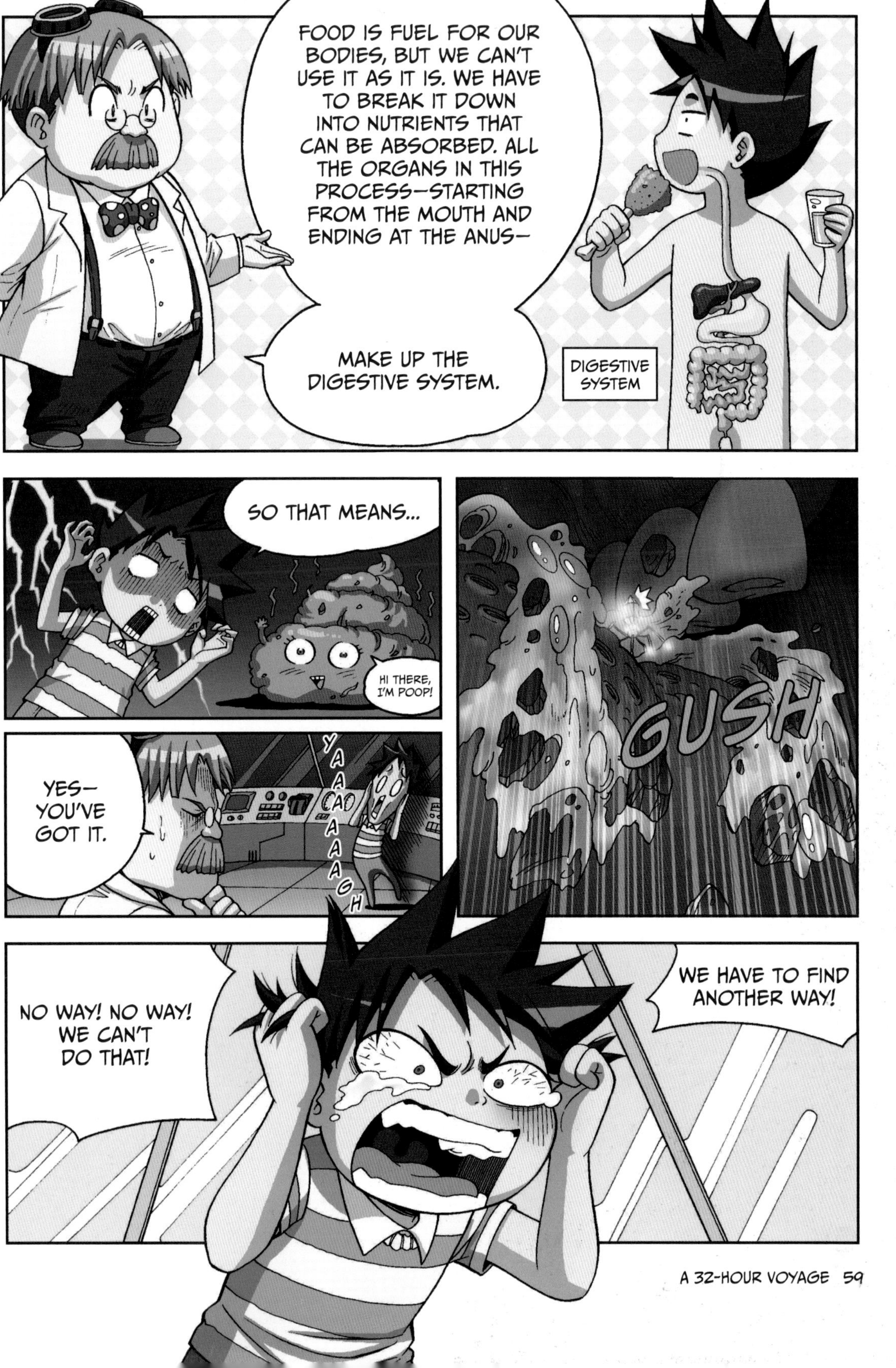

FOOD IS FUEL FOR OUR BODIES, BUT WE CAN'T USE IT AS IT IS. WE HAVE TO BREAK IT DOWN INTO NUTRIENTS THAT CAN BE ABSORBED. ALL THE ORGANS IN THIS PROCESS—STARTING FROM THE MOUTH AND ENDING AT THE ANUS—
MAKE UP THE DIGESTIVE SYSTEM.
DIGESTIVE SYSTEM
SO THAT MEANS...
HI THERE, I'M POOP!
GUSH
YES—YOU'VE GOT IT.
YAAAAAAAAAGH
NO WAY! NO WAY! WE CAN'T DO THAT!
WE HAVE TO FIND ANOTHER WAY!

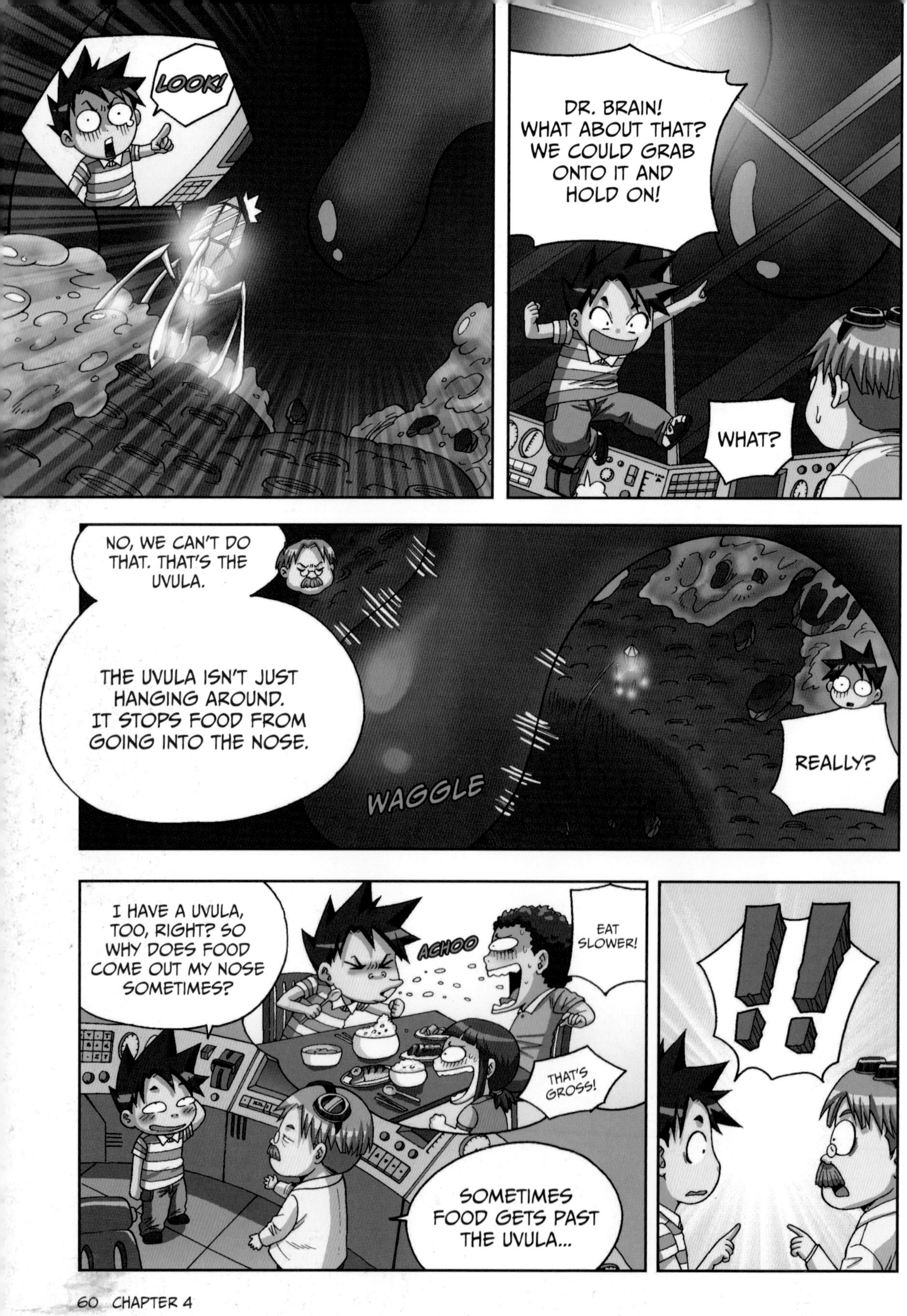

LOOK!
DR. BRAIN! WHAT ABOUT THAT? WE COULD GRAB ONTO IT AND HOLD ON!
WHAT?
NO, WE CAN'T DO THAT. THAT'S THE UVULA.
THE UVULA ISN'T JUST HANGING AROUND. IT STOPS FOOD FROM GOING INTO THE NOSE.
WAGGLE
REALLY?
I HAVE A UVULA, TOO, RIGHT? SO WHY DOES FOOD COME OUT MY NOSE SOMETIMES?
ACHOO
EAT SLOWER!
THAT'S GROSS!
SOMETIMES FOOD GETS PAST THE UVULA...
!!

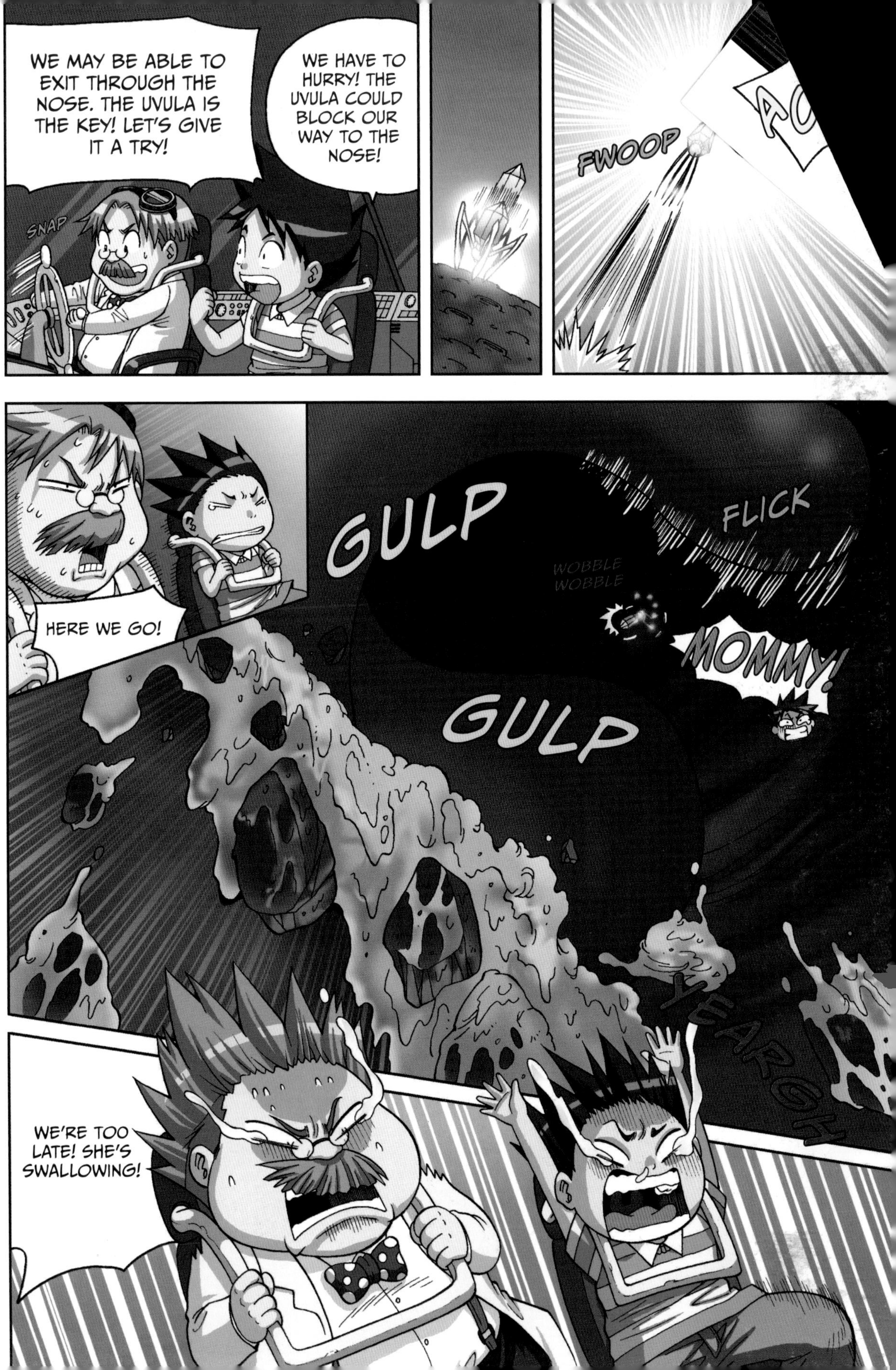
WE MAY BE ABLE TO EXIT THROUGH THE NOSE. THE UVULA IS THE KEY! LET'S GIVE IT A TRY!
WE HAVE TO HURRY! THE UVULA COULD BLOCK OUR WAY TO THE NOSE!
SNAP
FWOOP
HERE WE GO!
GULP
FLICK
WOBBLE WOBBLE
MOMMY!
GULP
YEARGH
WE'RE TOO LATE! SHE'S SWALLOWING!

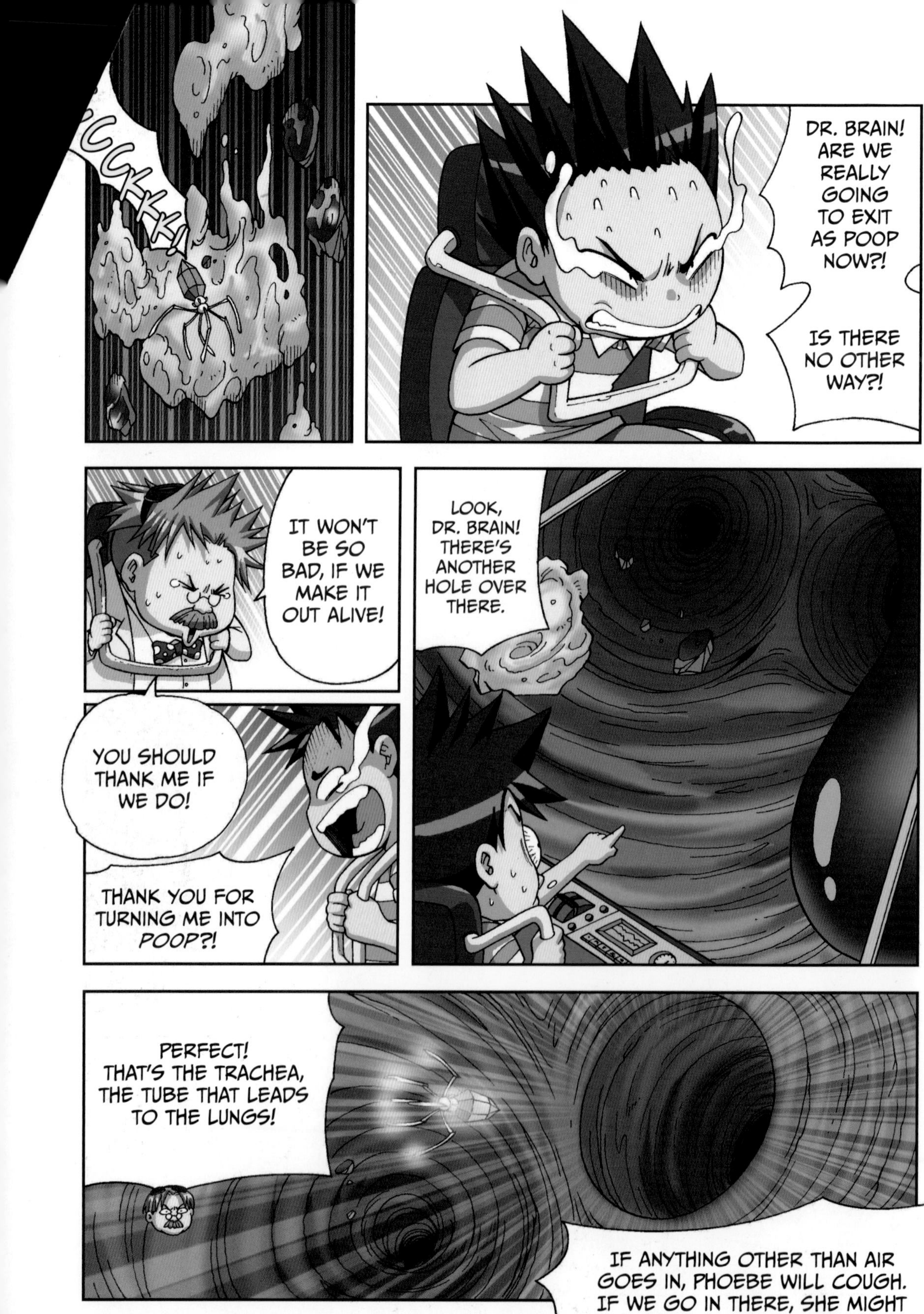
DR. BRAIN! ARE WE REALLY GOING TO EXIT AS POOP NOW?!
IS THERE NO OTHER WAY?!
IT WON'T BE SO BAD, IF WE MAKE IT OUT ALIVE!
YOU SHOULD THANK ME IF WE DO!
THANK YOU FOR TURNING ME INTO *POOP*?!
LOOK, DR. BRAIN! THERE'S ANOTHER HOLE OVER THERE.
PERFECT! THAT'S THE TRACHEA, THE TUBE THAT LEADS TO THE LUNGS!
IF ANYTHING OTHER THAN AIR GOES IN, PHOEBE WILL COUGH. IF WE GO IN THERE, SHE MIGHT SPIT US BACK OUT!

SMACK

YIPE!

IT JUST CLOSED!

OH NO! I FORGOT ABOUT THE EPIGLOTTIS!

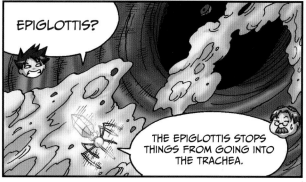

EPIGLOTTIS?

THE EPIGLOTTIS STOPS THINGS FROM GOING INTO THE TRACHEA.

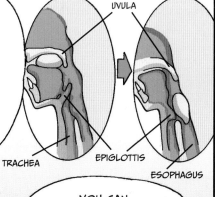

THE EPIGLOTTIS IS A LITTLE FLAP— WHEN IT'S OPEN, AIR GOES INTO THE LUNGS, BUT IT CLOSES WHEN FOOD PASSES THROUGH TO MAKE SURE THAT IT GOES INTO THE ESOPHAGUS INSTEAD.

UVULA

TRACHEA

EPIGLOTTIS

ESOPHAGUS

YOU CAN CHOKE IF FOOD GOES INTO THE TRACHEA.

YOU CHOKE WHEN THE EPIGLOTTIS CLOSES TOO LATE AND FOOD GETS INTO YOUR LUNGS.

COUGH COUGH

OH MAN, IT HURTS WHEN THAT HAPPENS...

I CAN'T DO THAT TO PHOEBE. I CAN HANDLE THE DIGESTIVE SYSTEM— I'M THE KING OF SURVIVAL!

SO HOW FAR DO WE STILL HAVE TO GO?

STAY POSITIVE!

A 32-HOUR VOYAGE 63

ABOUT 9 METERS...
WHAT?!
THAT'S IMPOSSIBLE! PHOEBE'S BARELY 1.5 METERS TALL! HOW CAN THE DIGESTIVE SYSTEM BE 9 METERS LONG?!
WHAT'S THE POINT OF EXPLAINING? YOU'LL SEE FOR YOURSELF SOON ENOUGH.
SHRUG
HOW LONG WILL IT TAKE? 50 MINUTES? A FEW HOURS?
SOB
IT TAKES ABOUT 32 HOURS TO GET FROM THE MOUTH TO THE ANUS.
TICK
TICK
TOCK
TOCK
NO
OO
32 HOURS?!

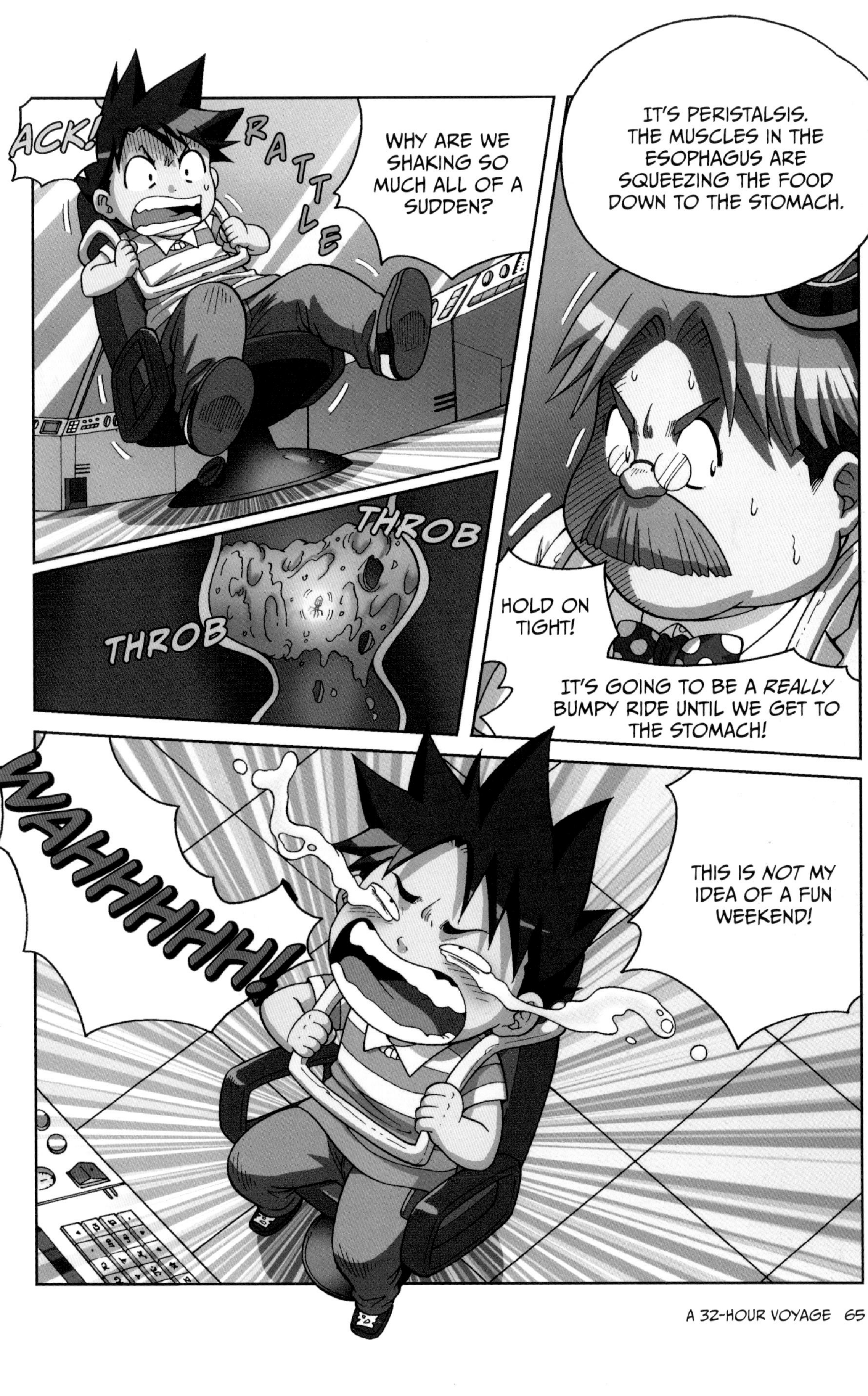
ACK!
RATTLE
WHY ARE WE SHAKING SO MUCH ALL OF A SUDDEN?
IT'S PERISTALSIS. THE MUSCLES IN THE ESOPHAGUS ARE SQUEEZING THE FOOD DOWN TO THE STOMACH.
THROB
THROB
HOLD ON TIGHT!
IT'S GOING TO BE A *REALLY* BUMPY RIDE UNTIL WE GET TO THE STOMACH!
WAHHHHHH!
THIS IS *NOT* MY IDEA OF A FUN WEEKEND!

DIGESTIVE SYSTEM

WHAT'S IN YOUR GULLET?

We use nearly 40 muscles to chew and swallow. It's a highly coordinated and complex symphony of events. Some actions in this part of digestion are deliberate, but many things happen without us even thinking about it.

PHARYNX

Your throat (or pharynx) is divided into three parts: the nasopharynx, oropharynx, and laryngopharynx. The nasopharynx is the top part of the pharynx that goes from your nose to the back of your mouth. This passage is where air travels when you breathe through your nose. The oropharynx, right below the nasopharynx, is near your mouth. Both food and air travel through this part of the pharynx. The nasopharynx and oropharynx meet at the laryngopharynx. Next, the pharynx splits into two passages: one tube for food called the *esophagus* and one for air called the *trachea*.

OROPHARYNX
NASOPHARYNX
LARYNGOPHARYNX
ESOPHAGUS
EPIGLOTTIS
TRACHEA

STRUCTURE OF THE THROAT

TONSILS

The tonsils are on both sides of the throat—you can see them in the mirror when you open your mouth wide. Sometimes when you catch a cold or get a fever, they swell up and you get a sore throat. Your tonsils are the first line of defense for stopping harmful bacteria in your food or in the air. That's why they get inflamed when bacteria or viruses enter the body. The pain is a sign that your tonsils are doing their job correctly!

PALATE (ROOF OF MOUTH)
UVULA
TONSIL
TONGUE

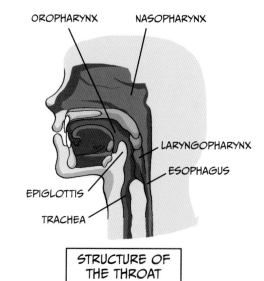

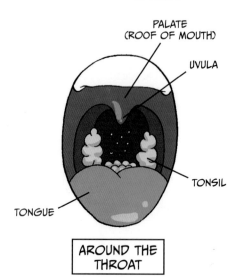

AROUND THE THROAT

Tonsillectomies (the removal of the tonsils) are the most common surgical procedure for children. This surgery becomes necessary when the swollen tonsils make breathing or swallowing difficult. Tonsillitis (an inflammation of the tonsils) that keeps coming back can also prompt the surgery.

UVULA AND EPIGLOTTIS

Your uvula is the small, fingerlike part at the back of your mouth. You can see it dangling when you open your mouth wide. Near the uvula, there is a tube that runs from your nose to your mouth. The uvula stops any food or drinks from getting in that tube and going into your nose. It doesn't happen too often, but food can come out your nose if you eat too quickly.

Your epiglottis is a flap that covers the trachea. Most of the time, it's open and lets air go into the trachea as you breathe, but it closes to block any food from going into the lungs as you swallow. We don't feel it, but we take a quick breath when we swallow. If food goes into the trachea because the epiglottis wasn't fast enough, you'll cough and try to spit it out. This is what happens when we say, "Food went down the wrong pipe."

ESOPHAGUS

Your esophagus uses its muscles, starting from the top, to push food down to the stomach—this kind of movement is called *peristalsis*. Peristalsis is very strong. It can send food down to the stomach even when you are upside down.

CAN YOU REALLY SWALLOW UPSIDE DOWN?
DON'T WORRY—THE ESOPHAGUS WILL TAKE CARE OF THAT!

THE TERROR OF THE STOMACH ACID

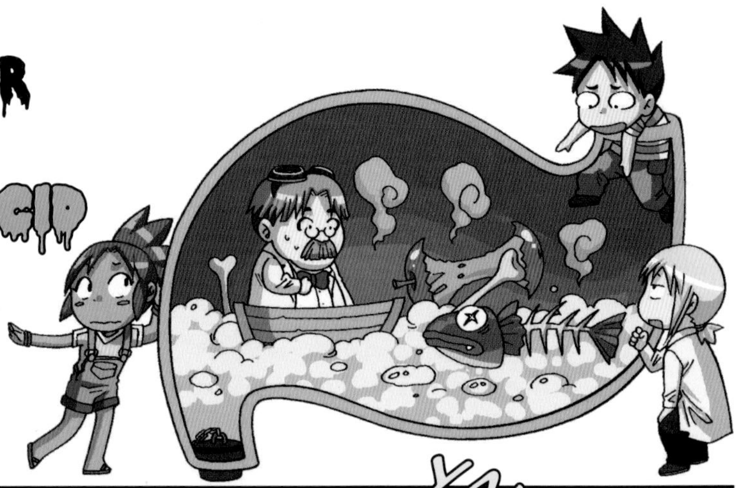

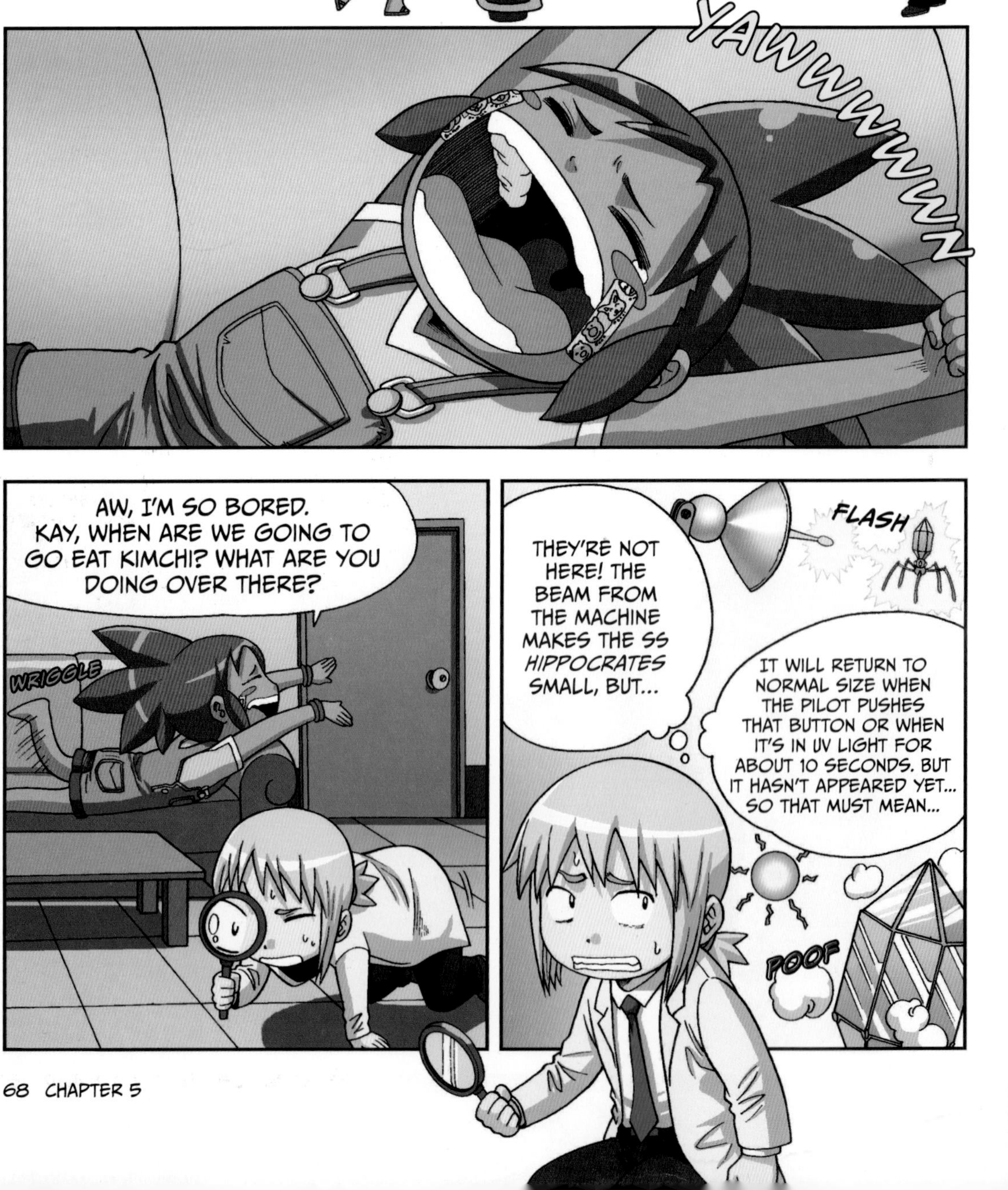

YAWWWWWWN
AW, I'M SO BORED. KAY, WHEN ARE WE GOING TO GO EAT KIMCHI? WHAT ARE YOU DOING OVER THERE?
WRIGGLE
THEY'RE NOT HERE! THE BEAM FROM THE MACHINE MAKES THE SS *HIPPOCRATES* SMALL, BUT...
FLASH
IT WILL RETURN TO NORMAL SIZE WHEN THE PILOT PUSHES THAT BUTTON OR WHEN IT'S IN UV LIGHT FOR ABOUT 10 SECONDS. BUT IT HASN'T APPEARED YET... SO THAT MUST MEAN...
POOF

COME ON, I'M SO BORED! WHERE IS GEO?!
GRRRRRR
YOU ATE HIM!
WHAT DO I DO NOW? SHOULD I TELL PHOEBE?
BLEARGH!
GEO IS INSIDE ME?!
NO, NO, NO. MAYBE I SHOULD REPORT IT TO OUR BOSS...
SHAKE SHAKE
THUMP
YOU EXPERIMENTED WITHOUT PERMISSION?! YOU'RE BOTH FIRED!
WHY ME? WHY DO THESE THINGS HAPPEN TO ME?
AND IF THEY THINK WE EXPERIMENTED ON HUMANS...
NO! NO!
IT'S NOT MY FAULT! SHE ATE THEM ALL BY HERSELF!
NEVER!
Medical Association
HUMAN RIGHTS
DOOM

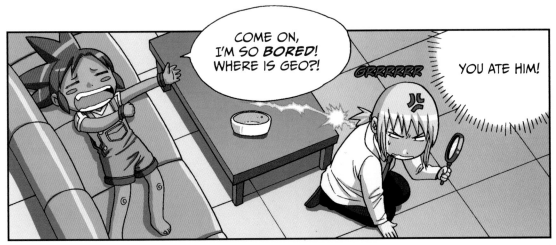

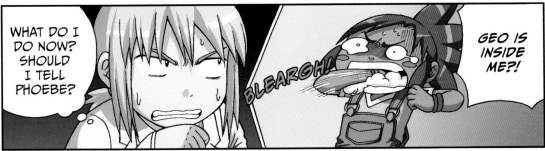

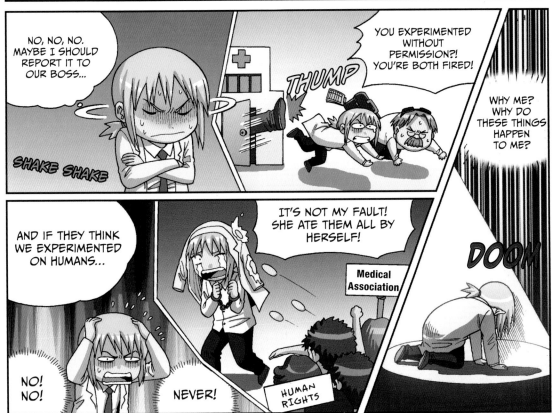

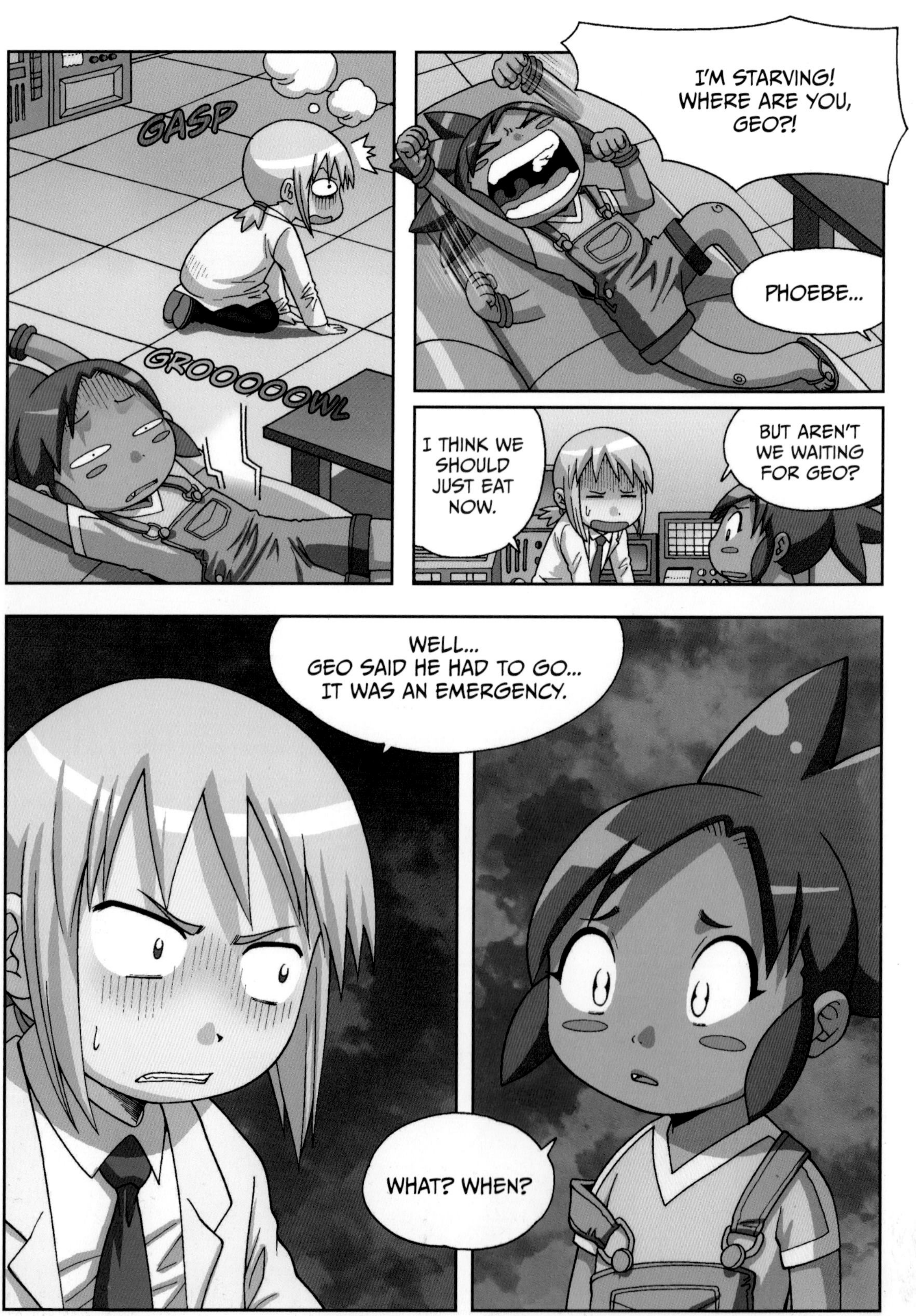
GASP
GROOOOOOWL
I'M STARVING! WHERE ARE YOU, GEO?!
PHOEBE...
BUT AREN'T WE WAITING FOR GEO?
I THINK WE SHOULD JUST EAT NOW.
WELL... GEO SAID HE HAD TO GO... IT WAS AN EMERGENCY.
WHAT? WHEN?

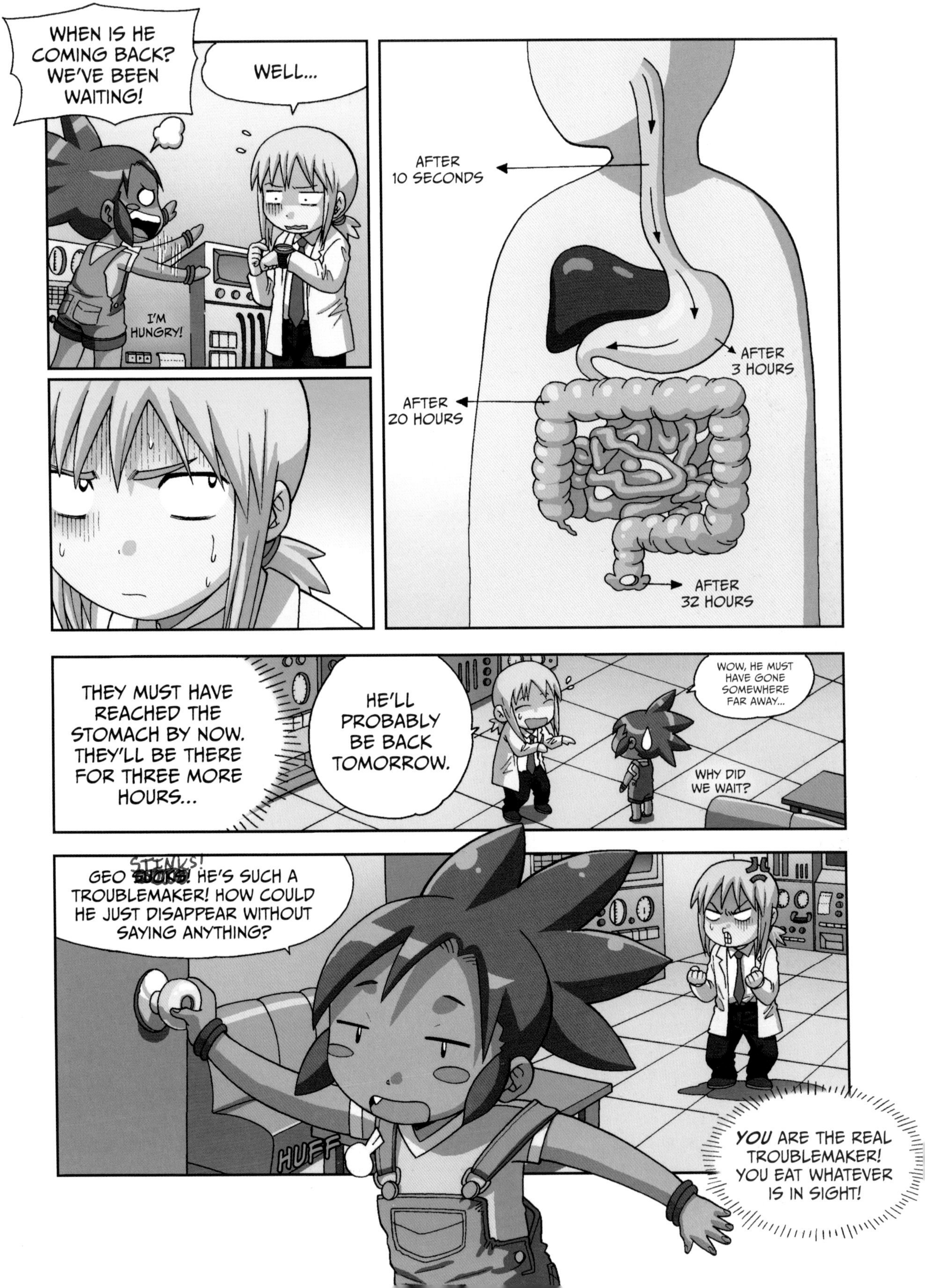
WHEN IS HE COMING BACK? WE'VE BEEN WAITING!
WELL...
I'M HUNGRY!
AFTER 10 SECONDS
AFTER 3 HOURS
AFTER 20 HOURS
AFTER 32 HOURS
THEY MUST HAVE REACHED THE STOMACH BY NOW. THEY'LL BE THERE FOR THREE MORE HOURS...
HE'LL PROBABLY BE BACK TOMORROW.
WOW, HE MUST HAVE GONE SOMEWHERE FAR AWAY...
WHY DID WE WAIT?
GEO ~~SUCKS~~ STINKS! HE'S SUCH A TROUBLEMAKER! HOW COULD HE JUST DISAPPEAR WITHOUT SAYING ANYTHING?
HUFF
YOU ARE THE REAL TROUBLEMAKER! YOU EAT WHATEVER IS IN SIGHT!

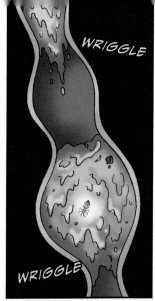

WRIGGLE

WRIGGLE

PHOEBE PROBABLY HAS NO IDEA WE'RE IN HERE, HUH?

SIGH

THUD

WHAT IS THAT?

I THINK WE'VE ARRIVED AT THE CARDIA. IT'S THE ENTRANCE TO THE STOMACH.

CARDIA?

CARDIA

PYLORUS

IT'S LIKE A DOOR TO THE STOMACH. IT'S USUALLY CLOSED, BUT IT OPENS FOR FOOD.

THE STOMACH HAS A DOOR?

BUT THE FOOD ALREADY CAN'T GET INTO THE NOSE OR TRACHEA.

FWAP

FWAP

STOMACH

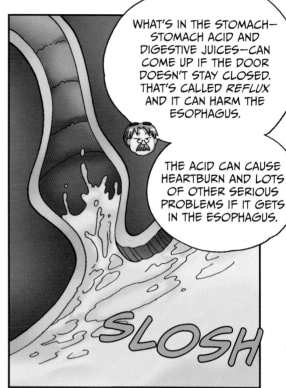

WHAT'S IN THE STOMACH— STOMACH ACID AND DIGESTIVE JUICES—CAN COME UP IF THE DOOR DOESN'T STAY CLOSED. THAT'S CALLED *REFLUX* AND IT CAN HARM THE ESOPHAGUS.

THE ACID CAN CAUSE HEARTBURN AND LOTS OF OTHER SERIOUS PROBLEMS IF IT GETS IN THE ESOPHAGUS.

SLOSH

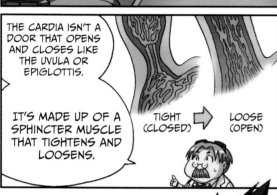

THE CARDIA ISN'T A DOOR THAT OPENS AND CLOSES LIKE THE UVULA OR EPIGLOTTIS.

IT'S MADE UP OF A SPHINCTER MUSCLE THAT TIGHTENS AND LOOSENS.

TIGHT (CLOSED)

LOOSE (OPEN)

ACID? LIKE WHAT WE USE TO MELT METAL IN CHEMISTRY EXPERIMENTS?

PSSSSSSST

THAT'S RIGHT! THE JUICE IN YOUR STOMACH IS A VERY STRONG ACID. IT STERILIZES FOOD BY KILLING BACTERIA.

WAIT!

WON'T THE *HIPPOCRATES* MELT WHEN IT TOUCHES THE STOMACH ACID?!

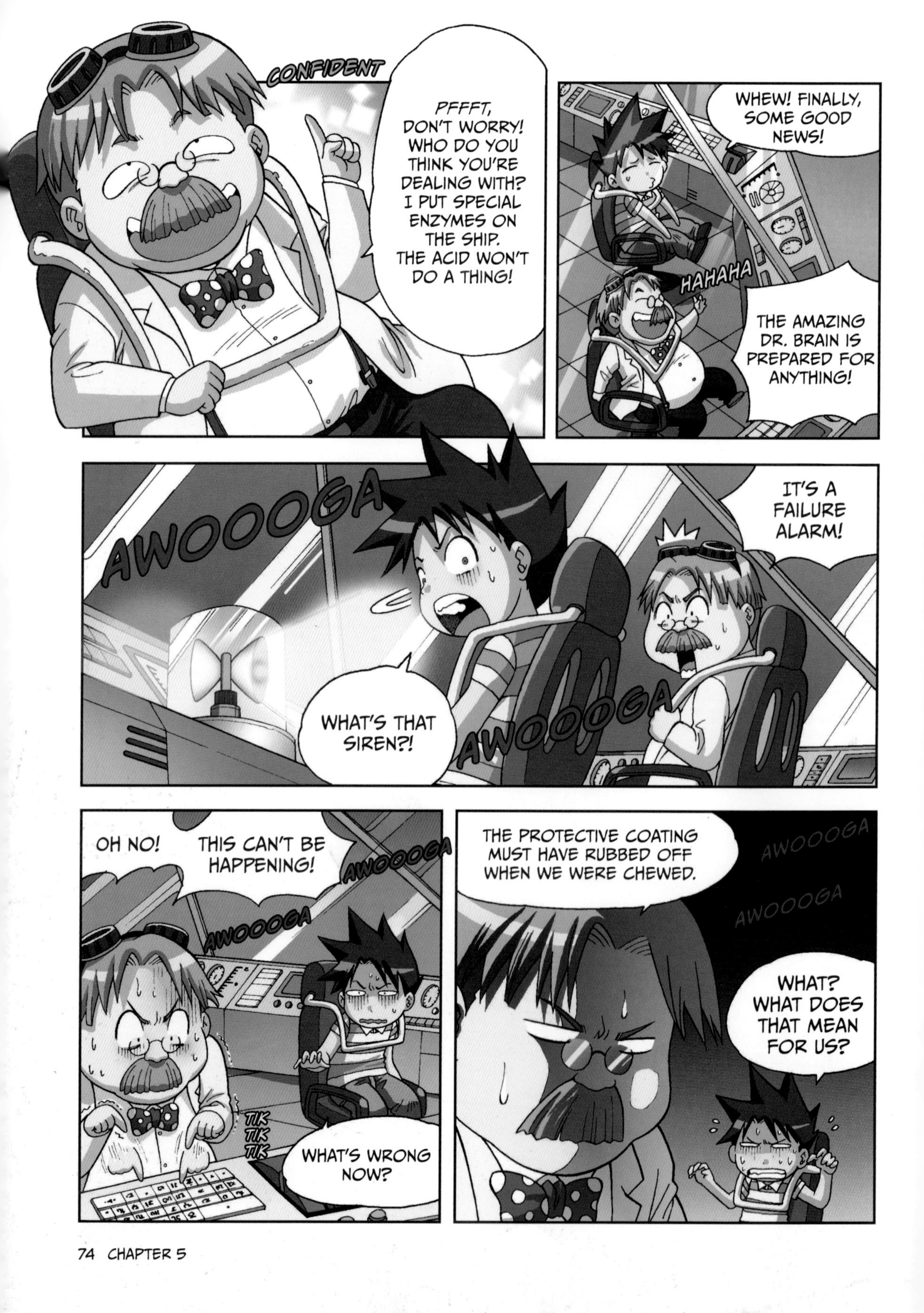
CONFIDENT
PFFFT, DON'T WORRY! WHO DO YOU THINK YOU'RE DEALING WITH? I PUT SPECIAL ENZYMES ON THE SHIP. THE ACID WON'T DO A THING!
WHEW! FINALLY, SOME GOOD NEWS!
HAHAHA
THE AMAZING DR. BRAIN IS PREPARED FOR ANYTHING!
AWOOOGA
WHAT'S THAT SIREN?!
AWOOOGA
IT'S A FAILURE ALARM!
OH NO!
THIS CAN'T BE HAPPENING!
AWOOOGA
AWOOOGA
TIK TIK TIK
WHAT'S WRONG NOW?
THE PROTECTIVE COATING MUST HAVE RUBBED OFF WHEN WE WERE CHEWED.
AWOOOGA
AWOOOGA
WHAT? WHAT DOES THAT MEAN FOR US?

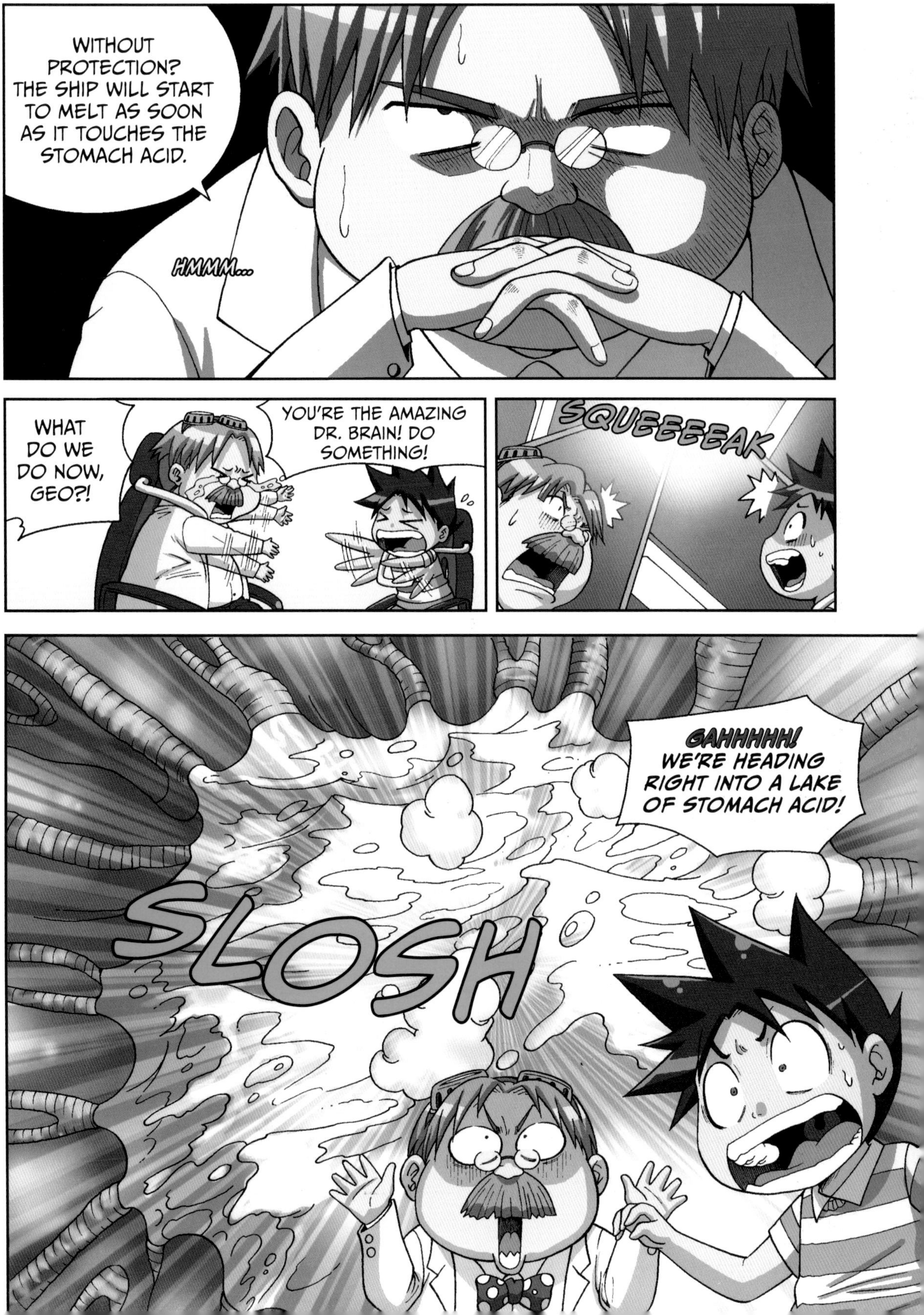
WITHOUT PROTECTION? THE SHIP WILL START TO MELT AS SOON AS IT TOUCHES THE STOMACH ACID.
HMMM...
WHAT DO WE DO NOW, GEO?!
YOU'RE THE AMAZING DR. BRAIN! DO SOMETHING!
SQUEEEEEAK
GAHHHHH! WE'RE HEADING RIGHT INTO A LAKE OF STOMACH ACID!
SLOSH

DIGESTIVE SYSTEM

WHAT'S A SPHINCTER GOOD FOR?

The food that you've swallowed moves down the esophagus and then travels through the stomach, small intestine, and large intestine—in that order. Your body absorbs nutrients from the food as it travels along this path. The leftover food scraps exit the body as feces, or waste. If any food moves backward along the path or moves forward too quickly, the digestive system goes into chaos. To prevent this from happening, our body has doors between the digestive organs—called *sphincters*.

ESOPHAGUS
CARDIA
PYLORUS
STOMACH
LARGE INTESTINE
SMALL INTESTINE
ILEOCECAL VALVE
ANUS

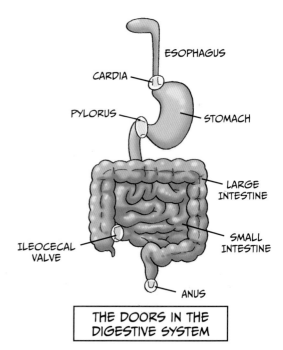

THE DOORS IN THE DIGESTIVE SYSTEM

DOORS IN THE DIGESTIVE SYSTEM

A sphincter is a ring-shaped muscle that loosens and tightens to open and close the pathways between organs. There are about 40 sphincter muscles in the body, and they keep food moving through the digestive system in the right direction and at the right time. The best-known sphincters in our bodies must be the two at the anus, which we use to empty our bowels (to poop). It would be a real disaster if any of our sphincter muscles didn't work!

CARDIA, THE ENTRANCE TO THE STOMACH

The cardia (and its partner sphincter, the lower esophageal sphincter) is near where the esophagus meets the stomach. If the cardia weakens or doesn't close the whole way, whatever is in your stomach will come back up the esophagus, including some stomach acid. The acid might leave a bitter taste in your mouth, and it can also hurt your esophagus and make it swell. When that happens, it feels like your chest is burning. This is called *heartburn*, or *reflux esophagitis*.

To prevent heartburn, it's best to not eat too much or the wrong kinds of food. Avoid food with caffeine, like cola and chocolate, and try not to eat greasy food or eat late at night.

PYLORUS, THE EXIT FROM THE STOMACH

The pylorus is the door between your stomach and the small intestine. This sphincter muscle holds food in your stomach and gives you enough time to completely digest your food. The pylorus also shuts tightly when you vomit so that only what's in your stomach comes out.

ILEOCECAL VALVE, THE EXIT FROM THE SMALL INTESTINE

The ileocecal valve is the sphincter muscle between your small intestine and large intestine. You can find it where the ileum (the last part of your small intestine) and the appendix (the beginning of your large intestine) meet. The valve keeps food scraps in the large intestine from going back into the small intestine. This way, bacteria from the large intestine can't get into the small intestine and make you sick.

ANUS

There are two sphincters in the anus, and they help you get rid of feces, the food scraps in the rectum delivered by the large intestine. One is the internal anal sphincter (inside the body). The other is the external anal sphincter (outside of the body). When the rectum is full, the internal anal sphincter opens. This is when you feel like you have to go to the bathroom. It's called the *defecation reflex*. When we are babies (under two years old), we poop whenever the defecation reflex happens. When we are older, we can decide when to go by controlling the external anal sphincter.

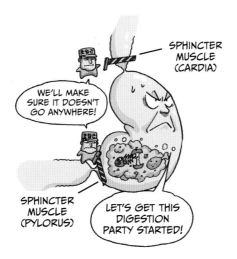

SPHINCTER MUSCLE (CARDIA)

WE'LL MAKE SURE IT DOESN'T GO ANYWHERE!

SPHINCTER MUSCLE (PYLORUS)

LET'S GET THIS DIGESTION PARTY STARTED!

HELICOBACTER PYLORI

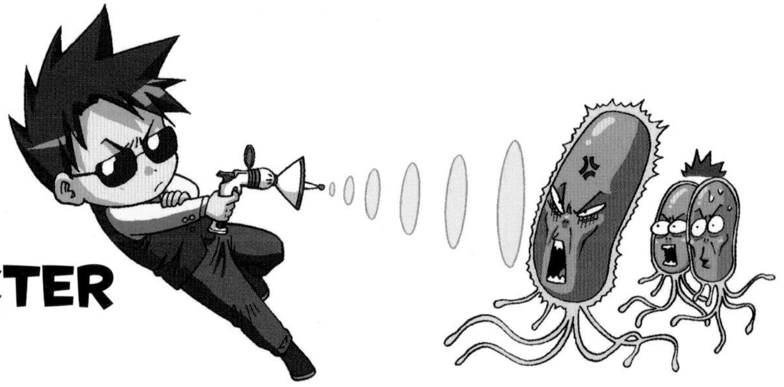

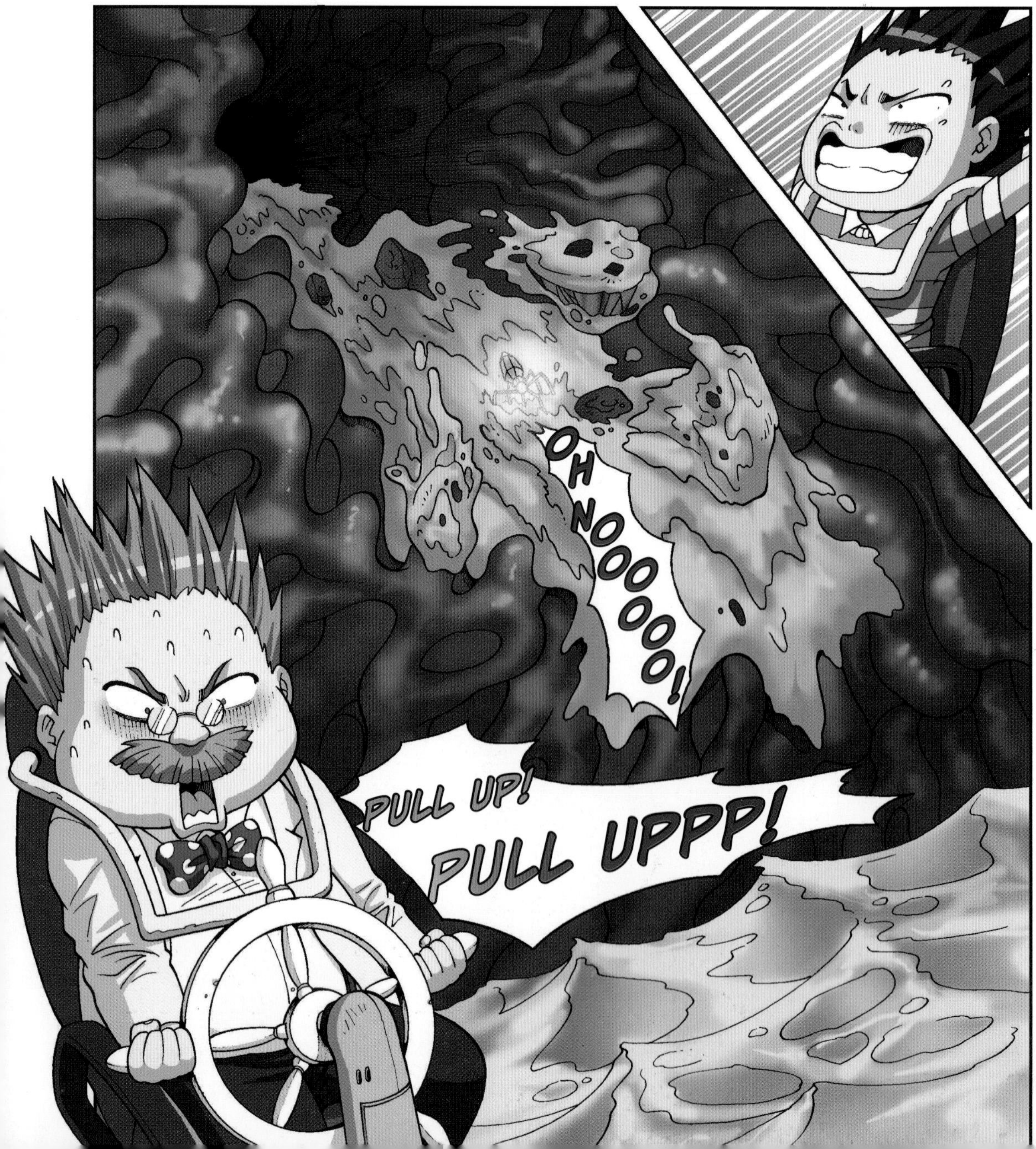
OH NOOOOOOO!
PULL UP!
PULL UPPP!

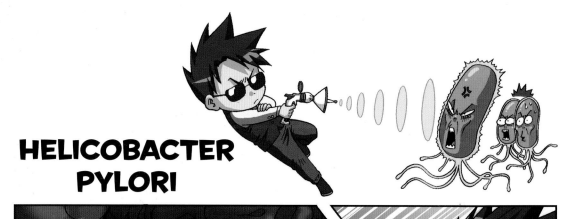

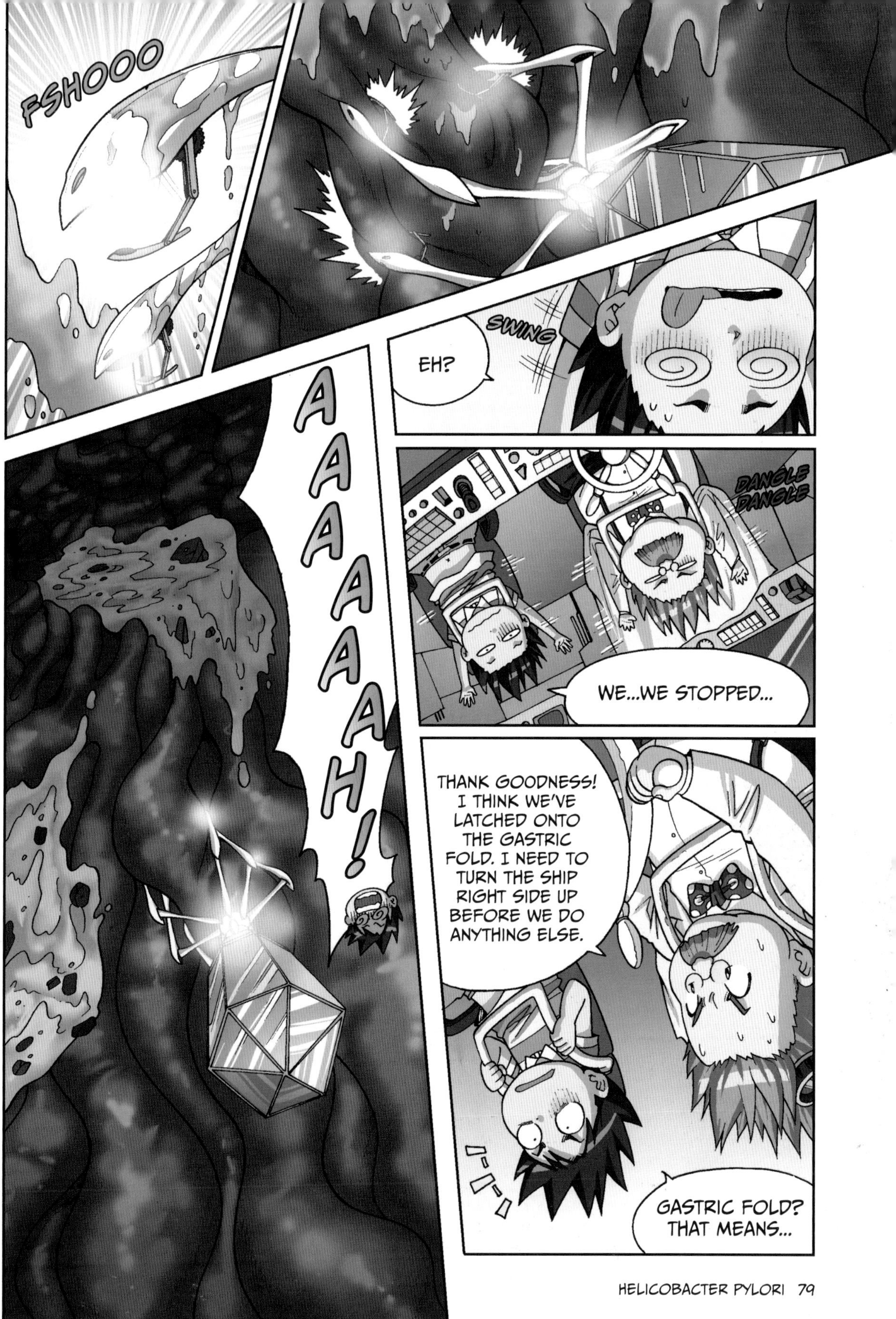
FSHOOO
SWING
EH?
AAAAAAAH!
DANGLE DANGLE
WE...WE STOPPED...
THANK GOODNESS! I THINK WE'VE LATCHED ONTO THE GASTRIC FOLD. I NEED TO TURN THE SHIP RIGHT SIDE UP BEFORE WE DO ANYTHING ELSE.
GASTRIC FOLD? THAT MEANS...

GROWWWWWWWWL
WE'RE IN THE *STOMACH*?!
SKITTER SCREECH
SPLAAAAAAASH

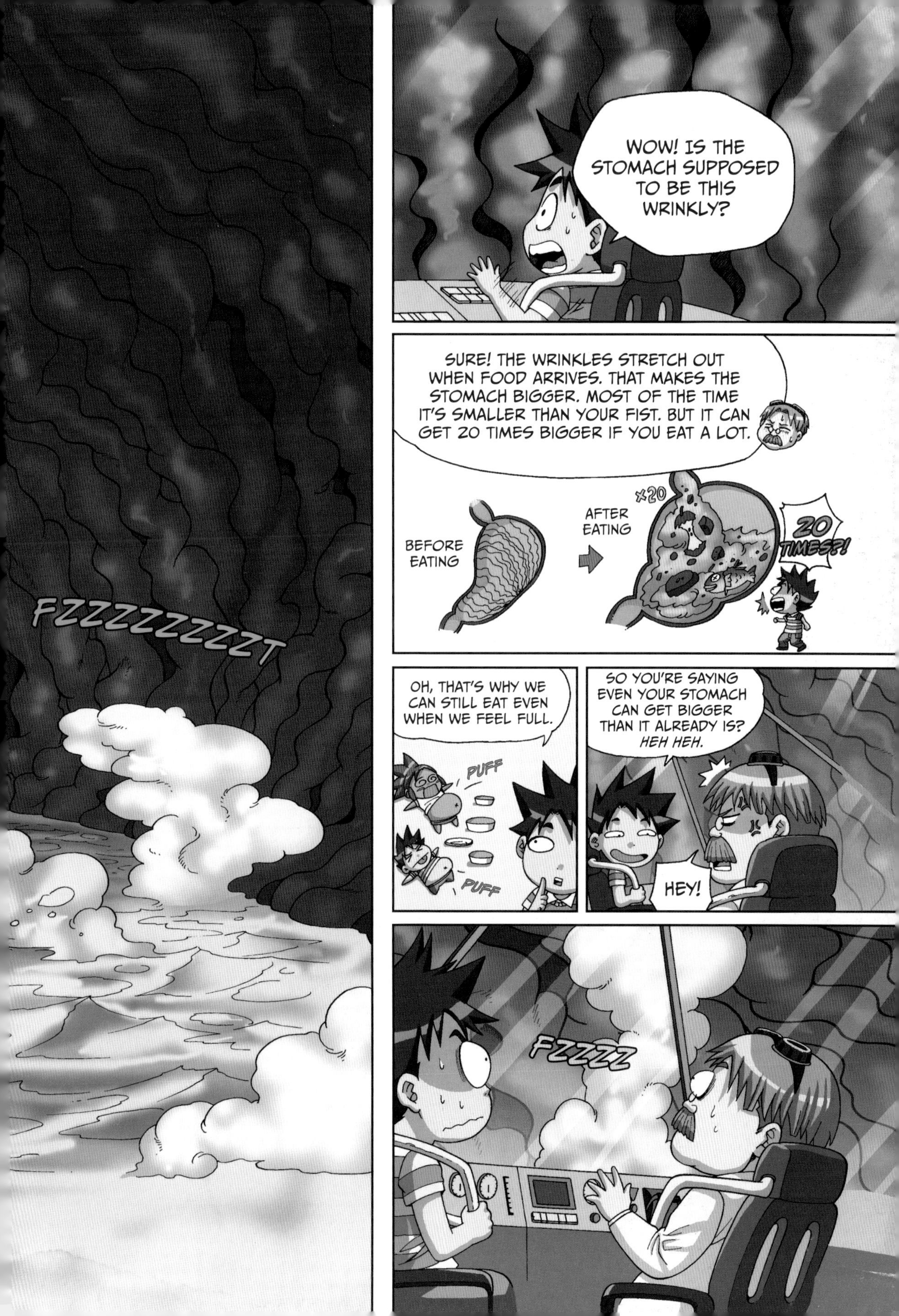
FZZZZZZZZZT
WOW! IS THE STOMACH SUPPOSED TO BE THIS WRINKLY?
SURE! THE WRINKLES STRETCH OUT WHEN FOOD ARRIVES. THAT MAKES THE STOMACH BIGGER. MOST OF THE TIME IT'S SMALLER THAN YOUR FIST. BUT IT CAN GET 20 TIMES BIGGER IF YOU EAT A LOT.
BEFORE EATING
AFTER EATING
×20
20 TIMES?!
OH, THAT'S WHY WE CAN STILL EAT EVEN WHEN WE FEEL FULL.
PUFF
PUFF
SO YOU'RE SAYING EVEN YOUR STOMACH CAN GET BIGGER THAN IT ALREADY IS? HEH HEH.
HEY!
FZZZZ

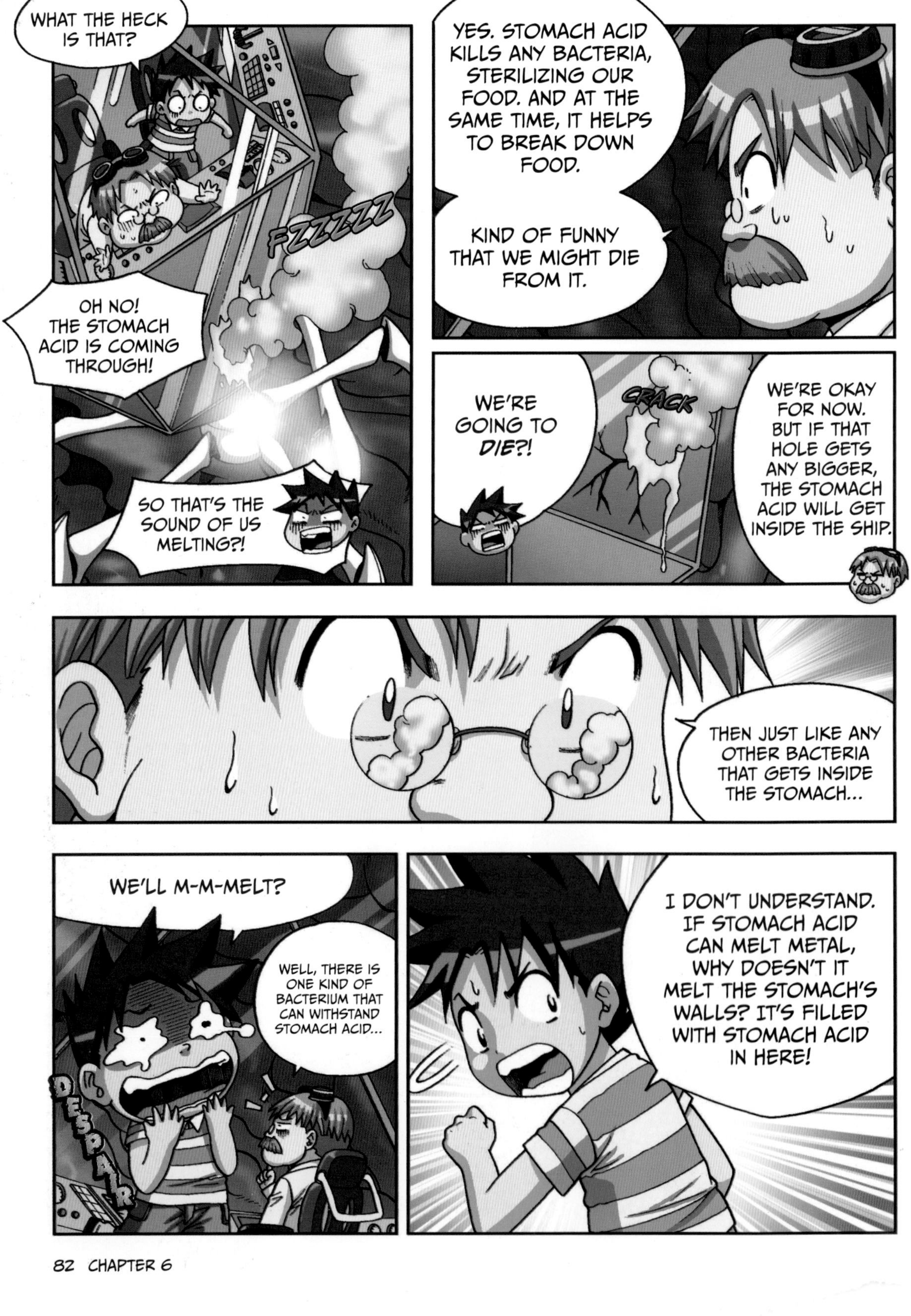
WHAT THE HECK IS THAT?
FZZZZZ
OH NO! THE STOMACH ACID IS COMING THROUGH!
SO THAT'S THE SOUND OF US MELTING?!
YES. STOMACH ACID KILLS ANY BACTERIA, STERILIZING OUR FOOD. AND AT THE SAME TIME, IT HELPS TO BREAK DOWN FOOD.
KIND OF FUNNY THAT WE MIGHT DIE FROM IT.
WE'RE GOING TO *DIE*?!
CRACK
WE'RE OKAY FOR NOW. BUT IF THAT HOLE GETS ANY BIGGER, THE STOMACH ACID WILL GET INSIDE THE SHIP.
THEN JUST LIKE ANY OTHER BACTERIA THAT GETS INSIDE THE STOMACH...
WE'LL M-M-MELT?
DESPAIR
WELL, THERE IS ONE KIND OF BACTERIUM THAT CAN WITHSTAND STOMACH ACID...
I DON'T UNDERSTAND. IF STOMACH ACID CAN MELT METAL, WHY DOESN'T IT MELT THE STOMACH'S WALLS? IT'S FILLED WITH STOMACH ACID IN HERE!

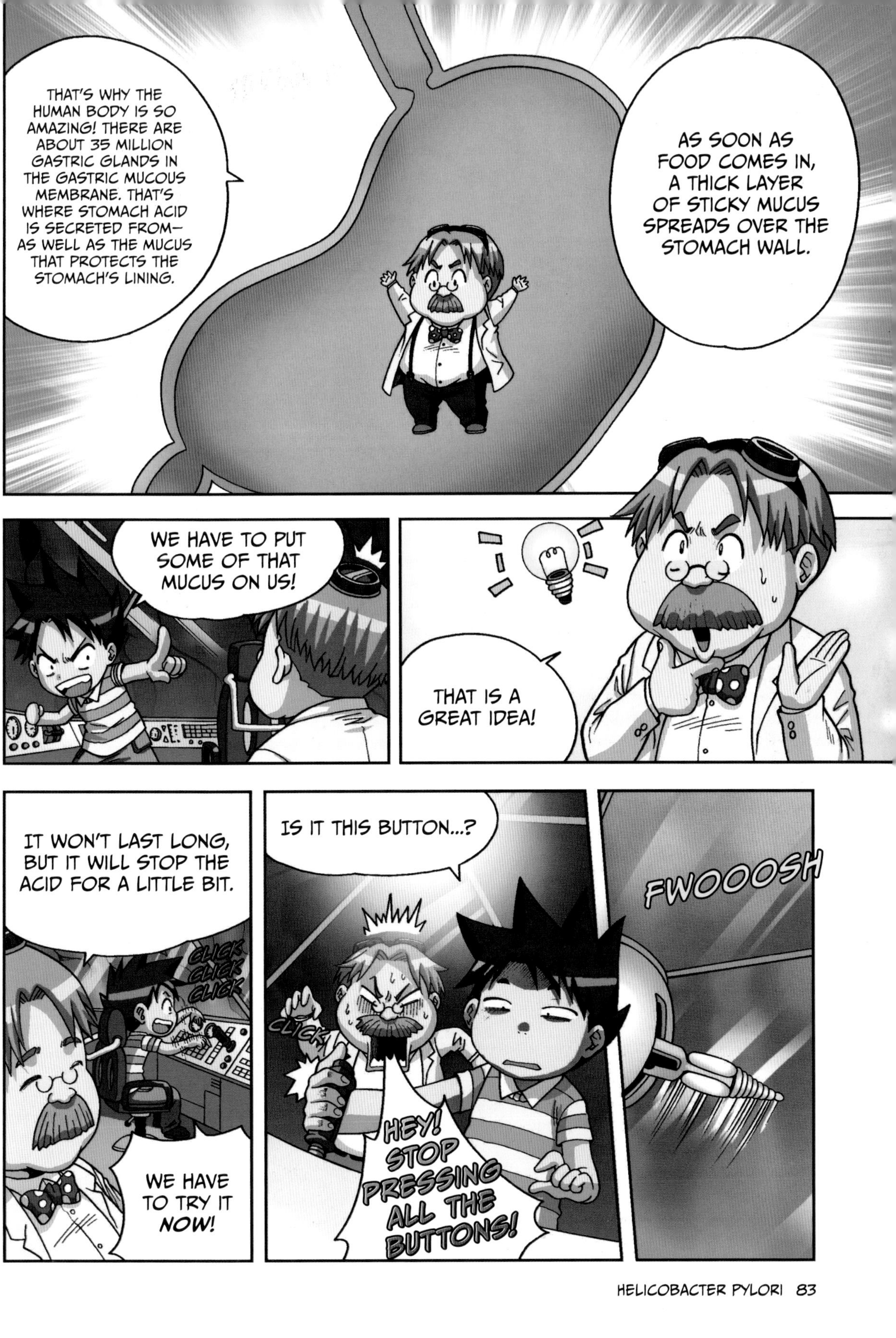

THAT'S WHY THE HUMAN BODY IS SO AMAZING! THERE ARE ABOUT 35 MILLION GASTRIC GLANDS IN THE GASTRIC MUCOUS MEMBRANE. THAT'S WHERE STOMACH ACID IS SECRETED FROM— AS WELL AS THE MUCUS THAT PROTECTS THE STOMACH'S LINING.
AS SOON AS FOOD COMES IN, A THICK LAYER OF STICKY MUCUS SPREADS OVER THE STOMACH WALL.
WE HAVE TO PUT SOME OF THAT MUCUS ON US!
THAT IS A GREAT IDEA!
IT WON'T LAST LONG, BUT IT WILL STOP THE ACID FOR A LITTLE BIT.
CLICK CLICK CLICK
WE HAVE TO TRY IT NOW!
IS IT THIS BUTTON...?
CLICK
HEY! STOP PRESSING ALL THE BUTTONS!
FWOOOSH

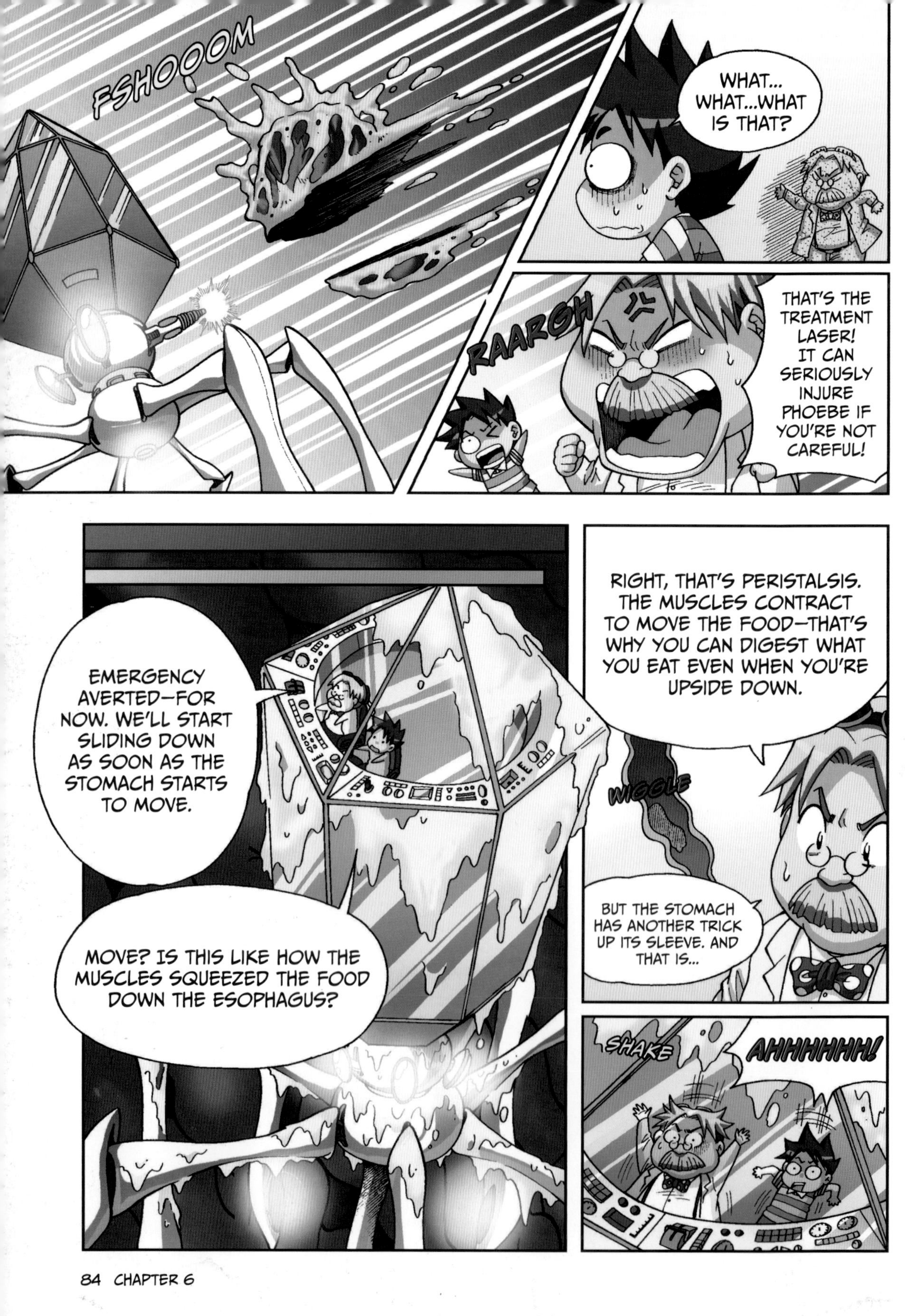
FSHOOOM
WHAT... WHAT...WHAT IS THAT?
RAARGH
THAT'S THE TREATMENT LASER! IT CAN SERIOUSLY INJURE PHOEBE IF YOU'RE NOT CAREFUL!
EMERGENCY AVERTED—FOR NOW. WE'LL START SLIDING DOWN AS SOON AS THE STOMACH STARTS TO MOVE.
MOVE? IS THIS LIKE HOW THE MUSCLES SQUEEZED THE FOOD DOWN THE ESOPHAGUS?
RIGHT, THAT'S PERISTALSIS. THE MUSCLES CONTRACT TO MOVE THE FOOD—THAT'S WHY YOU CAN DIGEST WHAT YOU EAT EVEN WHEN YOU'RE UPSIDE DOWN.
WIGGLE
BUT THE STOMACH HAS ANOTHER TRICK UP ITS SLEEVE. AND THAT IS...
SHAKE
AHHHHHHH!

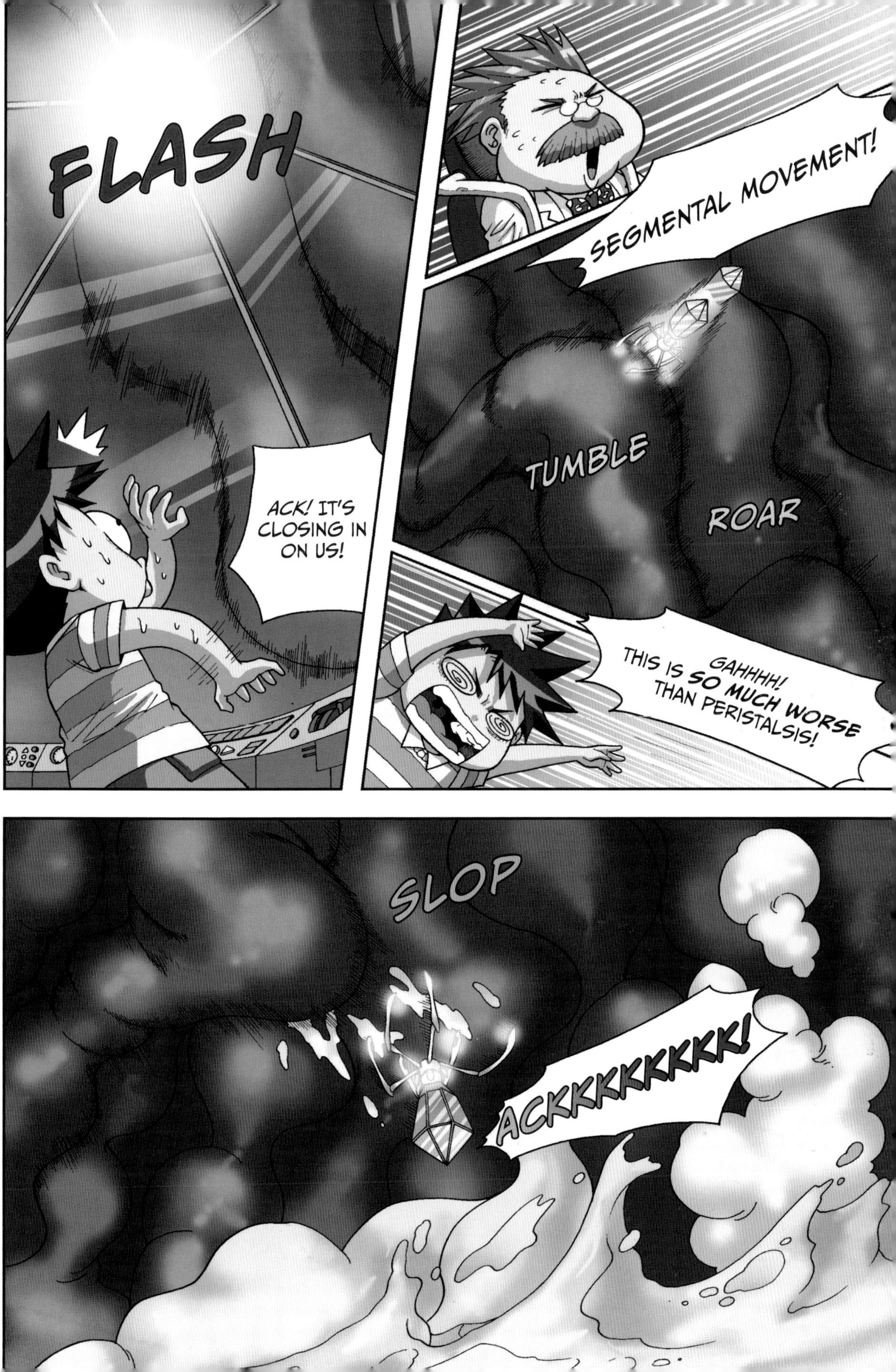
FLASH
SEGMENTAL MOVEMENT!
ACK! IT'S CLOSING IN ON US!
TUMBLE
ROAR
GAHHHH! THIS IS **SO MUCH WORSE** THAN PERISTALSIS!
SLOP
ACKKKKKKKK!

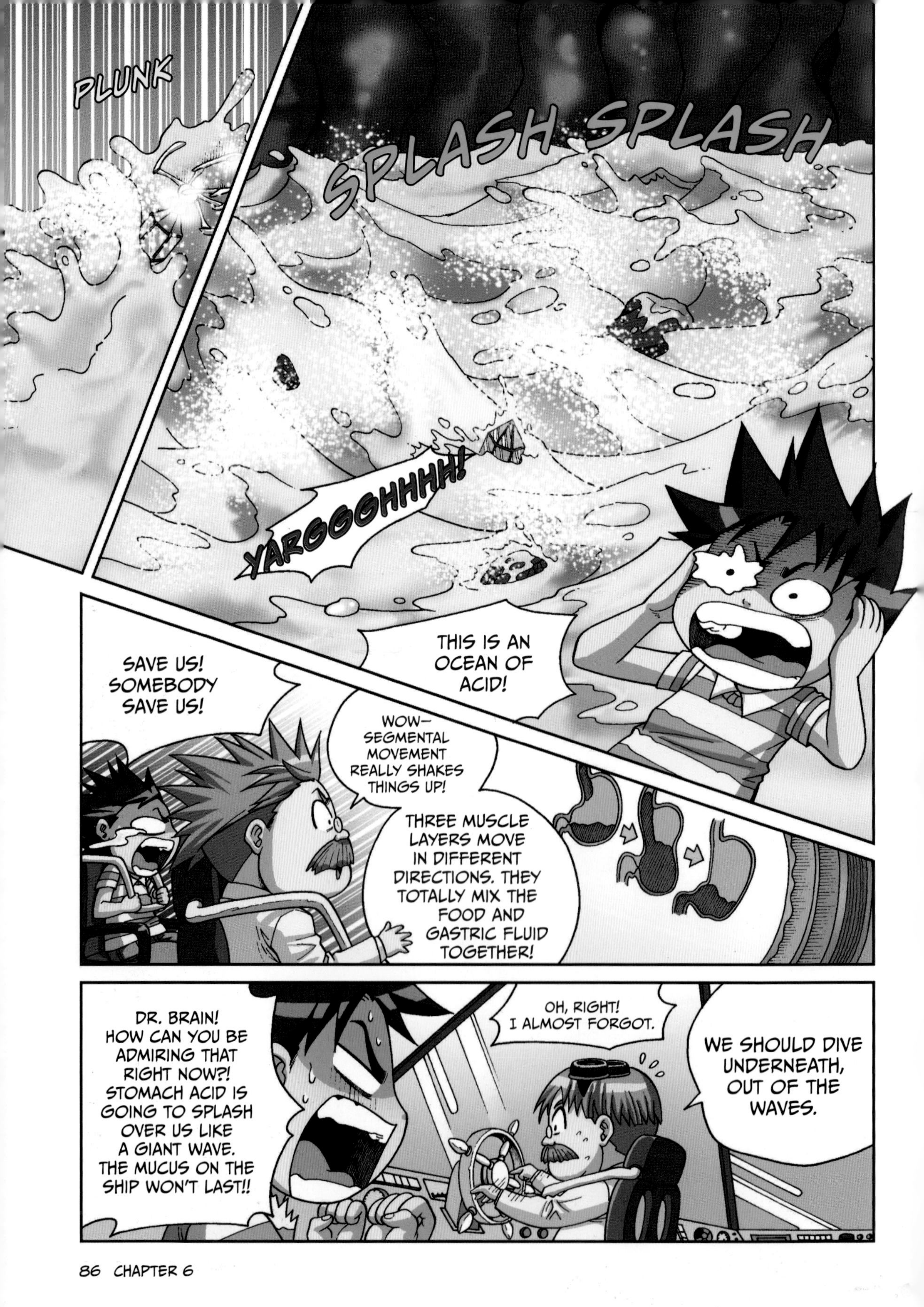
PLUNK
SPLASH SPLASH
YARGGGHHHH!
THIS IS AN OCEAN OF ACID!
SAVE US! SOMEBODY SAVE US!
WOW—SEGMENTAL MOVEMENT REALLY SHAKES THINGS UP!
THREE MUSCLE LAYERS MOVE IN DIFFERENT DIRECTIONS. THEY TOTALLY MIX THE FOOD AND GASTRIC FLUID TOGETHER!
DR. BRAIN! HOW CAN YOU BE ADMIRING THAT RIGHT NOW?! STOMACH ACID IS GOING TO SPLASH OVER US LIKE A GIANT WAVE. THE MUCUS ON THE SHIP WON'T LAST!!
OH, RIGHT! I ALMOST FORGOT.
WE SHOULD DIVE UNDERNEATH, OUT OF THE WAVES.

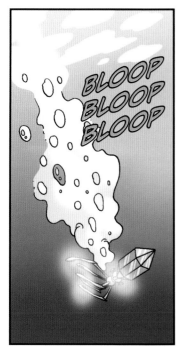

BLOOP
BLOOP
BLOOP

HEY, WHAT'S THAT?

IS THAT FOOD?

WRIGGLE WRIGGLE

NO, WAIT... IT'S *MOVING*!

THE MUCUS IS ALMOST ALL GONE. I SHOULD HAVE APPLIED A THICKER COAT...

DR. BRAIN! WHAT DO WE DO?!

I-I'M NOT SURE. IT'S ALREADY TOO LATE.

NO, NOT THAT! WE'RE GOING TO CRASH!

CRASH? WHAT ARE YOU TALKING ABOUT?!

BEEP BEEP

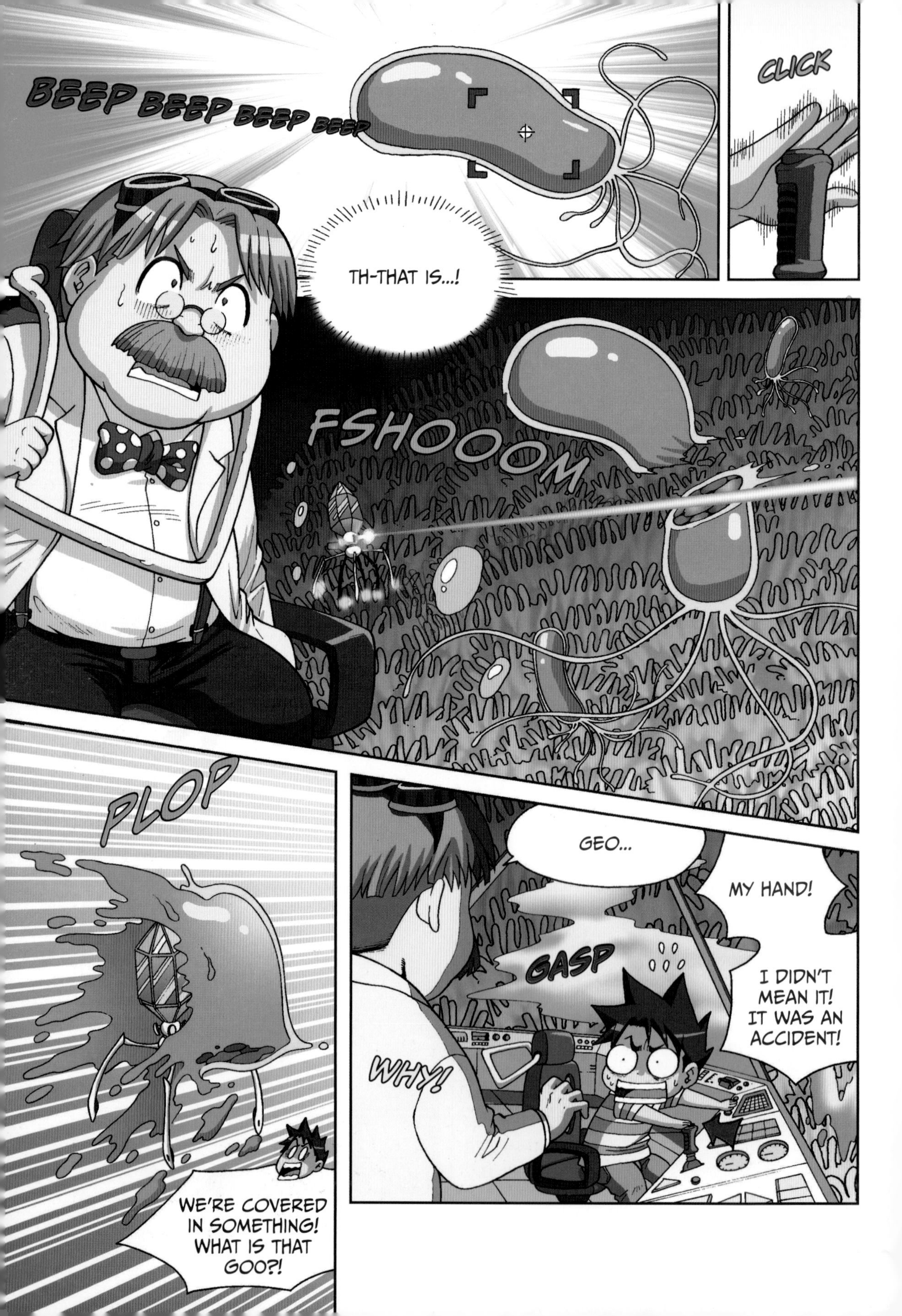
BEEP BEEP BEEP BEEP
CLICK
TH-THAT IS...!
FSHOOOM
PLOP
WE'RE COVERED IN SOMETHING! WHAT IS THAT GOO?!
GEO...
MY HAND!
GASP
I DIDN'T MEAN IT! IT WAS AN ACCIDENT!
WHY!

YOU'RE A GENIUS!

KING OF SURVIVAL! YOU REALLY DO KNOW HOW TO SAVE THE DAY!

HUG

WHAT?!

WE'LL GET THROUGH THIS IF YOU SHOOT THOSE THINGS WITH THE LASER!

WHAT DO YOU MEAN?

LOOK AT THAT! WE WERE IN DANGER JUST A MINUTE AGO BECAUSE WE LOST ALL OUR MUCUS. BUT THE ACID STOPPED WORKING ANYWAY! WHY?

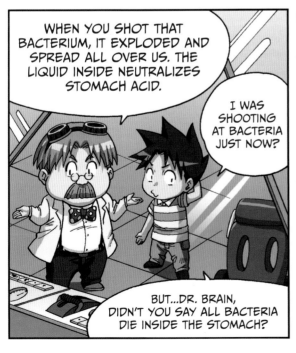

WHEN YOU SHOT THAT BACTERIUM, IT EXPLODED AND SPREAD ALL OVER US. THE LIQUID INSIDE NEUTRALIZES STOMACH ACID.

I WAS SHOOTING AT BACTERIA JUST NOW?

BUT...DR. BRAIN, DIDN'T YOU SAY ALL BACTERIA DIE INSIDE THE STOMACH?

WELL, THERE IS ONE KIND OF BACTERIUM THAT CAN WITHSTAND STOMACH ACID...

DESPAIR

SNAP

AHA! SO THIS IS THAT KIND OF BACTERIA!

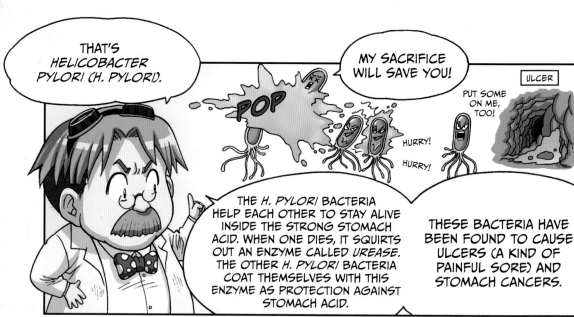

THAT'S *HELICOBACTER PYLORI* (H. PYLORI).

MY SACRIFICE WILL SAVE YOU!

POP

HURRY!

HURRY!

PUT SOME ON ME, TOO!

ULCER

THE *H. PYLORI* BACTERIA HELP EACH OTHER TO STAY ALIVE INSIDE THE STRONG STOMACH ACID. WHEN ONE DIES, IT SQUIRTS OUT AN ENZYME CALLED *UREASE*. THE OTHER *H. PYLORI* BACTERIA COAT THEMSELVES WITH THIS ENZYME AS PROTECTION AGAINST STOMACH ACID.

THESE BACTERIA HAVE BEEN FOUND TO CAUSE ULCERS (A KIND OF PAINFUL SORE) AND STOMACH CANCERS.

SO YOU'RE SAYING THE BACTERIA HAD TO BE STOPPED ANYWAY, RIGHT?

NOD

YES!

WHO* CLASSIFIED IT AS A GROUP 1 CARCINOGEN.

THEY'RE DANGEROUS. THE INFECTION RATE IS 20 TO 30 PERCENT IN MANY DEVELOPED COUNTRIES, AND IT'S EVEN HIGHER ELSEWHERE (50 PERCENT). USUALLY, PEOPLE GET THE BACTERIA AS KIDS—OFTEN FROM FAMILY MEMBERS. GOOD HYGIENE (WASHING YOUR HANDS AFTER GOING TO THE BATHROOM AND AGAIN BEFORE EATING) AND USING CLEAN WATER CAN HELP PREVENT IT.

GAS

GEO, THE FATE OF PHOEBE AND THE SS *HIPPOCRATES* IS IN YOUR HANDS NOW!

* WHO (WORLD HEALTH ORGANIZATION) IS AN AGENCY OF THE UNITED NATIONS THAT PROMOTES HEALTH.

BWAHAHAHA! YOU CAN TRUST ME! I AM ALSO THE KING OF VIDEO GAMES!
TA-DA
BEEP
BEEP
BEEP
BRING IT ON! I WILL PROTECT PHOEBE AND THE *HIPPOCRATES*!
POP
TAP TAP TAP TAP
POP

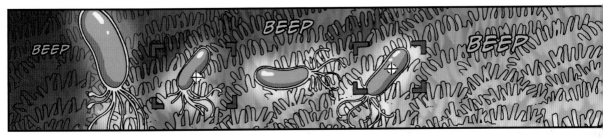

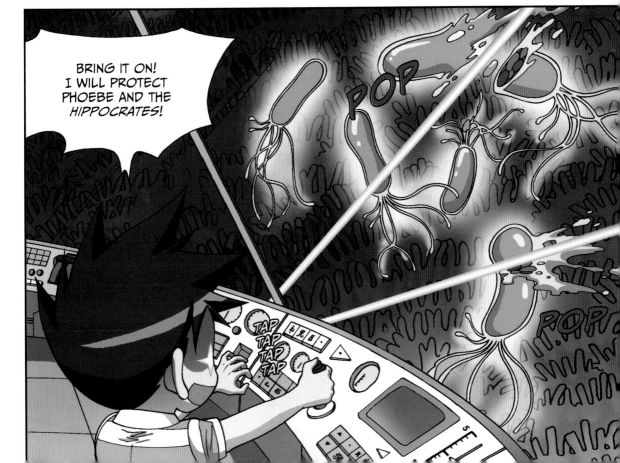

A REAL BELLY FULL

Your stomach is shaped a little like the letter *J*. You can find it just to the left of the center of your chest. A stomach without any food inside is a little wrinkly sack about the size of a fist. When food arrives, the wrinkles (called *rugae*) stretch out and the stomach can get a lot bigger—about 20 times larger when it's full!

SEGMENTAL MOVEMENT AND PERISTALSIS

Your stomach has three layers of muscles that are very strong and flexible. These muscles can move sideways, up and down, and diagonally to evenly mix food with gastric fluid in a process called *segmental movement*. When you hear your stomach growl, it's the sound of segmental movement mixing liquids, solids, and gases. Food is mixed for about 3 hours, and then it is sent to the small intestine using peristalsis. This is the same kind of movement that your esophagus uses to send food to your stomach.

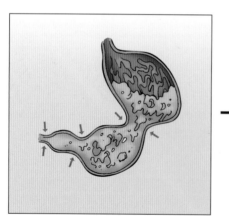

CAN MY STOMACH REALLY FIT ALL OF THIS?
YEAH, YEAH, DON'T WORRY ABOUT IT! THIS IS JUST THE SOUND OF MY STOMACH SWISHING AROUND FOOD.
GROWWWL

SEGMENTAL MOVEMENT Stomach muscles flex in many different directions to *mix* the food and gastric fluid.

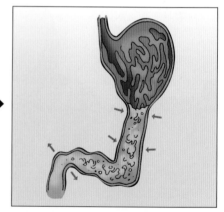

PERISTALSIS Stomach muscles flex to *move* food down to the small intestine.

GASTRIC FLUID AND MUCUS

Gastric fluid is made up of digestive enzymes like pepsin and lipase, which break down protein and fat, and an acid that is strong enough to melt metal. There is a good reason why your body makes such a strong acid. Your stomach kills most of the germs in your food with acid so you don't get sick. This acid also helps to break down foods, in preparation for the small intestine.

Why doesn't the acid melt your stomach? It has special protection: The inner wall of your stomach continuously releases mucus, which covers the entire inner wall and shields your stomach from being hurt by the acid.

H. PYLORI BACTERIA AND ULCERS

Stomach acid is strong enough to kill most bacteria, but in 1980 scientists found that some bacteria can actually live *inside* stomach acid. These *H. pylori* bacteria can make us sick with ulcers and inflammation of the stomach (gastritis). Gastritis can even lead to cancer.

Even though many people have these bacteria in their stomachs, most of them (more than 80 percent) don't get sick. And when people do get ulcers, doctors can help them with antibiotics, medicine that kills the bacteria.

To keep *H. pylori* bacteria out of your body, you should eat foods with plenty of vitamin C and practice good hygiene. Don't put your fingers in your mouth and wash your hands before you eat. Eating certain foods, including broccoli and garlic, may also help your body kill these bacteria.

© Yutaka Tsutsumi

H. pylori *bacterium*

INDIGESTION

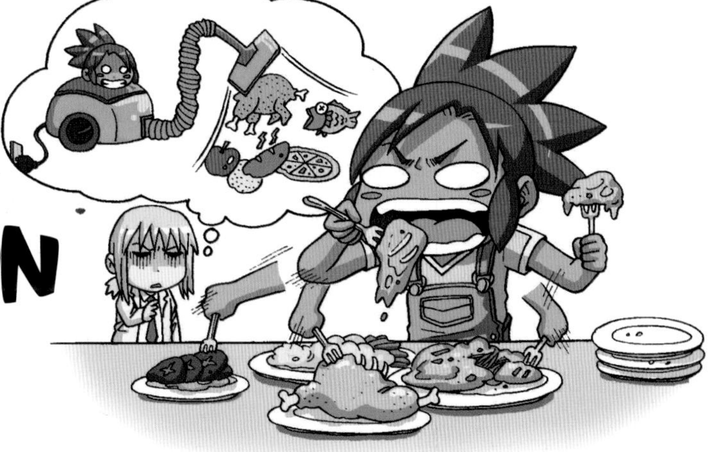

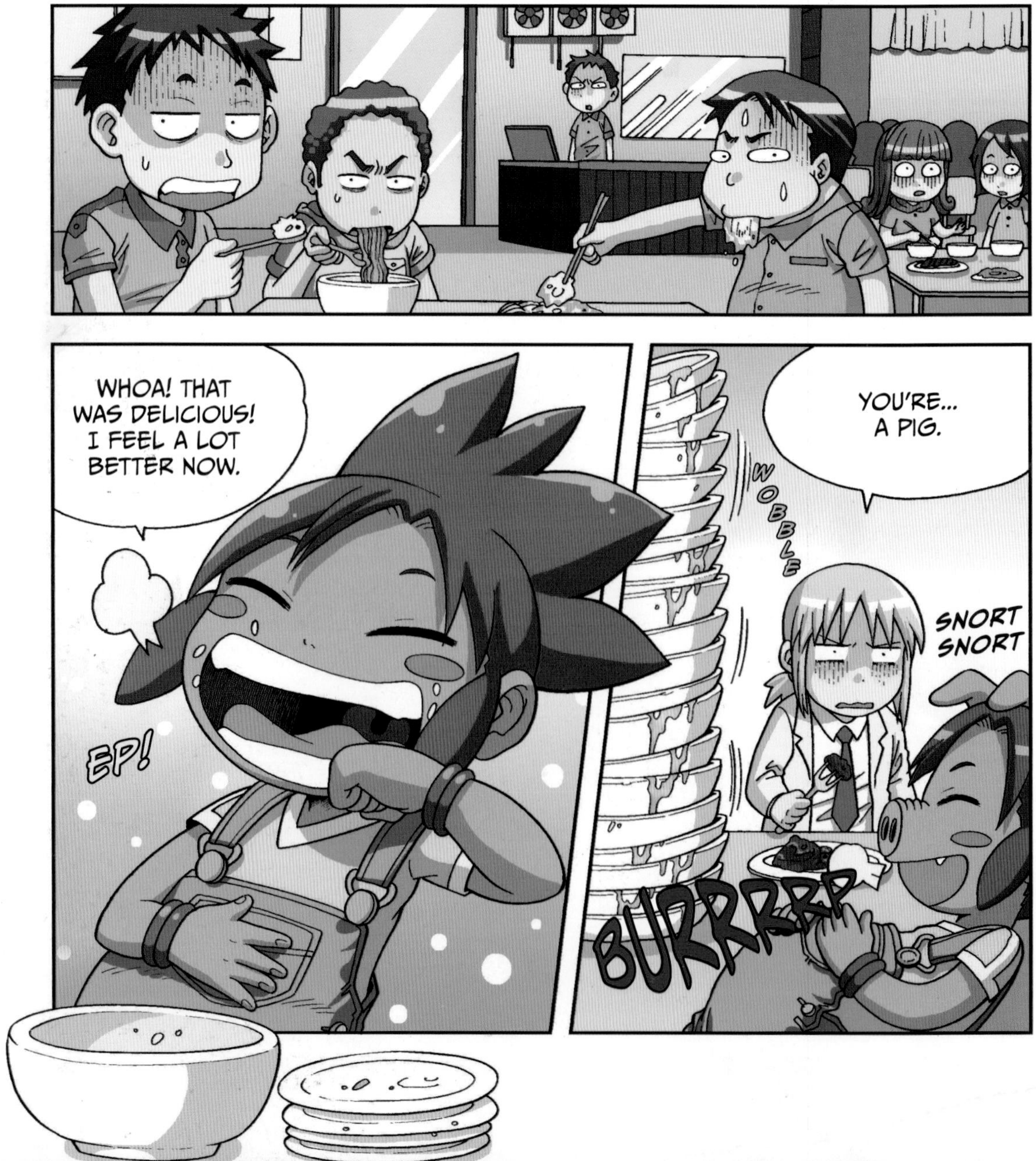
WHOA! THAT WAS DELICIOUS! I FEEL A LOT BETTER NOW.
EP!
YOU'RE... A PIG.
WOBBLE
SNORT SNORT
BURRRRP

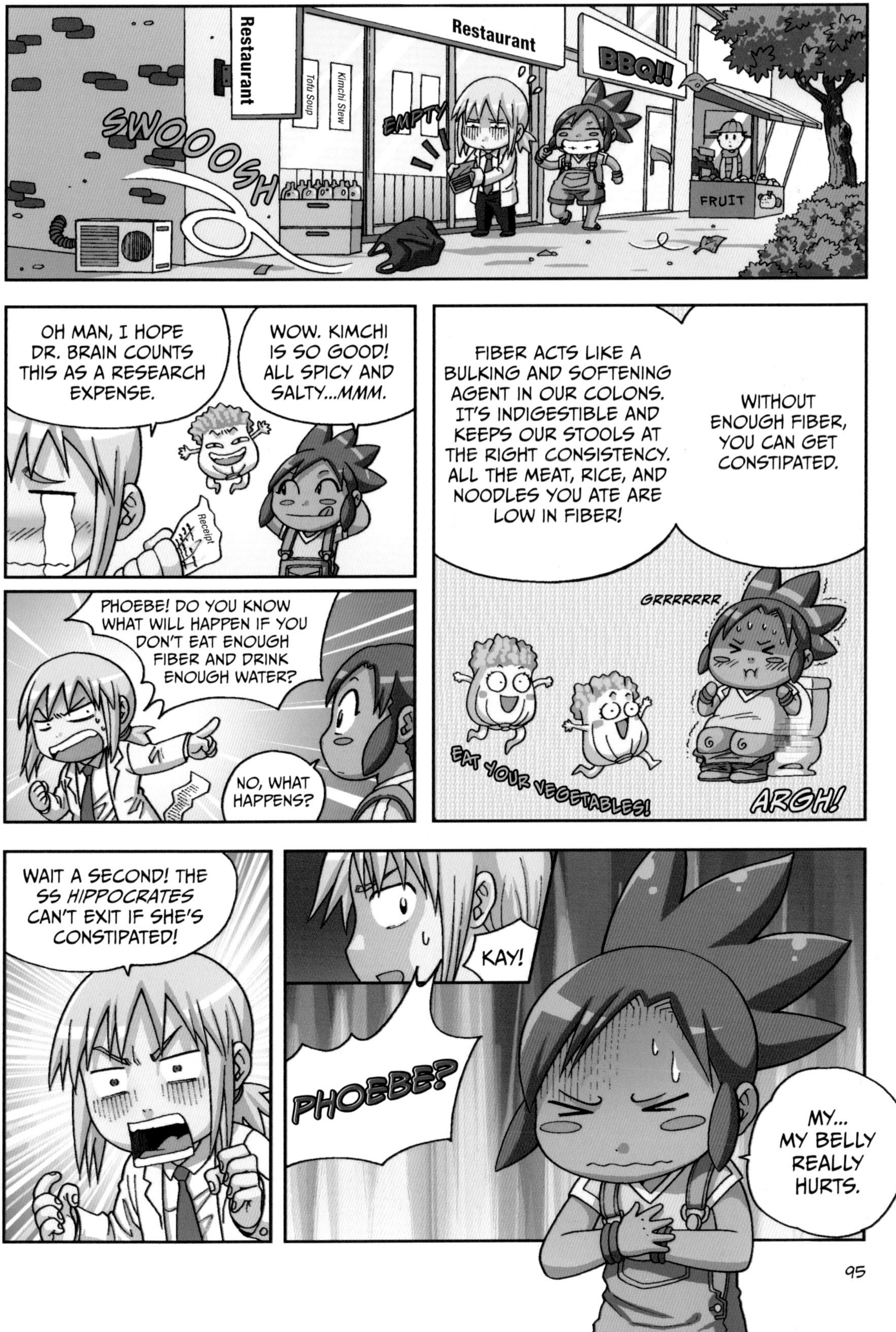
Restaurant
Restaurant
Tofu Soup
Kimchi Stew
BBQ!!
FRUIT
SWOOOSH
EMPTY
OH MAN, I HOPE DR. BRAIN COUNTS THIS AS A RESEARCH EXPENSE.
WOW. KIMCHI IS SO GOOD! ALL SPICY AND SALTY...MMM.
Receipt
FIBER ACTS LIKE A BULKING AND SOFTENING AGENT IN OUR COLONS. IT'S INDIGESTIBLE AND KEEPS OUR STOOLS AT THE RIGHT CONSISTENCY. ALL THE MEAT, RICE, AND NOODLES YOU ATE ARE LOW IN FIBER!
WITHOUT ENOUGH FIBER, YOU CAN GET CONSTIPATED.
GRRRRRRR
EAT YOUR VEGETABLES!
ARGH!
PHOEBE! DO YOU KNOW WHAT WILL HAPPEN IF YOU DON'T EAT ENOUGH FIBER AND DRINK ENOUGH WATER?
NO, WHAT HAPPENS?
WAIT A SECOND! THE SS HIPPOCRATES CAN'T EXIT IF SHE'S CONSTIPATED!
KAY!
PHOEBE?
MY... MY BELLY REALLY HURTS.

HOW LONG DO I HAVE TO KEEP SHOOTING?

CLICK CLICK CLICK

I THINK YOU CAN STOP NOW. I CAN BARELY SEE OUT THE WINDOW THANKS TO THIS THICK UREASE COATING.

SLOP

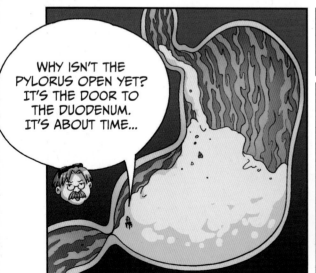

WHY ISN'T THE PYLORUS OPEN YET? IT'S THE DOOR TO THE DUODENUM. IT'S ABOUT TIME...

DO WE HAVE TO WAIT? CAN'T *WE* OPEN IT?

WE CAN'T OPEN THE DIGESTIVE SYSTEM DOORS WHENEVER WE WANT.

SO HOW DOES IT WORK?

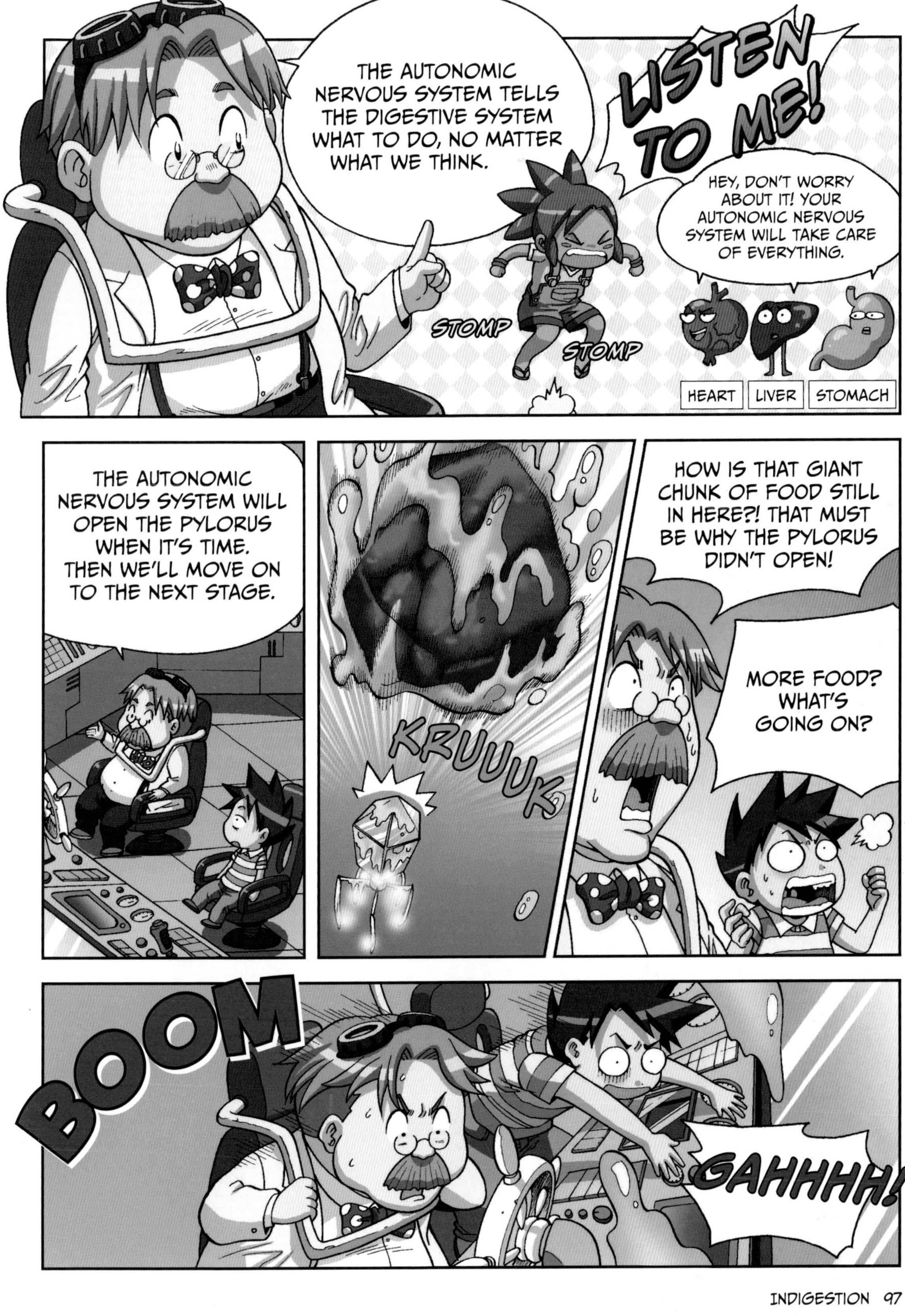
THE AUTONOMIC NERVOUS SYSTEM TELLS THE DIGESTIVE SYSTEM WHAT TO DO, NO MATTER WHAT WE THINK.
LISTEN TO ME!
HEY, DON'T WORRY ABOUT IT! YOUR AUTONOMIC NERVOUS SYSTEM WILL TAKE CARE OF EVERYTHING.
STOMP
STOMP
HEART
LIVER
STOMACH
THE AUTONOMIC NERVOUS SYSTEM WILL OPEN THE PYLORUS WHEN IT'S TIME. THEN WE'LL MOVE ON TO THE NEXT STAGE.
KRUUUK
HOW IS THAT GIANT CHUNK OF FOOD STILL IN HERE?! THAT MUST BE WHY THE PYLORUS DIDN'T OPEN!
MORE FOOD? WHAT'S GOING ON?
BOOM
GAHHHH!

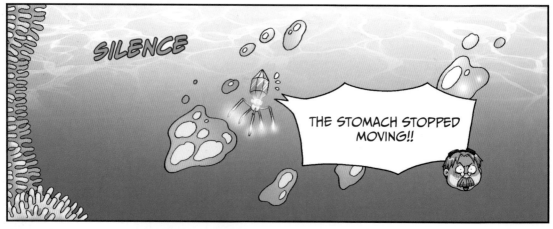

SILENCE

THE STOMACH STOPPED MOVING!!

DO YOU THINK SOMETHING WENT WRONG? MAYBE SOMETHING ELSE IS GOING ON OUT THERE.

I'D BETTER GO UP AND CHECK.

CLICK

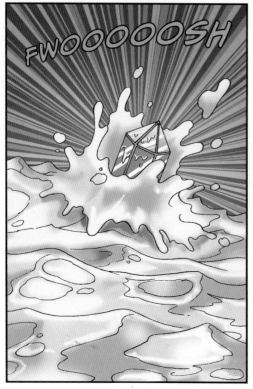

FWOOOOOOSH

IT'S LIKE THICK SOUP—IT'S NOT EASY TO MOVE IN THIS.

LOOK!

DR. BRAIN! LOOK OVER THERE!

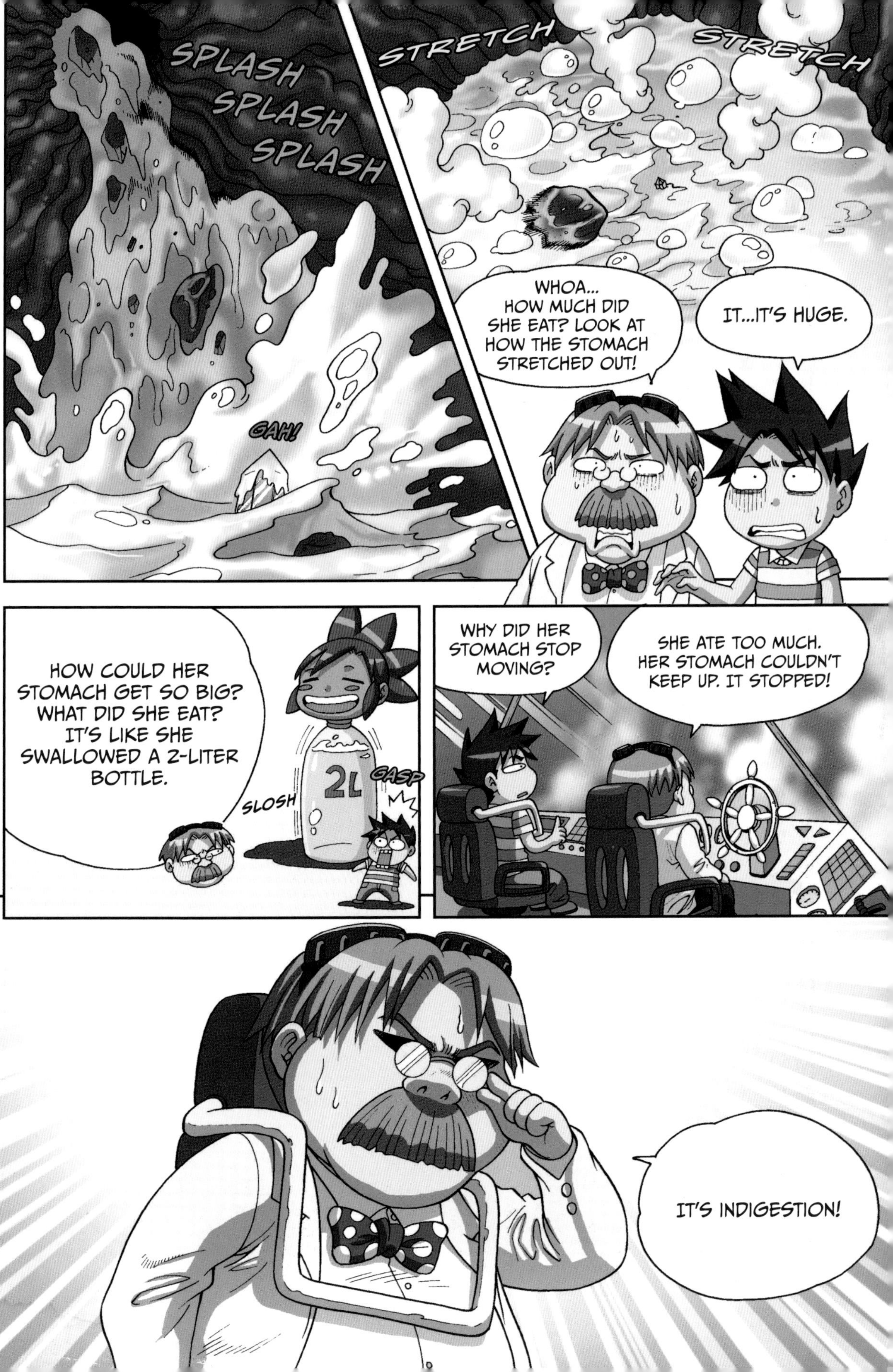
SPLASH
SPLASH
SPLASH
GAH!
STRETCH
STRETCH
WHOA... HOW MUCH DID SHE EAT? LOOK AT HOW THE STOMACH STRETCHED OUT!
IT...IT'S HUGE.
HOW COULD HER STOMACH GET SO BIG? WHAT DID SHE EAT? IT'S LIKE SHE SWALLOWED A 2-LITER BOTTLE.
2L
SLOSH
GASP
WHY DID HER STOMACH STOP MOVING?
SHE ATE TOO MUCH. HER STOMACH COULDN'T KEEP UP. IT STOPPED!
IT'S INDIGESTION!

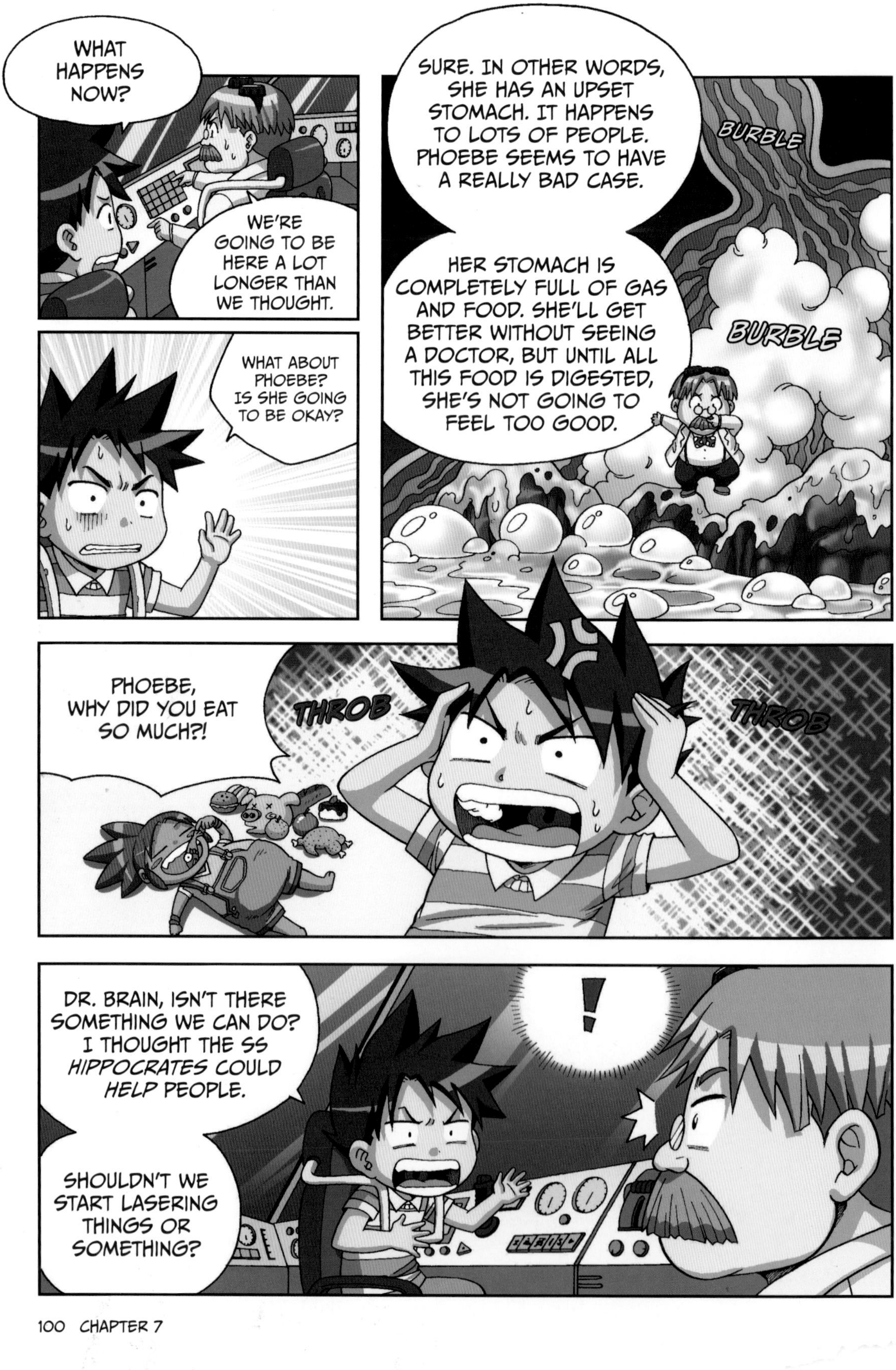
WHAT HAPPENS NOW?
WE'RE GOING TO BE HERE A LOT LONGER THAN WE THOUGHT.
SURE. IN OTHER WORDS, SHE HAS AN UPSET STOMACH. IT HAPPENS TO LOTS OF PEOPLE. PHOEBE SEEMS TO HAVE A REALLY BAD CASE.
BURBLE
HER STOMACH IS COMPLETELY FULL OF GAS AND FOOD. SHE'LL GET BETTER WITHOUT SEEING A DOCTOR, BUT UNTIL ALL THIS FOOD IS DIGESTED, SHE'S NOT GOING TO FEEL TOO GOOD.
BURBLE
WHAT ABOUT PHOEBE? IS SHE GOING TO BE OKAY?
PHOEBE, WHY DID YOU EAT SO MUCH?!
THROB
THROB
DR. BRAIN, ISN'T THERE SOMETHING WE CAN DO? I THOUGHT THE SS *HIPPOCRATES* COULD *HELP* PEOPLE.
SHOULDN'T WE START LASERING THINGS OR SOMETHING?
!

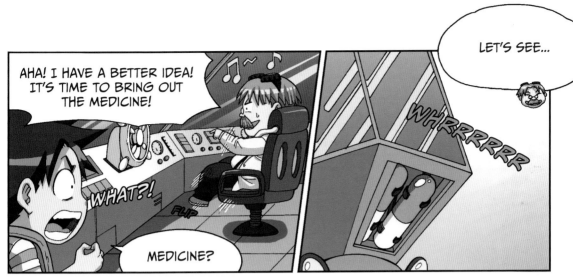

AHA! I HAVE A BETTER IDEA! IT'S TIME TO BRING OUT THE MEDICINE!

WHAT?!

FLIP

MEDICINE?

LET'S SEE...

WHRRRRRR

THANK GOODNESS I BROUGHT THE DRUG WE NEED!

IT'S NOT DANGEROUS, IS IT?

I'M WORRIED...

HAHA, DON'T YOU WORRY! THIS DIGESTIVE MEDICINE, SIMETHICONE, WORKS TO RELIEVE BLOATING. IT WILL HELP THE STOMACH MOVE AND GET RID OF GAS.

PHOEBE WILL FEEL A LOT BETTER ONCE SHE BURPS AND GETS RID OF THIS GAS.

TIK TIK

OH, SO THAT'S WHAT A BURP IS.

ALL RIGHT, GET READY. I'LL NEED YOUR HELP TO MAKE SURE THE DRUG IS ABSORBED QUICKLY.

ME?

101

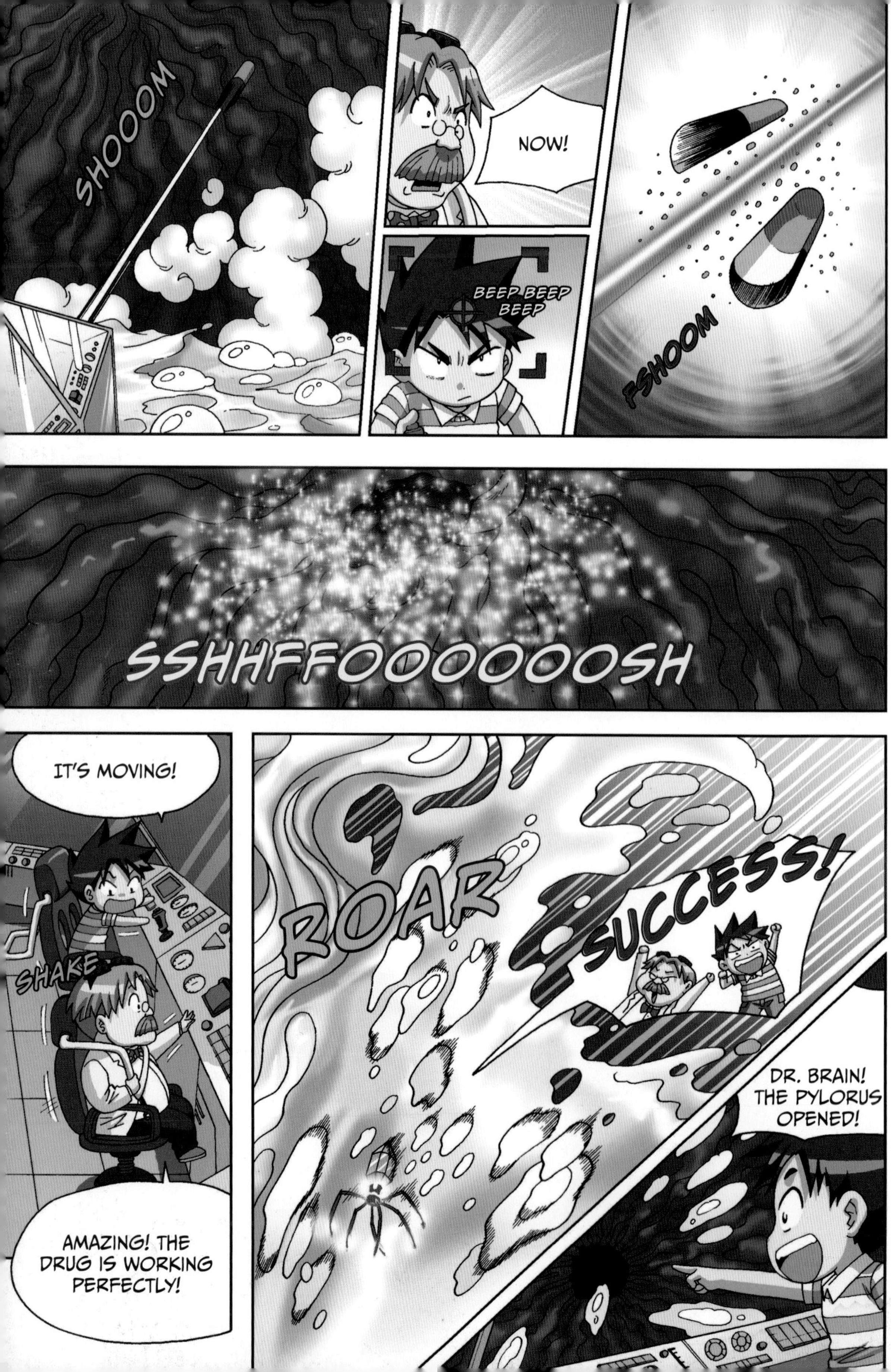

SHOOOM
NOW!
BEEP BEEP BEEP
FSHOOM
SSHHFFOOOOOOOSH
IT'S MOVING!
SHAKE
AMAZING! THE DRUG IS WORKING PERFECTLY!
ROAR
SUCCESS!
DR. BRAIN! THE PYLORUS OPENED!

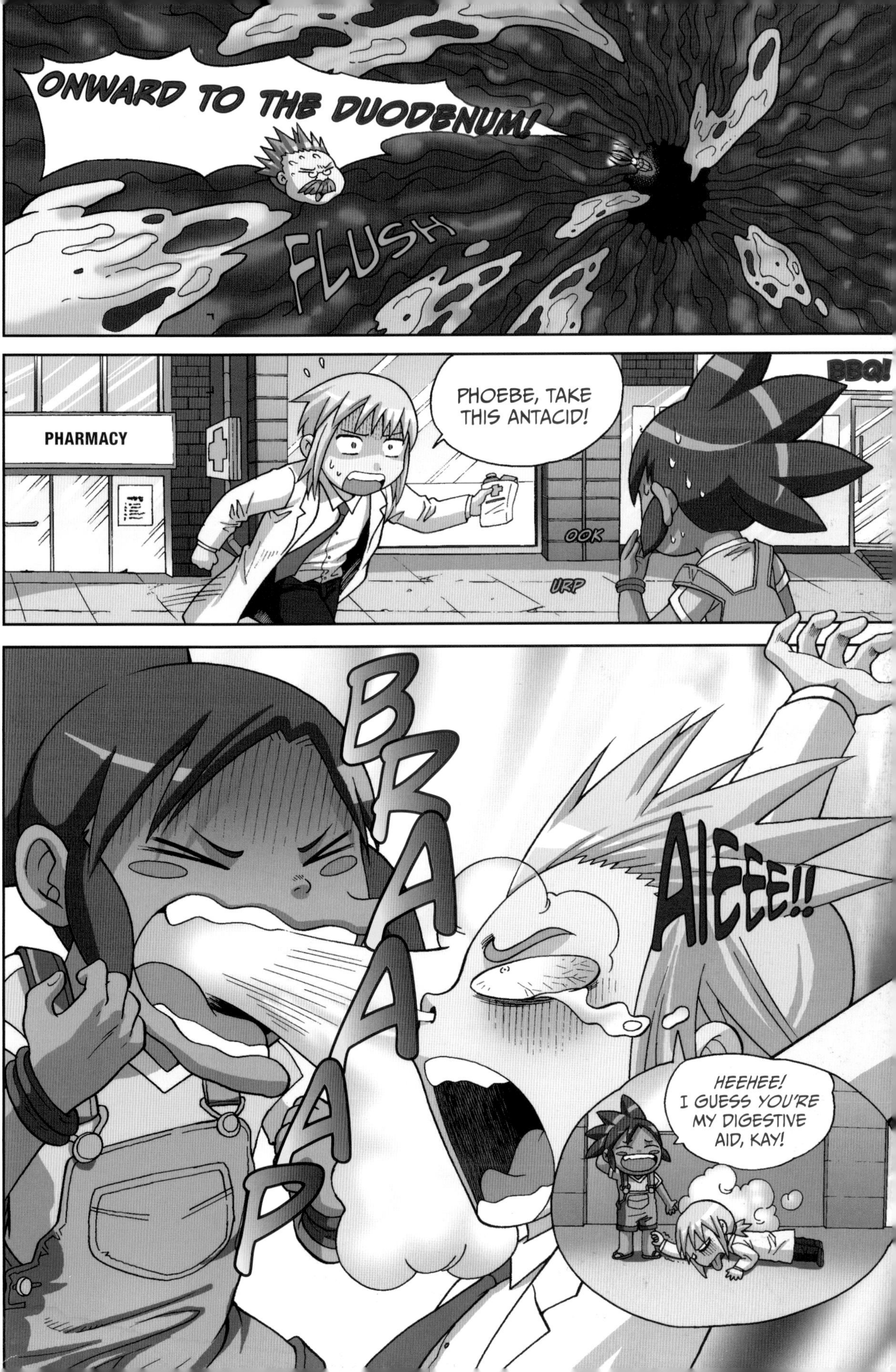
ONWARD TO THE DUODENUM!
FLUSH
PHARMACY
PHOEBE, TAKE THIS ANTACID!
BBQ!
OOK
URP
BRAAAAP
AIEEE!!
HEEHEE! I GUESS YOU'RE MY DIGESTIVE AID, KAY!

AN UPSET STOMACH

If you feel sick, bloated, or gassy right after eating, you may have indigestion. This happens when something goes wrong in your stomach or intestines. People often get indigestion because of bad eating habits, like eating too much or eating too quickly. There are some common sense steps you can take to keep indigestion away. Don't eat more than you need, and don't eat 2 to 3 hours before bedtime. Avoid foods that are too spicy or greasy and drinks that have lots of caffeine.

DIGESTIVE MEDICINES

You can fix most small digestion problems with medicines, like antacids, pink bismuth, and drugs that actually block the production of stomach acid. Antacids, like Tums or Rolaids, are a quick fix that make stomach acid weaker. Pink bismuth, like Pepto-Bismol or Kaopectate, works as an anti-inflammatory, antacid, and anti-microbial agent. Anti-secretory drugs, like Zantac or Prilosec, stop your stomach from making as much acid. As helpful as these treatments can be, if you take them too often, your body will need them all the time and your digestive system won't work as well anymore. It's best to take digestive medicine only when you have to.

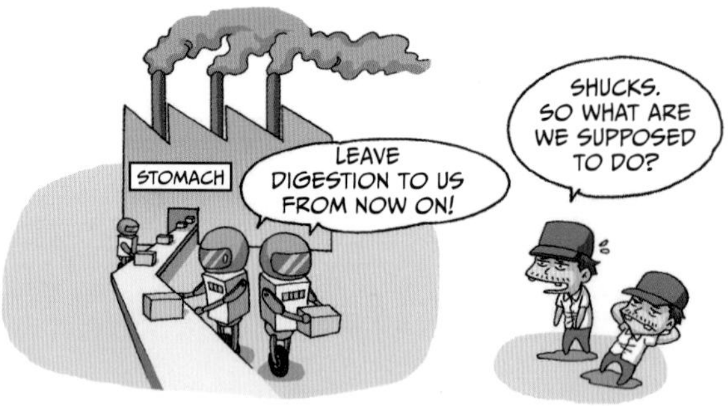
STOMACH
LEAVE DIGESTION TO US FROM NOW ON!
SHUCKS. SO WHAT ARE WE SUPPOSED TO DO?

OTHER COMMON DIGESTIVE PROBLEMS

When you have indigestion, you should feel better after you eat a few healthy meals. But you have to be careful—some stomach problems might feel like indigestion but are much more serious! If you get indigestion a lot, see a doctor. The doctor will find out what is wrong and help you.

GASTRITIS AND STOMACH ULCERS

Gastritis is an inflammation of the lining in your stomach. It can happen when the mucous lining of your stomach wears down. The inflammation can make you feel pain in your belly.

If it gets worse, gastritis can turn into a stomach ulcer, a very painful sore in the stomach's wall. With an ulcer, you may even see blood in your feces. People who are really stressed out or who drink lots of alcohol can get ulcers, but people

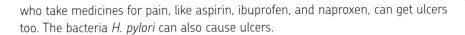

who take medicines for pain, like aspirin, ibuprofen, and naproxen, can get ulcers too. The bacteria *H. pylori* can also cause ulcers.

GASTROENTERITIS (INTESTINAL INFLAMMATION)

Gastroenteritis is a serious infection inside the intestine. It can be caused by some bacteria, parasites, or viruses, so good hygiene can prevent this infection. If you have a fever along with abdominal pain or vomiting, the best thing to do is to go to a doctor right away for a checkup. People who have gastroenteritis should drink lots of water.

I HAVE HEARTBURN BECAUSE OF YOU, DR. BRAIN!

JUST RELAX, KAY! YOUR STOMACH WILL GET WORSE IF YOU'RE STRESSED OUT.

APPENDICITIS

Appendicitis is an infection in the appendix. Your appendix is at the bottom of the cecum, the start of the large intestine. If you have appendicitis, you will get a stomachache first. The stomachache might move to the right and down low on your belly. With time, this pain will get worse, and you might feel sick to your stomach and lose your appetite. You might throw up or get a fever, too. You can lose your life if you have appendicitis and don't go to a doctor. The infection can spread to your peritoneum—the lining of your abdominal cavity, where lots of your organs are. Doctors can treat appendicitis very easily; they just remove the appendix in surgery.

 ERUCTATION AND FLATULENCE

Eructation (burping) is when you let out gas through your mouth. This gas is from the air that came into your stomach along with food when you swallowed. Flatulence (farting) is when gas is released through the anus. This gas is produced when the bacteria in your large intestine break down food scraps. The large intestine makes about 7–10 liters of gas each day. Only 0.6 liters of it turns into flatulence. The rest is reabsorbed by the mucous membrane.

BURP

POOPPFFT

THAT IS TOXIC!

PARTY CRASHER AT THE DUODENUM

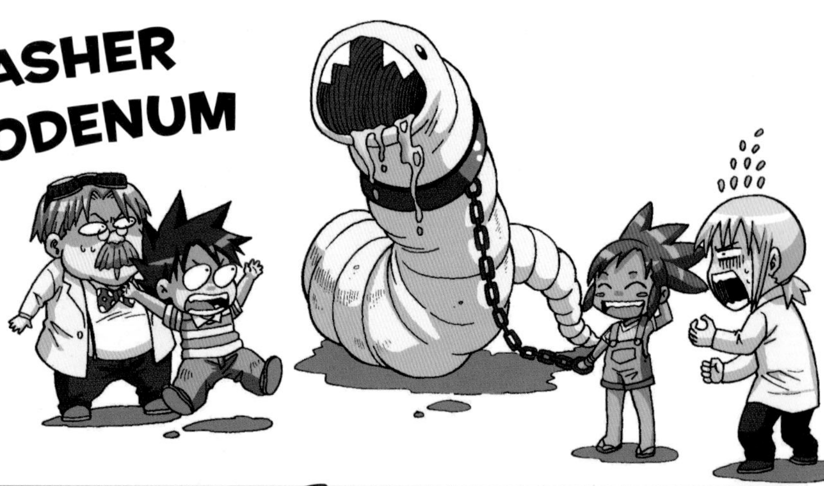

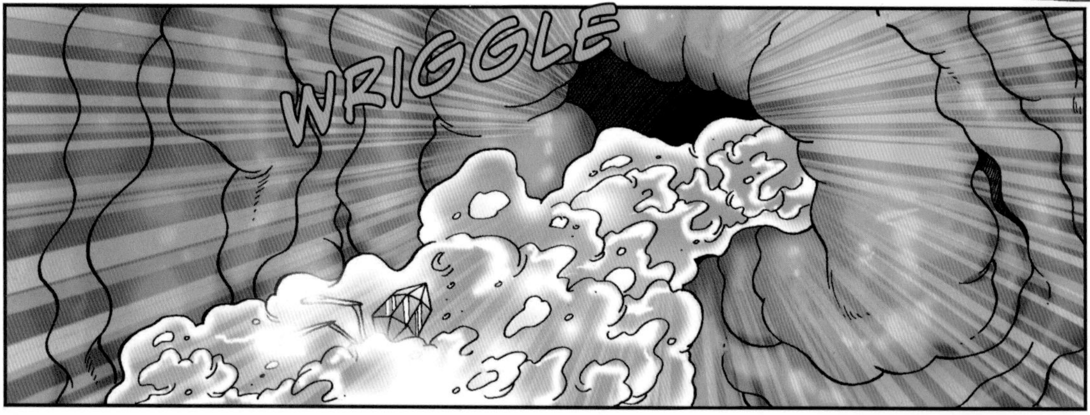
WRIGGLE

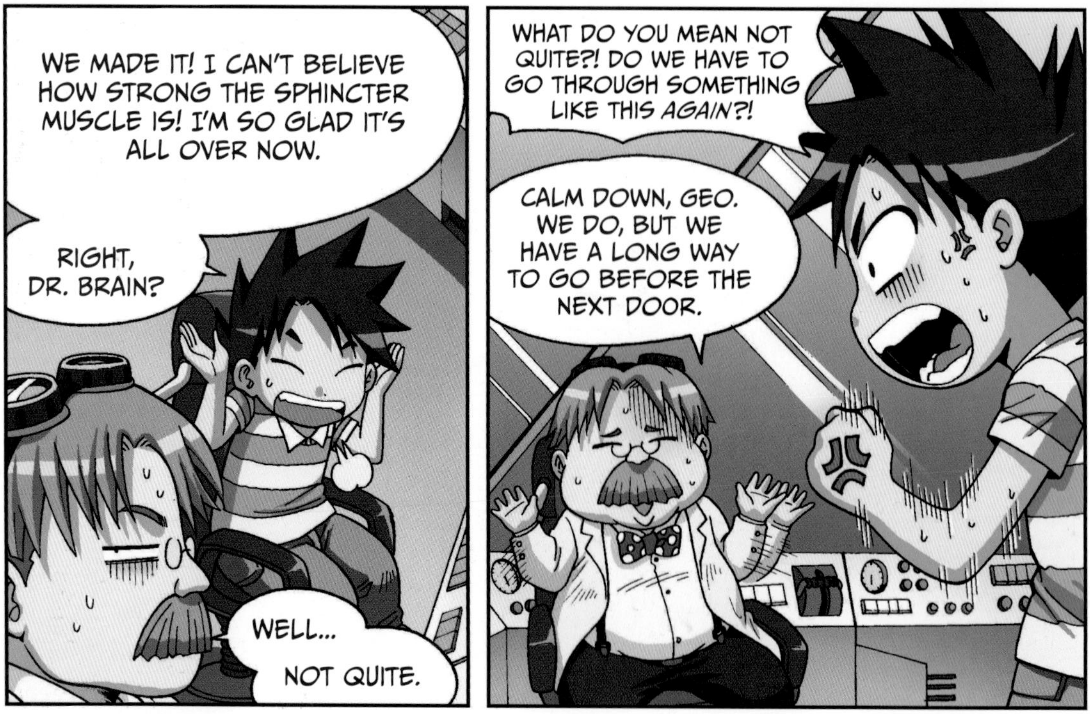
WE MADE IT! I CAN'T BELIEVE HOW STRONG THE SPHINCTER MUSCLE IS! I'M SO GLAD IT'S ALL OVER NOW.
RIGHT, DR. BRAIN?
WELL...
NOT QUITE.
WHAT DO YOU MEAN NOT QUITE?! DO WE HAVE TO GO THROUGH SOMETHING LIKE THIS *AGAIN*?!
CALM DOWN, GEO. WE DO, BUT WE HAVE A LONG WAY TO GO BEFORE THE NEXT DOOR.

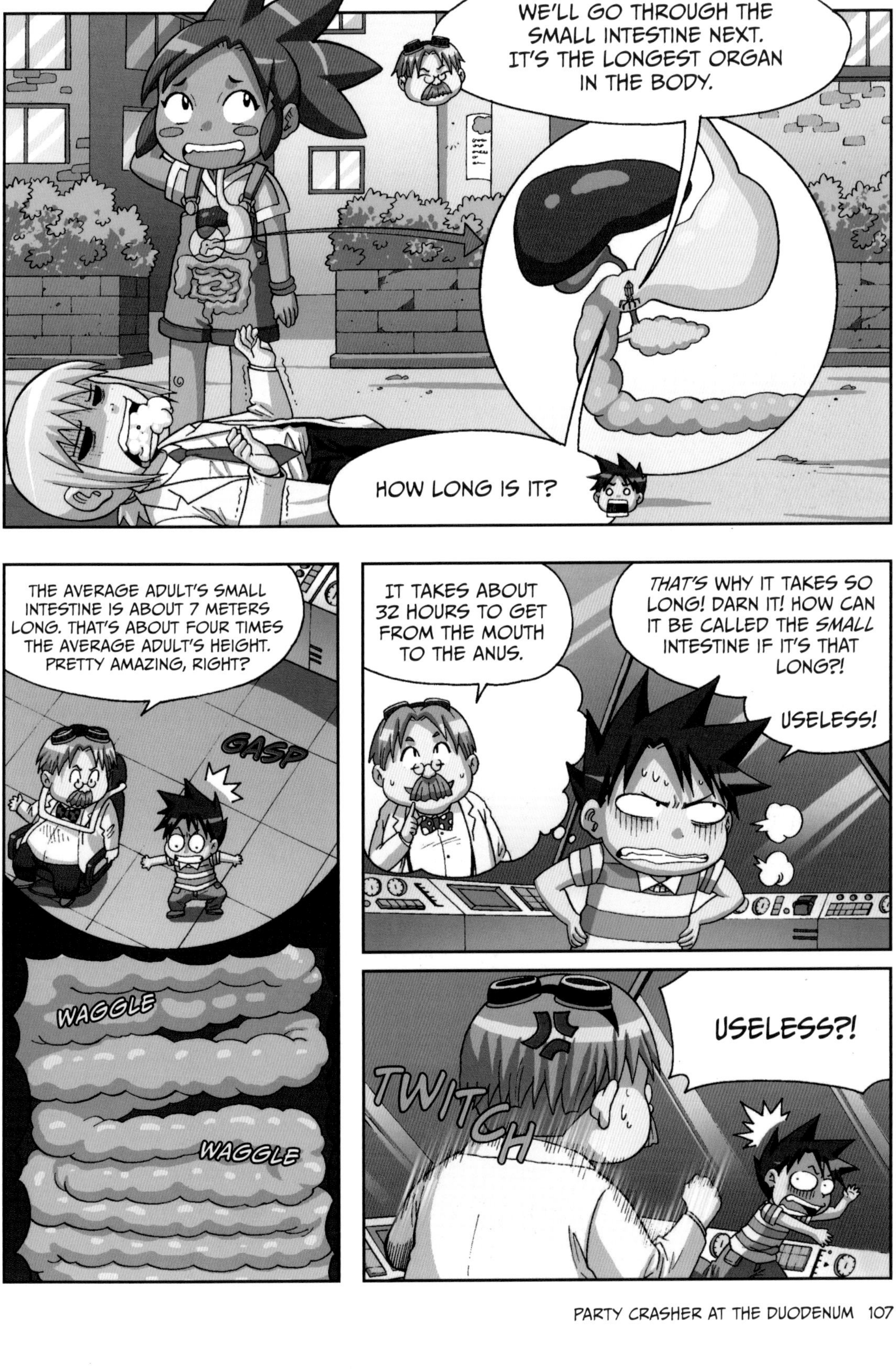
WE'LL GO THROUGH THE SMALL INTESTINE NEXT. IT'S THE LONGEST ORGAN IN THE BODY.
HOW LONG IS IT?
THE AVERAGE ADULT'S SMALL INTESTINE IS ABOUT 7 METERS LONG. THAT'S ABOUT FOUR TIMES THE AVERAGE ADULT'S HEIGHT. PRETTY AMAZING, RIGHT?
GASP
WAGGLE
WAGGLE
IT TAKES ABOUT 32 HOURS TO GET FROM THE MOUTH TO THE ANUS.
THAT'S WHY IT TAKES SO LONG! DARN IT! HOW CAN IT BE CALLED THE *SMALL* INTESTINE IF IT'S THAT LONG?!
USELESS!
USELESS?!
TWITCH

THERE IS ABSOLUTELY NOTHING USELESS IN THE HUMAN BODY!

EVEN THE SMALLEST CELL PLAYS AN IMPORTANT ROLE IN KEEPING US ALIVE AND MOVING!

THE SMALL INTESTINE IS VERY LONG BECAUSE THAT IS WHERE THE MOST IMPORTANT STEP OF DIGESTION HAPPENS. FOOD IS BROKEN DOWN AND THE NUTRIENTS ARE ABSORBED INTO THE BODY.

WITHOUT THE SMALL INTESTINE, YOUR BODY COULDN'T GET THE NUTRIENTS IT NEEDS. YOU WOULDN'T HAVE ANY ENERGY TO SURVIVE. IT WOULDN'T MATTER HOW MUCH YOU ATE.

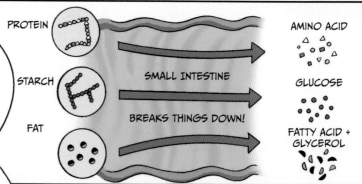

PROTEIN

STARCH

FAT

SMALL INTESTINE

BREAKS THINGS DOWN!

AMINO ACID

GLUCOSE

FATTY ACID + GLYCEROL

SMALL INTESTINE LABOR STRIKE!

I ATE *EVERYTHING*... BUT I STILL HAVE NO ENERGY...

HOW CAN YOU CALL THE SMALL INTESTINE USELESS WHEN IT PLAYS SUCH AN IMPORTANT ROLE!

NO, NO, NO! ISN'T IT WEIRD THAT IT'S CALLED A *SMALL* INTESTINE, BUT IT'S THE LONGEST ORGAN IN THE BODY?

THERE'S NOTHING STRANGE ABOUT THAT. IT'S NARROWER THAN THE LARGE INTESTINE. IT'S JUST REALLY *LONG!*

SMALL LARGE

STRETCH

LONG SHORT

OH— I GET IT!

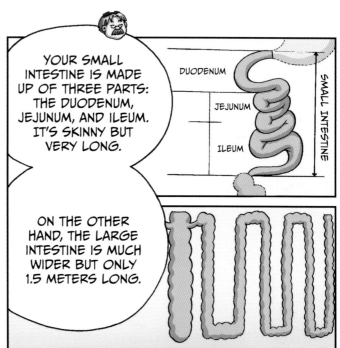

YOUR SMALL INTESTINE IS MADE UP OF THREE PARTS: THE DUODENUM, JEJUNUM, AND ILEUM. IT'S SKINNY BUT VERY LONG.

DUODENUM

JEJUNUM

ILEUM

SMALL INTESTINE

ON THE OTHER HAND, THE LARGE INTESTINE IS MUCH WIDER BUT ONLY 1.5 METERS LONG.

NOW WE'LL GO THROUGH THE SMALL INTESTINE AND LARGE INTESTINE TO—

ACK!

DR. BRAIN! THERE'S A STRANGE YELLOW LIQUID POURING OUT BEHIND YOU!

IT'S STARTING!

TAKE A GOOD LOOK. WE'RE IN THE FIRST PART OF THE SMALL INTESTINE, CALLED THE *DUODENUM.*

SPLOSHHHHHH

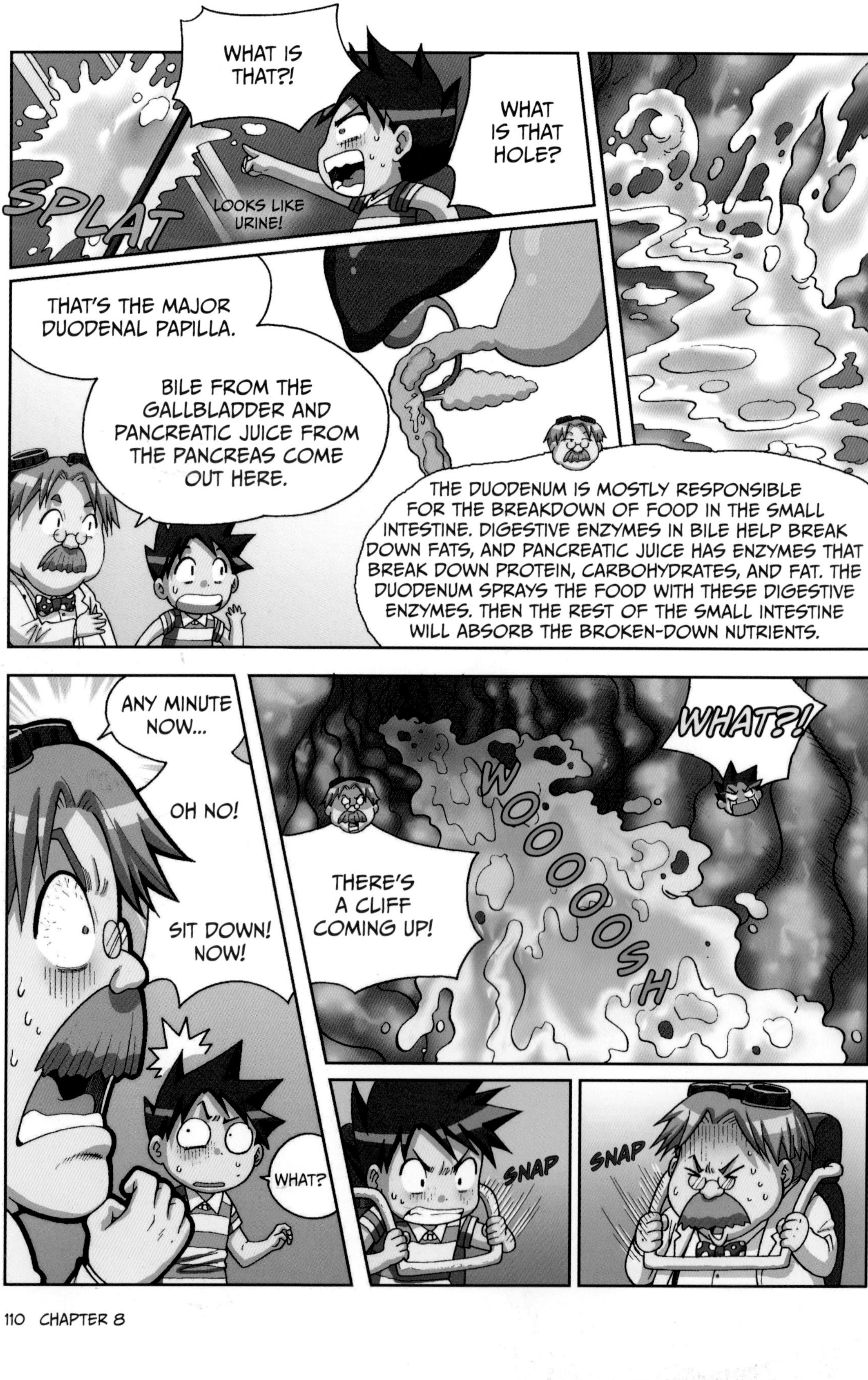

WHAT IS THAT?!
WHAT IS THAT HOLE?
SPLAT
LOOKS LIKE URINE!
THAT'S THE MAJOR DUODENAL PAPILLA.
BILE FROM THE GALLBLADDER AND PANCREATIC JUICE FROM THE PANCREAS COME OUT HERE.
THE DUODENUM IS MOSTLY RESPONSIBLE FOR THE BREAKDOWN OF FOOD IN THE SMALL INTESTINE. DIGESTIVE ENZYMES IN BILE HELP BREAK DOWN FATS, AND PANCREATIC JUICE HAS ENZYMES THAT BREAK DOWN PROTEIN, CARBOHYDRATES, AND FAT. THE DUODENUM SPRAYS THE FOOD WITH THESE DIGESTIVE ENZYMES. THEN THE REST OF THE SMALL INTESTINE WILL ABSORB THE BROKEN-DOWN NUTRIENTS.
ANY MINUTE NOW...
OH NO!
SIT DOWN! NOW!
WHAT?
WHAT?!
WOOOOOOSH
THERE'S A CLIFF COMING UP!
SNAP
SNAP

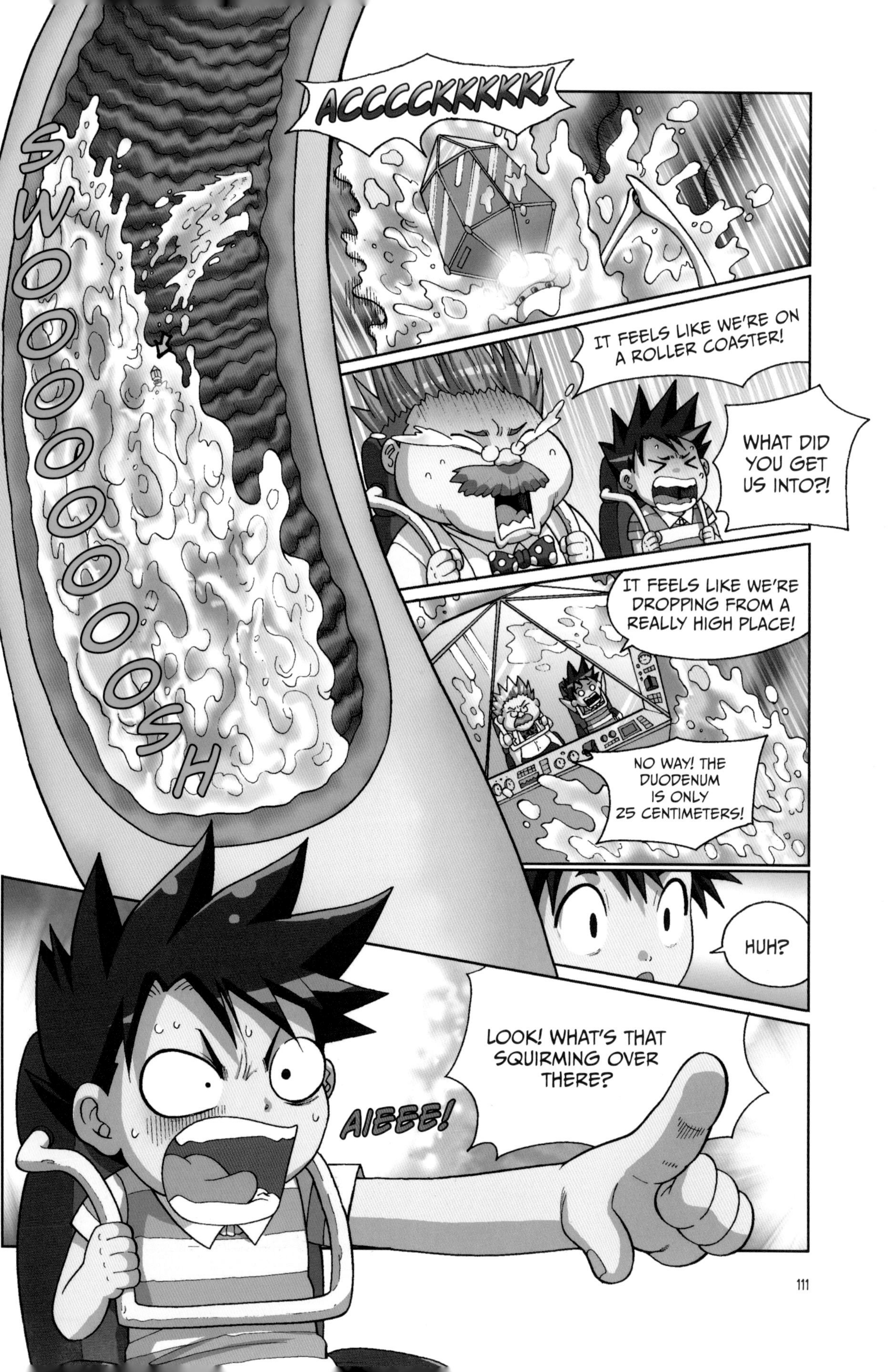

SWOOOOOOOOSH
ACCCCKKKKK!
IT FEELS LIKE WE'RE ON A ROLLER COASTER!
WHAT DID YOU GET US INTO?!
IT FEELS LIKE WE'RE DROPPING FROM A REALLY HIGH PLACE!
NO WAY! THE DUODENUM IS ONLY 25 CENTIMETERS!
HUH?
LOOK! WHAT'S THAT SQUIRMING OVER THERE?
AIEEE!

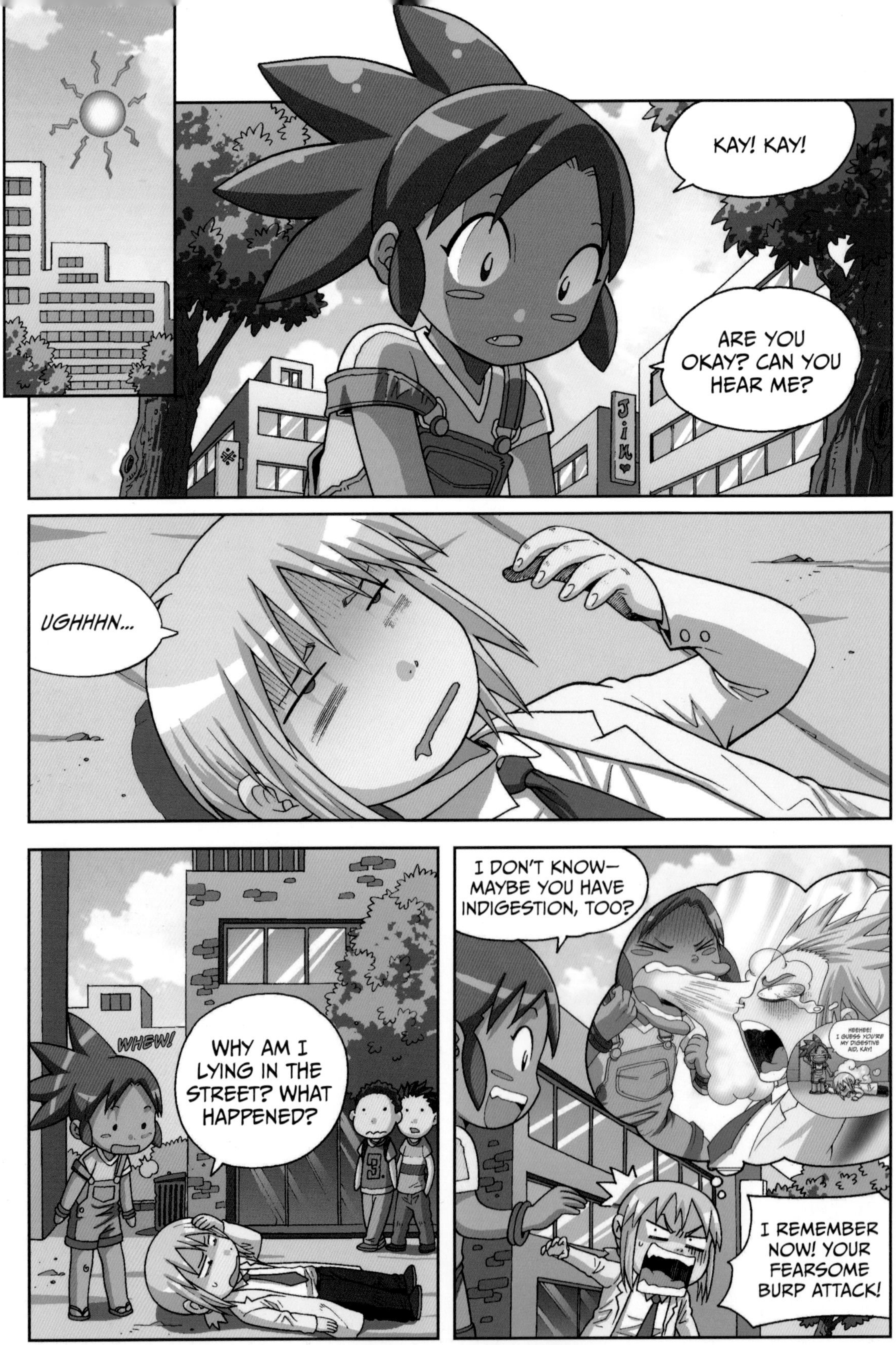
KAY! KAY!
ARE YOU OKAY? CAN YOU HEAR ME?
UGHHHN...
WHEW!
WHY AM I LYING IN THE STREET? WHAT HAPPENED?
I DON'T KNOW— MAYBE YOU HAVE INDIGESTION, TOO?
HEEHEE! I GUESS YOU'RE MY DIGESTIVE AID, KAY!
I REMEMBER NOW! YOUR FEARSOME BURP ATTACK!

YOU EAT SO MUCH—NO WONDER YOU BURP LIKE A MOUNTAIN MAN. IT'S STRANGE THAT YOU'RE STILL SO THIN.

PHOEBE, ARE YOU SURE YOUR NUTRIENTS AREN'T BEING STOLEN OR SOMETHING?

TAP TAP

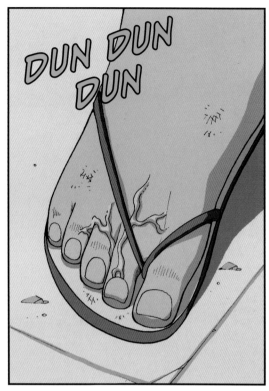

DUN DUN DUN

AUGH! WHAT IS THIS?!

THIS IS DEFINITELY WHERE A HOOKWORM BURROWED IN!

SPLAK

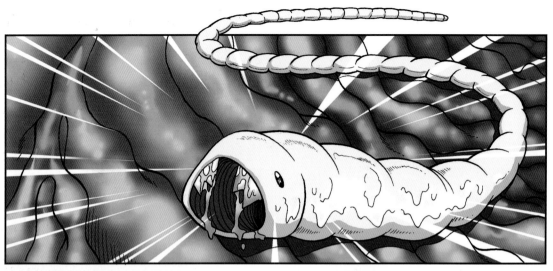

SHE HAS PARASITES TOO?

PA-PA-PARASITE?

EW!

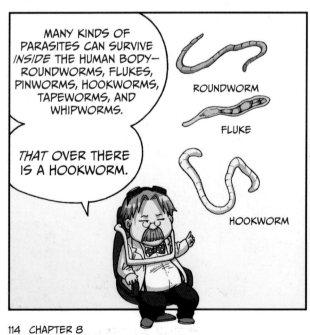

MANY KINDS OF PARASITES CAN SURVIVE *INSIDE* THE HUMAN BODY— ROUNDWORMS, FLUKES, PINWORMS, HOOKWORMS, TAPEWORMS, AND WHIPWORMS.

THAT OVER THERE IS A HOOKWORM.

ROUNDWORM

FLUKE

HOOKWORM

BUT WHAT IS IT DOING HERE?

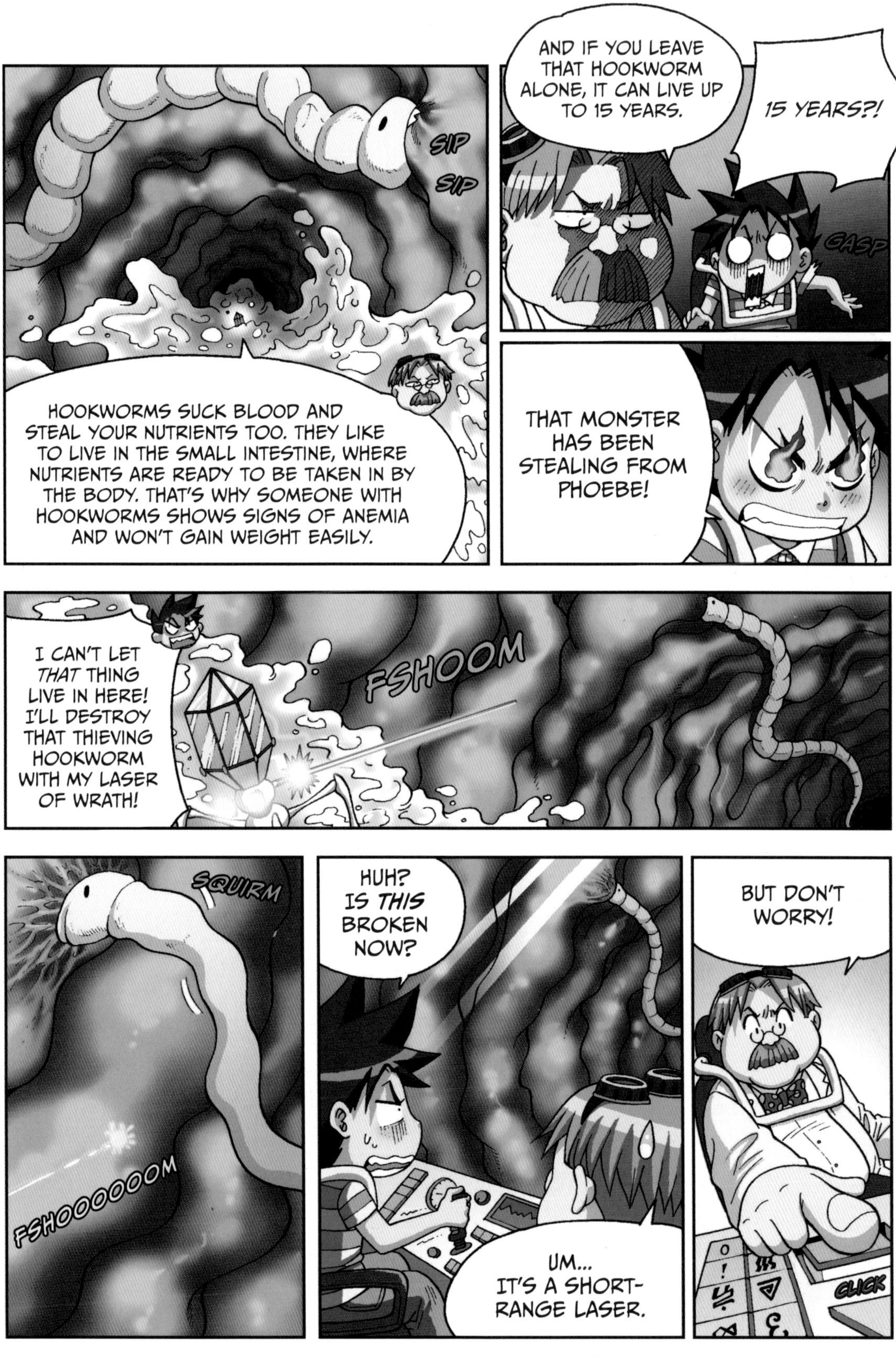
SIP
SIP
HOOKWORMS SUCK BLOOD AND STEAL YOUR NUTRIENTS TOO. THEY LIKE TO LIVE IN THE SMALL INTESTINE, WHERE NUTRIENTS ARE READY TO BE TAKEN IN BY THE BODY. THAT'S WHY SOMEONE WITH HOOKWORMS SHOWS SIGNS OF ANEMIA AND WON'T GAIN WEIGHT EASILY.
AND IF YOU LEAVE THAT HOOKWORM ALONE, IT CAN LIVE UP TO 15 YEARS.
15 YEARS?!
GASP
THAT MONSTER HAS BEEN STEALING FROM PHOEBE!
I CAN'T LET *THAT* THING LIVE IN HERE! I'LL DESTROY THAT THIEVING HOOKWORM WITH MY LASER OF WRATH!
FSHOOM
SQUIRM
FSHOOOOOOM
HUH? IS *THIS* BROKEN NOW?
UM... IT'S A SHORT-RANGE LASER.
BUT DON'T WORRY!
CLICK

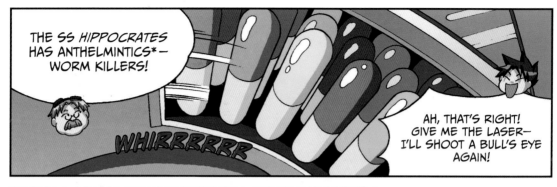

THE SS HIPPOCRATES HAS ANTHELMINTICS*— WORM KILLERS!
WHIRRRRRRR
AH, THAT'S RIGHT! GIVE ME THE LASER— I'LL SHOOT A BULL'S EYE AGAIN!
HOLD ON A SECOND. DIFFERENT PARASITES NEED DIFFERENT DRUGS.
WE NEED ALBENDAZOLE FOR HOOKWORMS.
CLICK CLICK
UH-OH!
SQUIRM
UH...
DARN IT, THAT'S THE ONLY DRUG WE'RE MISSING!
WHAT?!
BURROW BURROW
LOOK, IT'S TRYING TO ESCAPE!

* ANTHELMINTICS ARE ANTI-PARASITE DRUGS ALSO KNOWN AS *WORMERS* OR *DEWORMERS*.

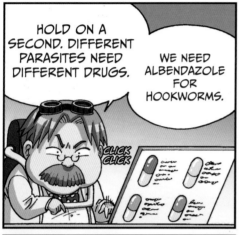

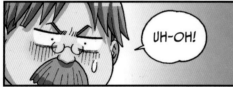

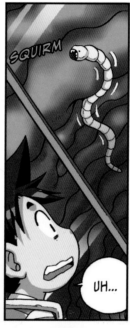

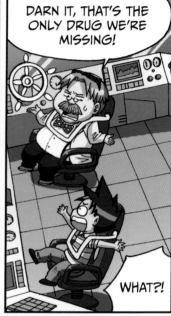

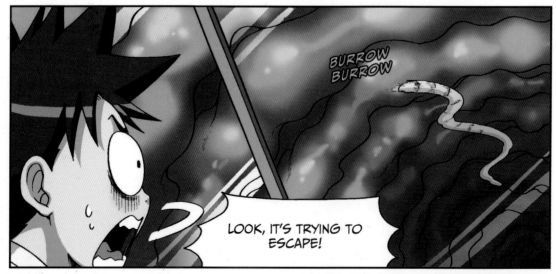

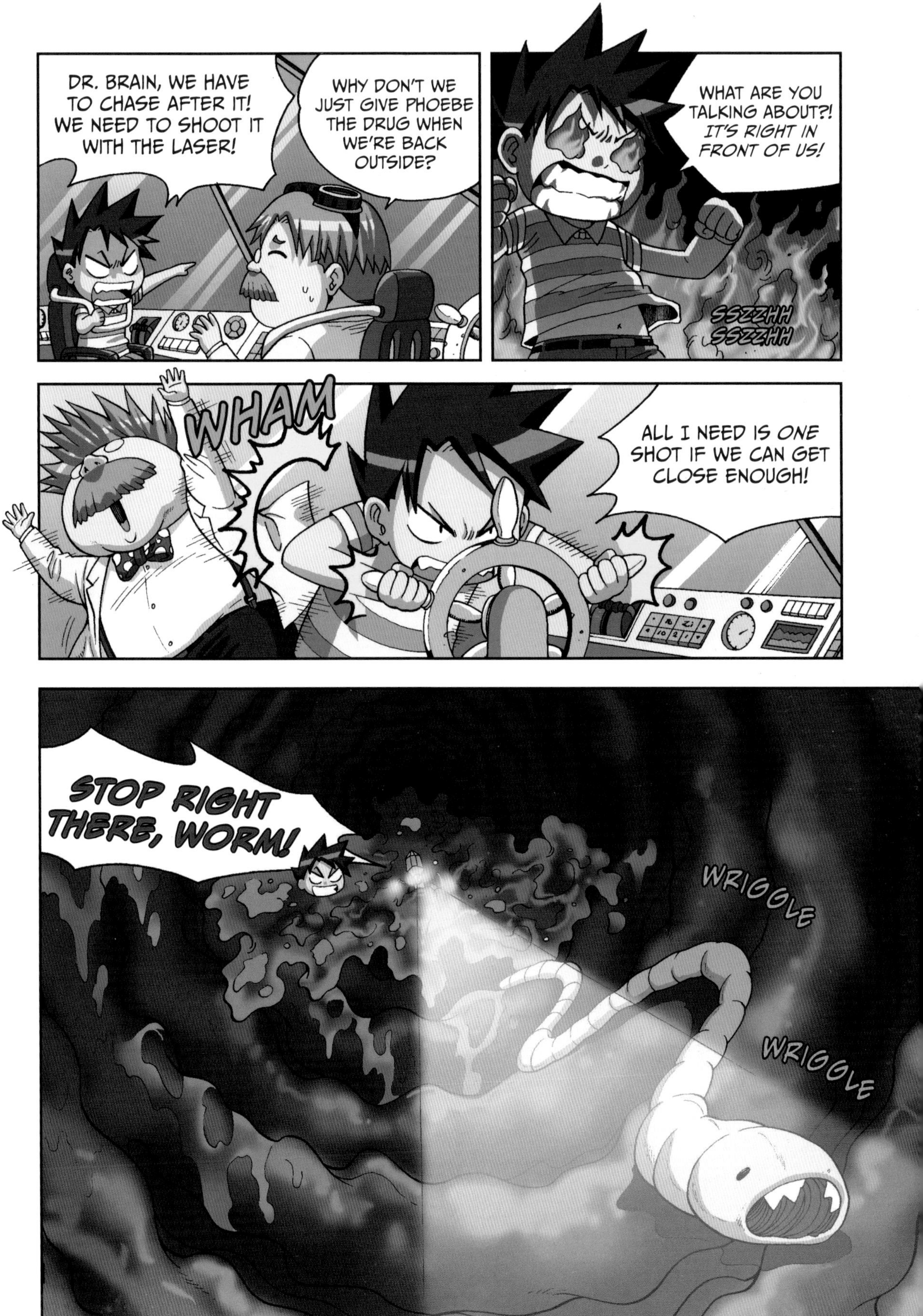

DR. BRAIN, WE HAVE TO CHASE AFTER IT! WE NEED TO SHOOT IT WITH THE LASER!
WHY DON'T WE JUST GIVE PHOEBE THE DRUG WHEN WE'RE BACK OUTSIDE?
WHAT ARE YOU TALKING ABOUT?! *IT'S RIGHT IN FRONT OF US!*
SSZZHH SSZZHH
WHAM
ALL I NEED IS *ONE* SHOT IF WE CAN GET CLOSE ENOUGH!
STOP RIGHT THERE, WORM!
WRIGGLE
WRIGGLE

SMALL INTESTINE, SUPER ABSORBER

After going through the stomach, food in your body goes to the small intestine. The length of this digestive organ is 6–7 meters long (about 20–23 feet)—quite long indeed. There are three parts to the small intestine: the duodenum, jejunum, and ileum. The small intestine breaks down food even more than the stomach does, and it absorbs nutrients to power the body. The leftover food scraps then go to the large intestine.

DIGESTION IN THE DUODENUM

The duodenum plays a big role in digestion, even though it is only about 25 centimeters (about 10 inches) long. It spurts important digestive fluids that help us digest food. The minor duodenal papilla and major duodenal papilla secrete bile and pancreatic juice.

Bile (produced by the liver) aids in breaking down the fat in food. Pancreatic juice (produced by the pancreas) and other intestinal juices help to digest protein, fat, and carbohydrates. This process of breaking down foods with enzymes is called *chemical digestion*. These fluids also protect the intestine by weakening the stomach acid that's been mixed with the food.

Then, the food goes down to the jejunum, where nutrient absorption begins in earnest.

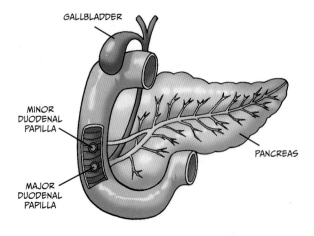

GALLBLADDER

MINOR
DUODENAL
PAPILLA

MAJOR
DUODENAL
PAPILLA

PANCREAS

STRUCTURE OF THE
DUODENUM

ABSORPTION IN THE JEJUNUM AND ILEUM

The nutrients broken down by digestive enzymes are absorbed by the jejunum and ileum, and they become energy for the body. In the jejunum and ileum, our villi—tiny, fingerlike things on the walls of the intestines—help absorb nutrients.

The epithelial cells in the intestine that make up your villi are some of the fastest growing in the whole body. The small intestine has a new lining about every four to five days!

MOVEMENTS OF THE SMALL INTESTINE

The small intestine moves in two ways. Segmental movement mixes the food and intestinal juice by squeezing together the sides of the small intestine's walls. This motion is like the segmental movement of the stomach, except the mixing happens all along the small intestine, at regular intervals (see page 135). After digestion is complete and all the nutrients have been absorbed, peristalsis sends the food scraps to the large intestine in a motion that's similar to the one used by the esophagus and stomach.

WHERE'S GEO?

GEO

VS.

THE PARASITES

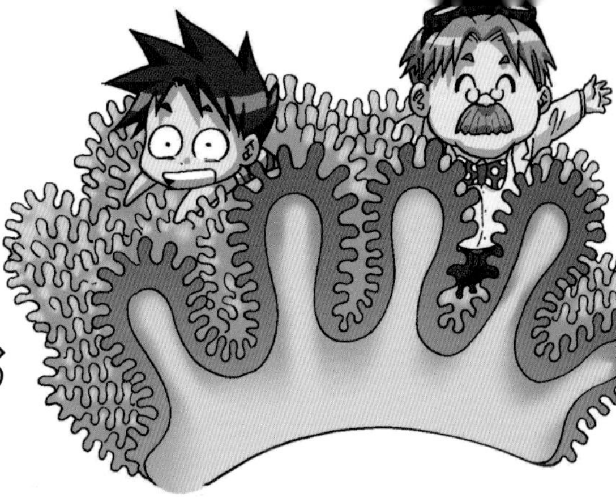

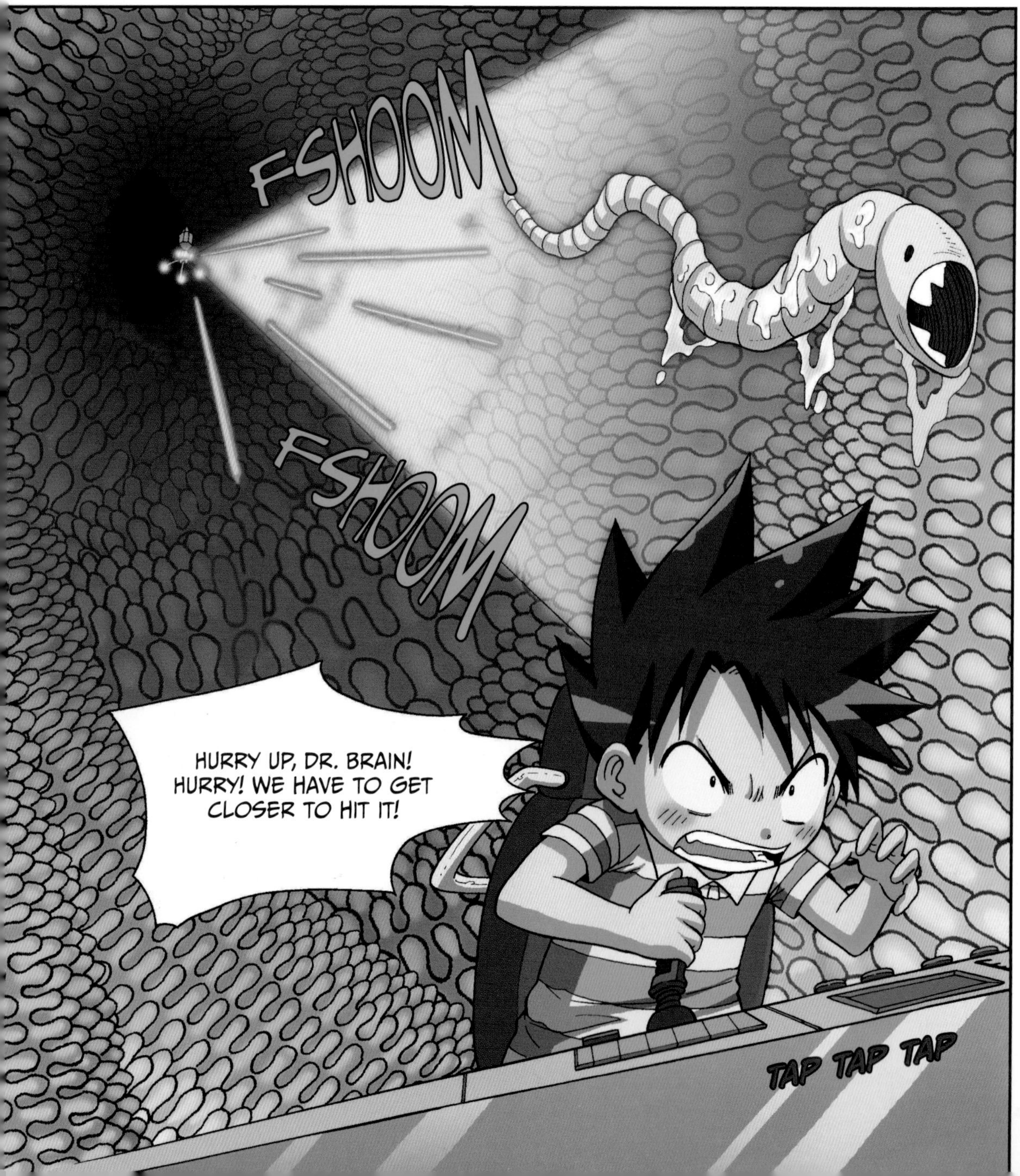
FSHOOM
FSHOOM
HURRY UP, DR. BRAIN! HURRY! WE HAVE TO GET CLOSER TO HIT IT!
TAP TAP TAP

THIS IS AS FAST AS WE CAN GO ON A CURVY ROAD LIKE THIS!
LOOK!
WATCH OUT!
!!
VOOSH
AHHHHH!
VROOOOOOOM
WE REALLY CAN'T GO FASTER THAN THIS IN THE SMALL INTESTINE.
OKAY, OKAY, FINE.

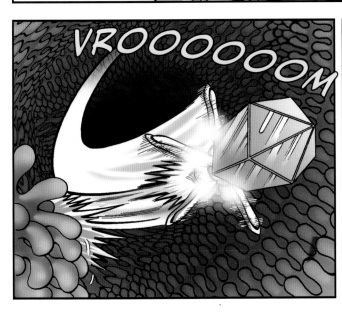

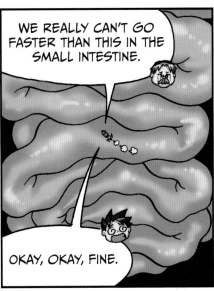

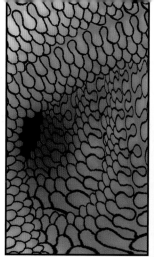

WHERE DID THAT THING GO?

WHRRR

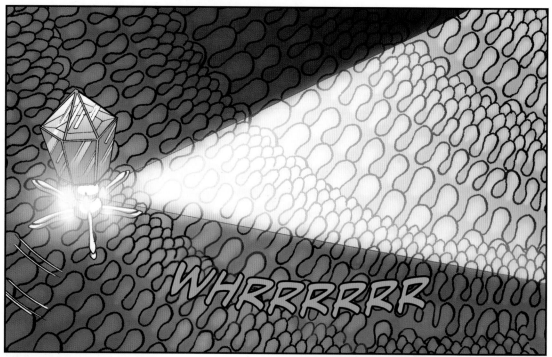

WHRRRRRR

IT COULD BE HIDING IN THE WRINKLY FOLDS. WHY IS IT SO WRINKLY HERE?

BECAUSE OF WHAT THE SMALL INTESTINE DOES. MORE WRINKLES MEANS HAVING MORE AREA TO ABSORB NUTRIENTS.

OH, I SEE.

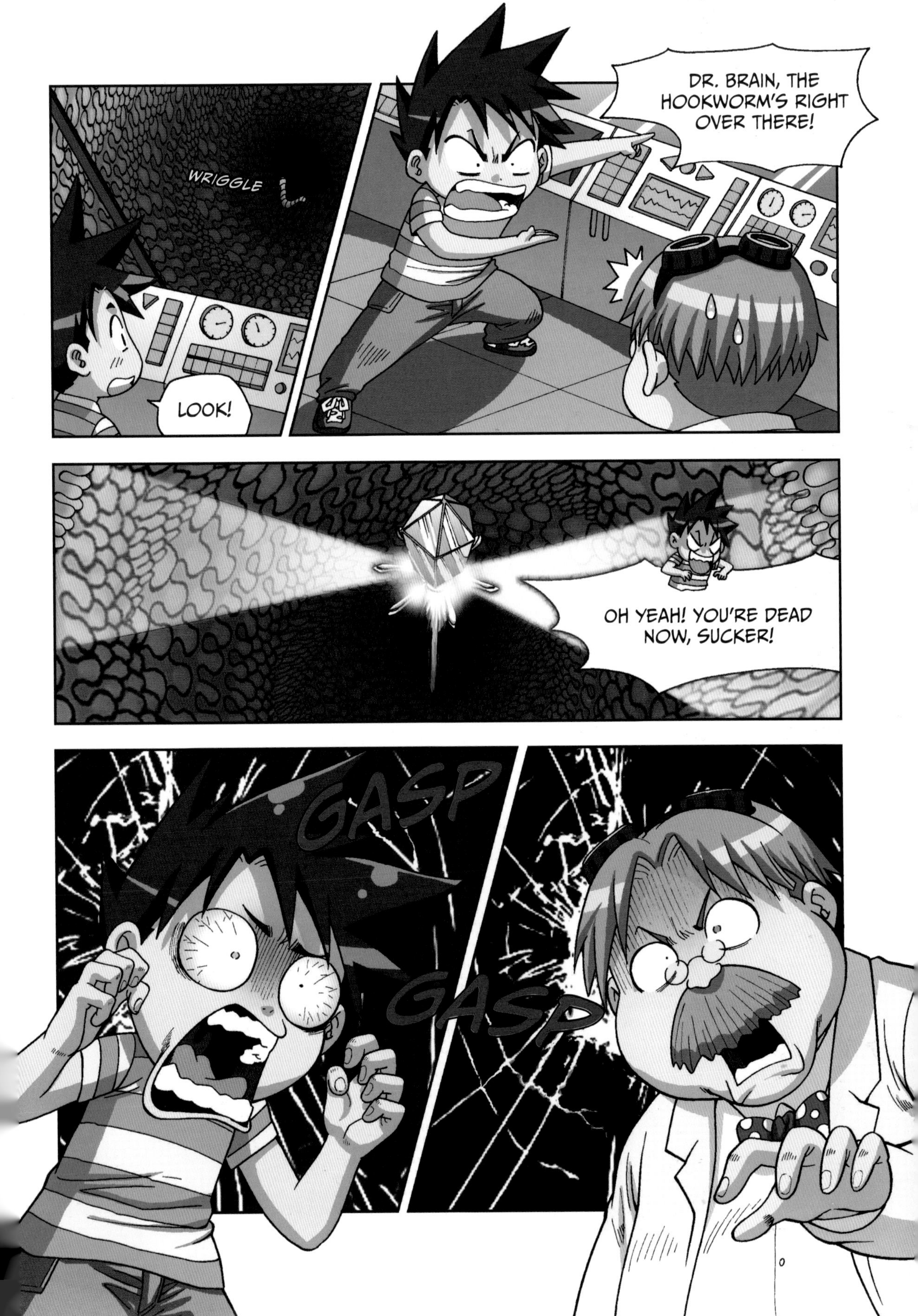
DR. BRAIN, THE HOOKWORM'S RIGHT OVER THERE!
WRIGGLE
LOOK!
OH YEAH! YOU'RE DEAD NOW, SUCKER!
GASP
GASP

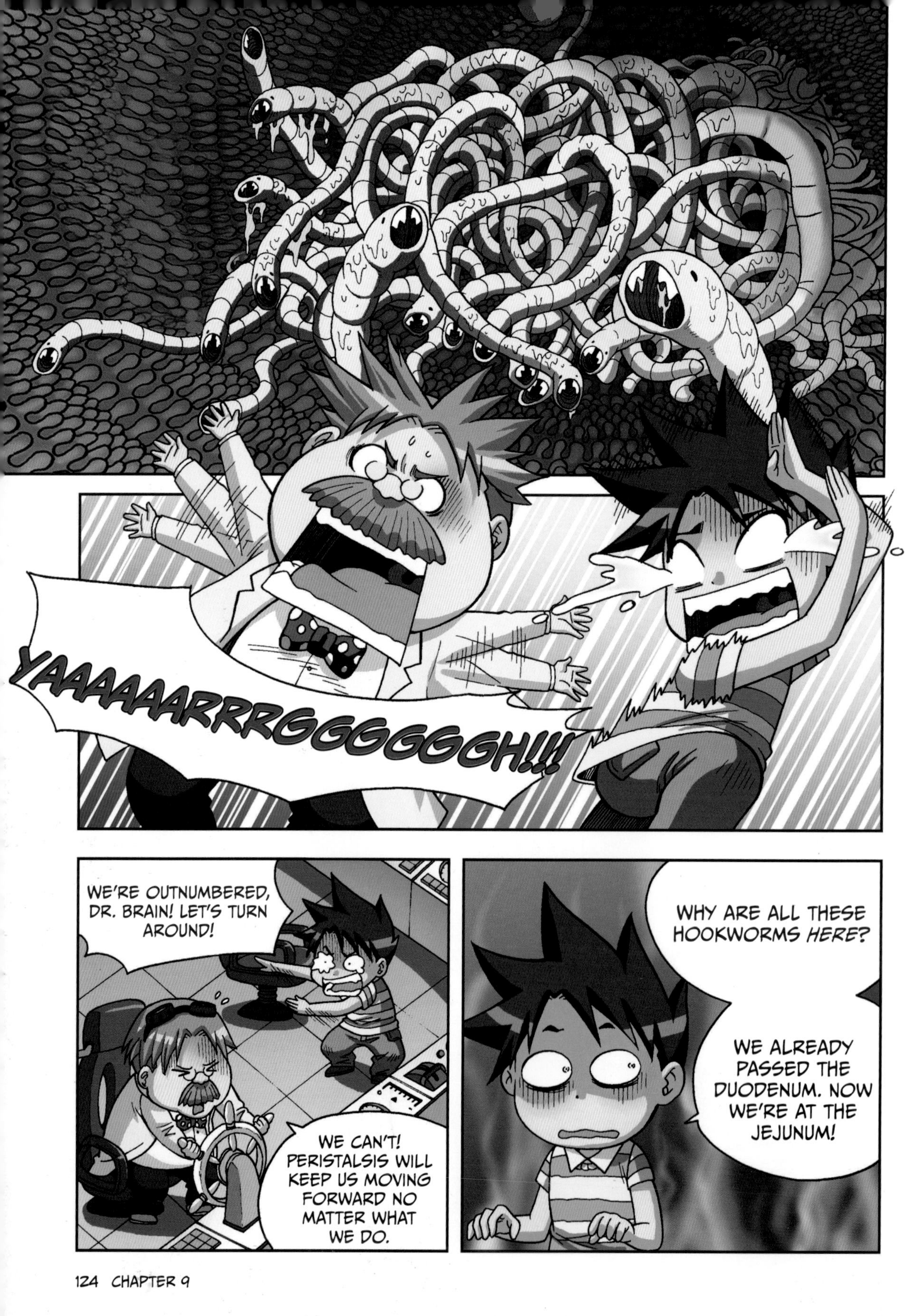
YAAAAAARRRGGGGGGGH!!!
WE'RE OUTNUMBERED, DR. BRAIN! LET'S TURN AROUND!
WE CAN'T! PERISTALSIS WILL KEEP US MOVING FORWARD NO MATTER WHAT WE DO.
WHY ARE ALL THESE HOOKWORMS HERE?
WE ALREADY PASSED THE DUODENUM. NOW WE'RE AT THE JEJUNUM!

PEOPLE FIRST FOUND HOOKWORMS IN THE DUODENUM IN 1838. THAT DOESN'T MEAN THAT'S THE ONLY PLACE THEY LIVE. MOST PARASITES LIVE IN THE JEJUNUM BECAUSE THAT'S WHERE MOST OF THE NUTRIENTS ARE!

OKAY...THERE IS NO NEED FOR US TO PANIC JUST BECAUSE WE'RE OUTNUMBERED.

WRIGGLE WRIGGLE

THINK OF SPAGHETTI... THINK OF SPAGHETTI...

WRIGGLE WRIGGLE

SHUDDER

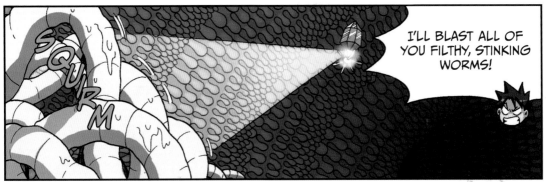

S Q U I R M

I'LL BLAST ALL OF YOU FILTHY, STINKING WORMS!

SWOOOOOOP

AUGH!!

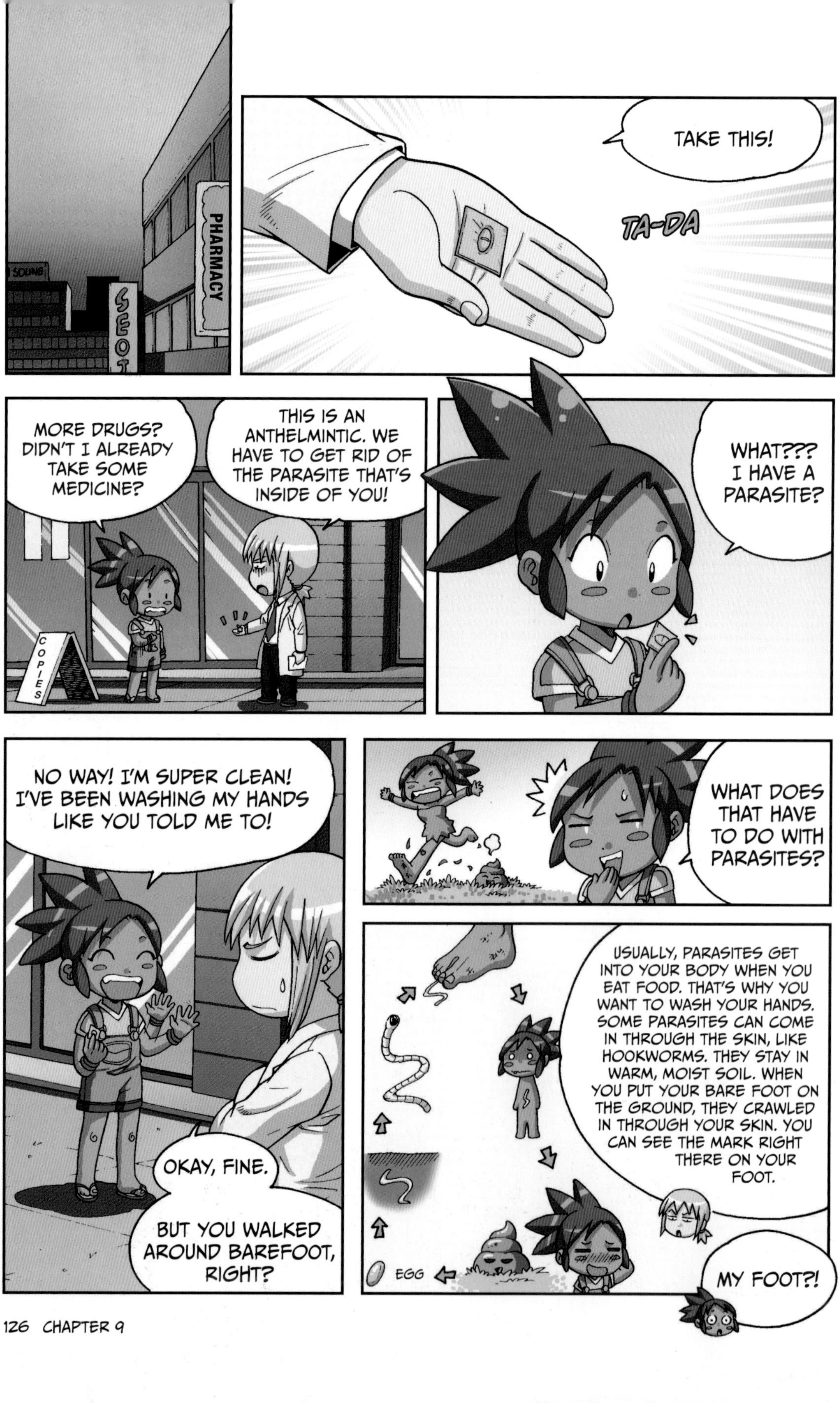

PHARMACY
SEOT
SOUND
TAKE THIS!
TA-DA
MORE DRUGS? DIDN'T I ALREADY TAKE SOME MEDICINE?
THIS IS AN ANTHELMINTIC. WE HAVE TO GET RID OF THE PARASITE THAT'S INSIDE OF YOU!
COPIES
WHAT??? I HAVE A PARASITE?
NO WAY! I'M SUPER CLEAN! I'VE BEEN WASHING MY HANDS LIKE YOU TOLD ME TO!
OKAY, FINE.
BUT YOU WALKED AROUND BAREFOOT, RIGHT?
WHAT DOES THAT HAVE TO DO WITH PARASITES?
USUALLY, PARASITES GET INTO YOUR BODY WHEN YOU EAT FOOD. THAT'S WHY YOU WANT TO WASH YOUR HANDS. SOME PARASITES CAN COME IN THROUGH THE SKIN, LIKE HOOKWORMS. THEY STAY IN WARM, MOIST SOIL. WHEN YOU PUT YOUR BARE FOOT ON THE GROUND, THEY CRAWLED IN THROUGH YOUR SKIN. YOU CAN SEE THE MARK RIGHT THERE ON YOUR FOOT.
EGG
MY FOOT?!

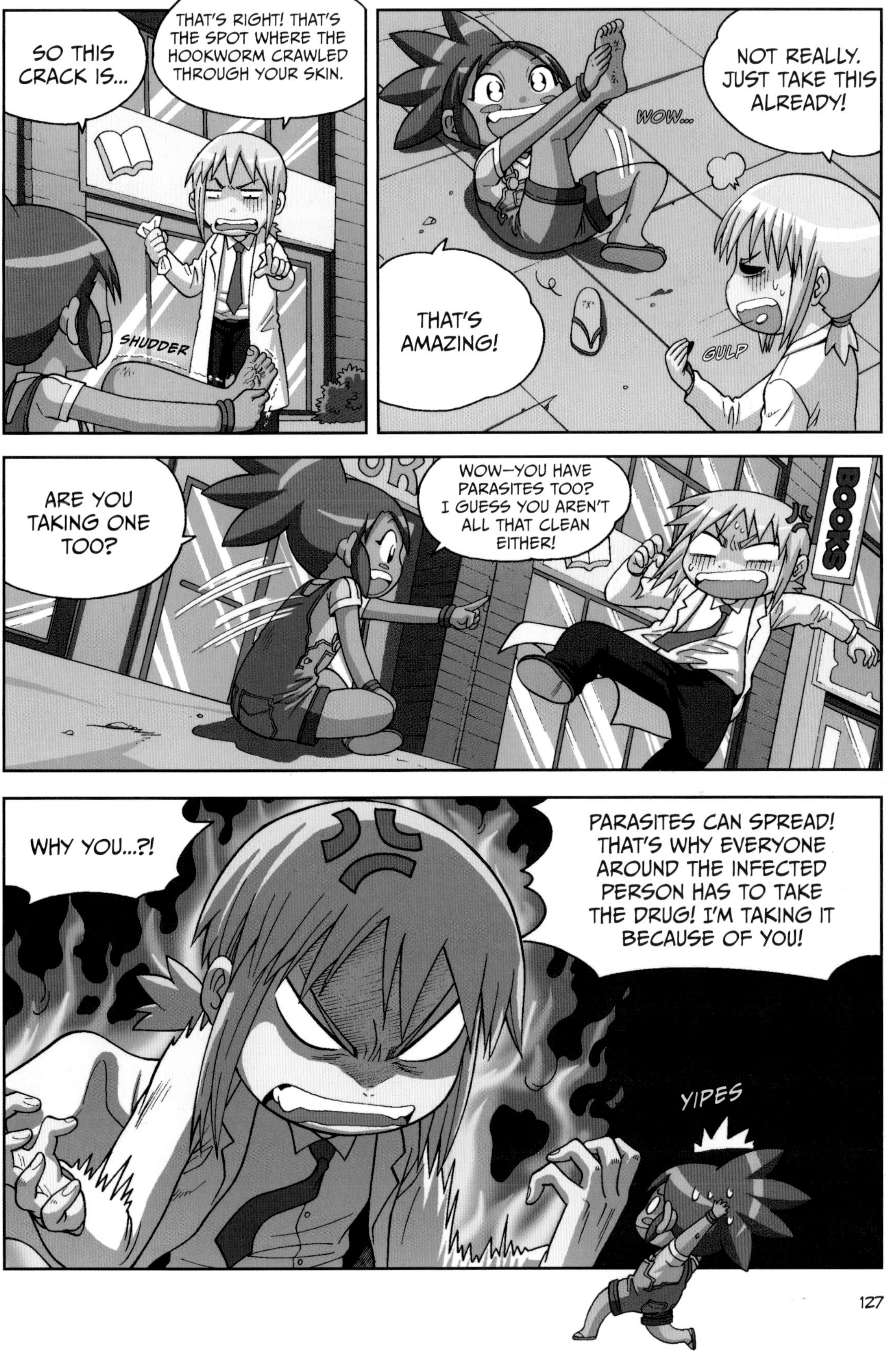
SO THIS CRACK IS...
THAT'S RIGHT! THAT'S THE SPOT WHERE THE HOOKWORM CRAWLED THROUGH YOUR SKIN.
SHUDDER
NOT REALLY. JUST TAKE THIS ALREADY!
WOW...
THAT'S AMAZING!
GULP
ARE YOU TAKING ONE TOO?
WOW—YOU HAVE PARASITES TOO? I GUESS YOU AREN'T ALL THAT CLEAN EITHER!
BOOKS
WHY YOU...?!
PARASITES CAN SPREAD! THAT'S WHY EVERYONE AROUND THE INFECTED PERSON HAS TO TAKE THE DRUG! I'M TAKING IT BECAUSE OF YOU!
YIPES

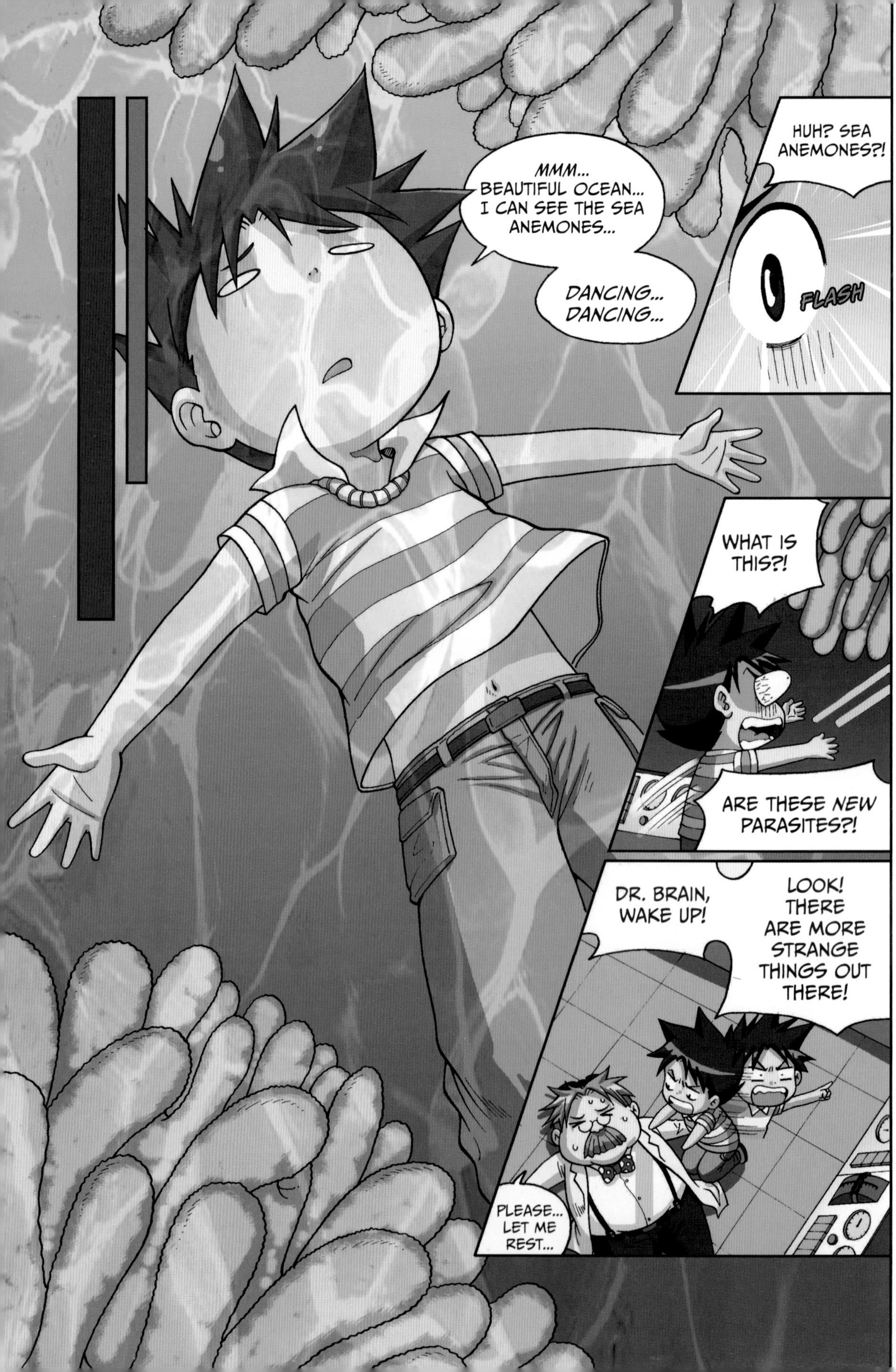
MMM... BEAUTIFUL OCEAN... I CAN SEE THE SEA ANEMONES...
DANCING... DANCING...
HUH? SEA ANEMONES?!
FLASH
WHAT IS THIS?!
ARE THESE *NEW* PARASITES?!
DR. BRAIN, WAKE UP!
LOOK! THERE ARE MORE STRANGE THINGS OUT THERE!
PLEASE... LET ME REST...

THOSE ARE JUST THE VILLI ON THE SMALL INTESTINE.

VILLI???

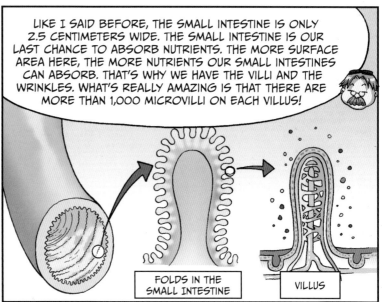

LIKE I SAID BEFORE, THE SMALL INTESTINE IS ONLY 2.5 CENTIMETERS WIDE. THE SMALL INTESTINE IS OUR LAST CHANCE TO ABSORB NUTRIENTS. THE MORE SURFACE AREA HERE, THE MORE NUTRIENTS OUR SMALL INTESTINES CAN ABSORB. THAT'S WHY WE HAVE THE VILLI AND THE WRINKLES. WHAT'S REALLY AMAZING IS THAT THERE ARE MORE THAN 1,000 MICROVILLI ON EACH VILLUS!

FOLDS IN THE SMALL INTESTINE

VILLUS

IF YOU STRETCHED OUT ALL THE VILLI, THEY COULD COVER A TENNIS COURT!

NOW DO YOU UNDERSTAND HOW THIS SEEMINGLY SMALL ORGAN CAN ABSORB ALL THOSE NUTRIENTS?

WOW. ARE YOU SAYING THERE'S SOMETHING *INSIDE THE BODY* THAT'S AS BIG AS A TENNIS COURT?

SO THEN WHY ARE WE IN THE VILLI?

WAIT, WE FORGOT ABOUT THE PARASITES!

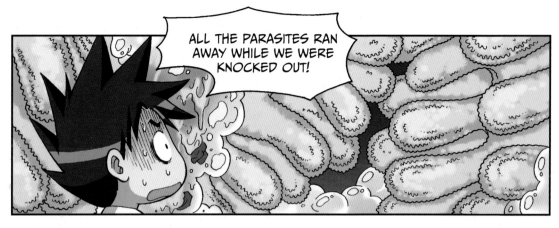

ALL THE PARASITES RAN AWAY WHILE WE WERE KNOCKED OUT!

I'M SO HUNGRY... ALWAYS HUNGRY... WHY...?

I'M SO SORRY, PHOEBE. I REALLY WANTED TO KILL ALL THE PARASITES FOR YOU...

HAHA! I'M STEALING ALL YOUR FOOD!

DON'T WORRY. WE'LL GIVE PHOEBE SOME ANTHELMINTICS WHEN WE GET OUT OF HERE.

WHAT?

IF SHE TAKES AN ANTHELMINTIC, THE PARASITES WILL EITHER DIE OR BECOME PARALYZED AND COME OUT AS POOP.

BUT PARASITE EGGS CAN COME OUT, TOO. SO WHEN YOU HAVE PARASITES, EVERYONE WHO LIVES WITH YOU SHOULD TAKE MEDICINE AS WELL. THAT WAY, THE PARASITES CAN'T SPREAD.

SHALL WE GET GOING AGAIN?

YES!

WHAT?!

CHILL

WHAT'S WRONG NOW?

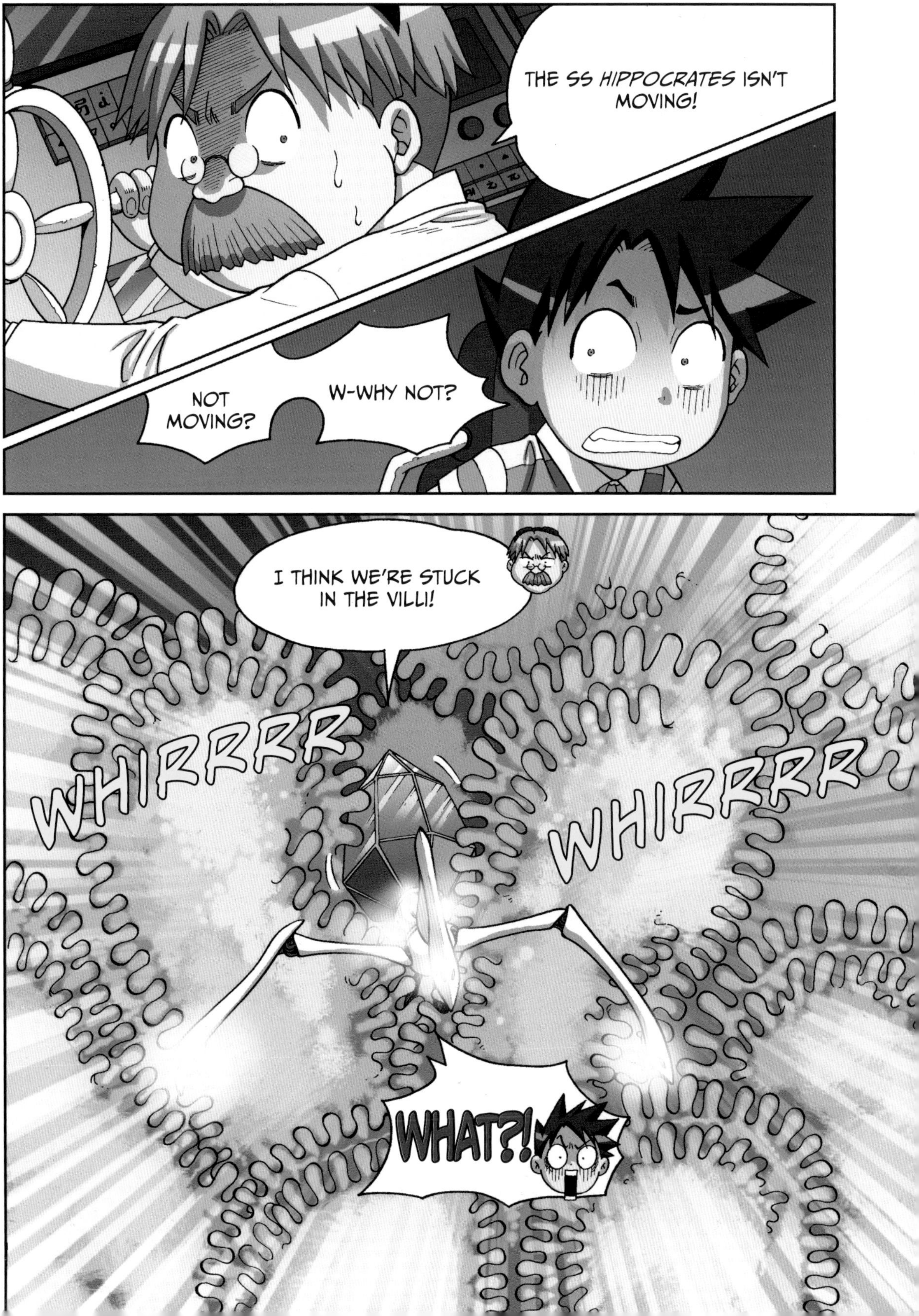
THE SS *HIPPOCRATES* ISN'T MOVING!
NOT MOVING?
W-WHY NOT?
I THINK WE'RE STUCK IN THE VILLI!
WHIRRRR
WHIRRRR
WHAT?!

PARASITES INSIDE THE BODY

Parasites are small organisms that live inside our bodies by stealing nutrients. Because these parasites take the energy our bodies need, they can make us sick or keep us from growing. Parasites have been around for a long time. Scientists have found writings by Egyptian doctors from more than 3,000 years ago that talk about parasites—and they are still with us today.

Parasites are a big health problem all over the world. The Center for Disease Control says that more than *one billion* people have some sort of worm infection. These parasites can be found in dirty soil, human waste, and uncooked food. They can be so small that we can't see them or meters long when fully grown. They can cause all kinds of sicknesses—in the digestive system, lungs, brain, or heart. But clean water and public health efforts (like creating sewers and educating people about parasites) can prevent parasite infections.

HOOKWORMS

Hookworms can live all over the small intestine. Hookworm eggs are in the poop of the people and animals they have infected. When the eggs hatch, baby parasites (larvae) grow in the soil. When they're ready, they invade the human body through any hands or feet that touch the soil. Inside our bodies, hookworms quickly grow into adults and move to the small intestine. From there, they hook their sharp teeth on the walls of the small intestine and suck up blood. This is why people with hookworms feel weak and tired, lose weight, get dizzy, have stomachaches, and don't feel like eating.

GROWTH OF HOOKWORMS

It takes about five days for hookworm eggs to hatch. After that, they turn into larvae and wait in the soil until an animal or person comes along. Then they grab on and crawl in through the skin. That's why hookworms are called *soil-transmitted helminths*.

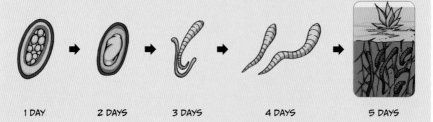

| 1 DAY | 2 DAYS | 3 DAYS | 4 DAYS | 5 DAYS |

Once inside the human body, the larvae go into the blood. When they get into the lungs, they can make you cough. The coughed-up larvae get swallowed. From there, they get into the small intestine where they grow into adults and steal your nutrients.

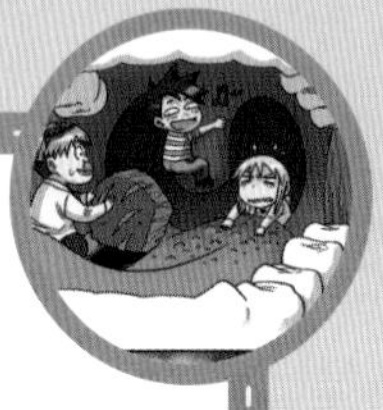

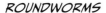

ROUNDWORMS

You can get roundworms (also called *ascaris*) if you eat vegetables with roundworm eggs in them. Roundworms live in the small intestine just like hookworms, but they are much larger—they can grow up to 40 centimeters (16 inches) long! You can get a high fever, dyspnea (have a hard time breathing), and pneumonia. They are scary parasites that can also go into your nose or ears. Sometimes, you find out you have roundworms by seeing them in your poop or by coughing one up.

PINWORMS

If your bottom itches even after a good bath or shower, you might have *pinworms*. Pinworms live inside the human body. They don't cause much harm, but they can make you very itchy and spread very easily. Pinworms can make it hard to sleep, so they can keep you from growing the way you should. That is why you should go to a doctor and take anthelmintics (drugs that get rid of parasites) if you have pinworms.

Pinworms are very common. Scientists think about 40 million people in the United States have them. Doctors can tell if someone has pinworms by putting a piece of Scotch tape on his or her bottom. Pinworm eggs will stick to the tape, which doctors can see with a microscope.

TAPEWORMS

Tapeworm infections come from uncooked fish, beef, or pork. Like hookworms, tapeworms hook their teeth into the wall of the small intestine and survive by sucking blood. They're flat, segmented worms that can grow to be 3–8 meters (10–26 feet) long! You can see if you have tapeworms when one or a few pieces of the tapeworm come out in your poop.

PREVENTION AND ANTHELMINTICS

The easiest way to avoid getting parasites is to *wash your hands* after going to the bathroom, after coming in from being outside, and right before eating. It's also important to never play in areas where there is any kind of animal poop, like dog parks, especially barefoot. Also, be sure not to eat any raw meat. If you live with anyone who has a parasite, you should also take the anthelmintics at the same time to keep from getting the parasite yourself.

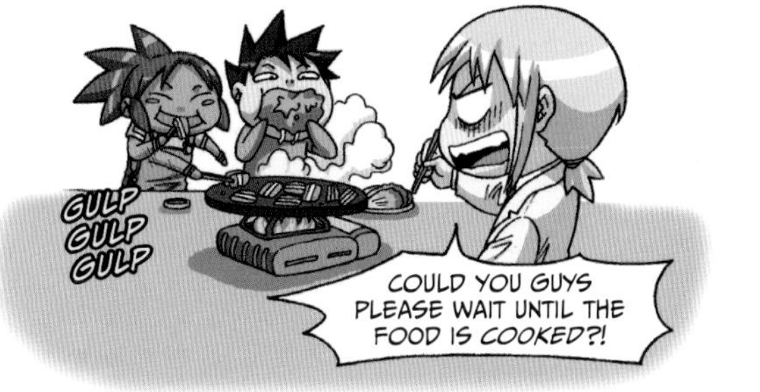
GULP
GULP
GULP
COULD YOU GUYS PLEASE WAIT UNTIL THE FOOD IS COOKED?!

In countries with a parasite problem, the World Health Organization recommends that everyone takes anthelmintics twice or three times a year, whether or not they have any signs of infection. It's a matter of prevention!

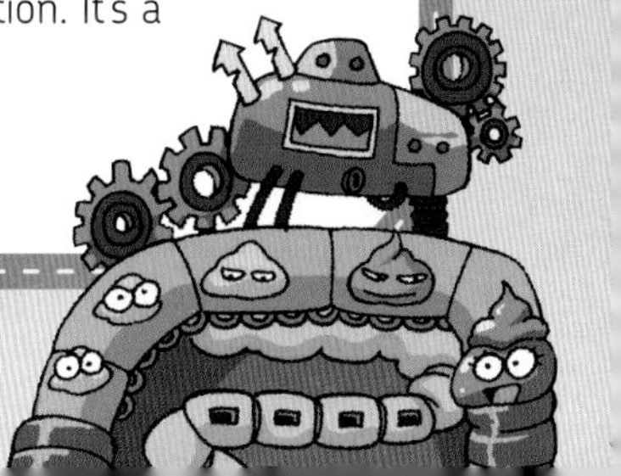

OUT OF JUICE

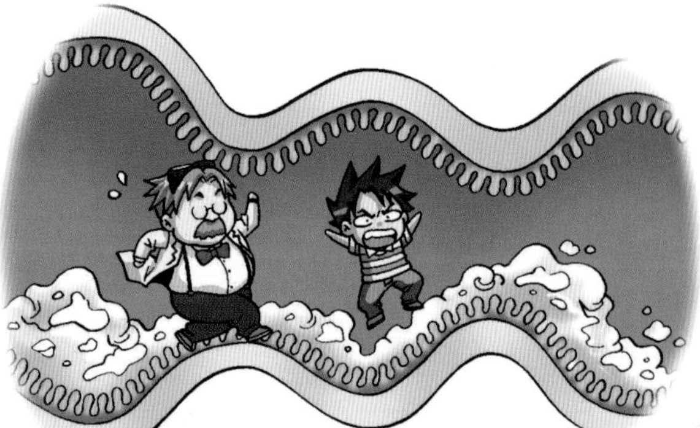

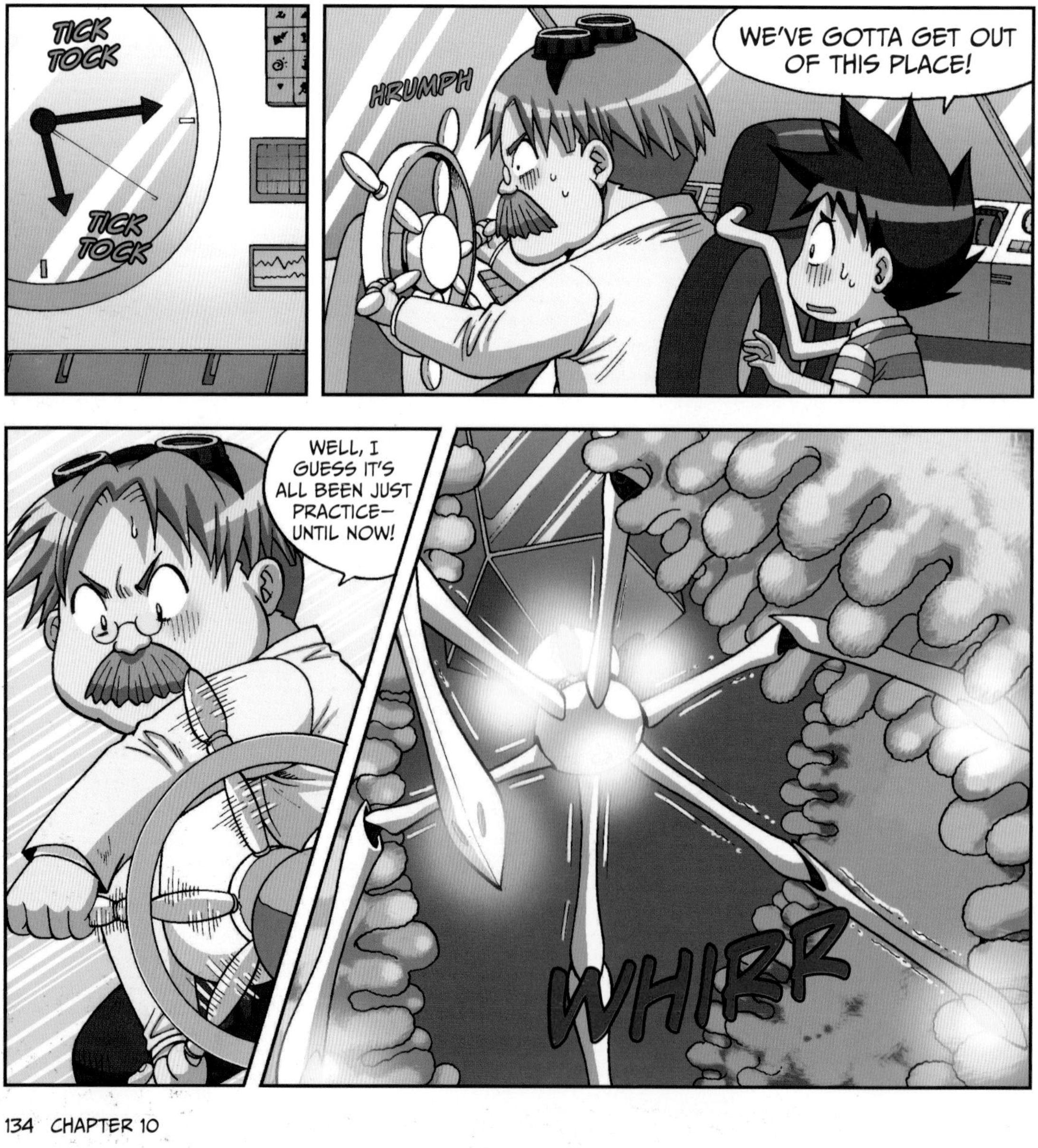
TICK TOCK
TICK TOCK
HRUMPH
WE'VE GOTTA GET OUT OF THIS PLACE!
WELL, I GUESS IT'S ALL BEEN JUST PRACTICE— UNTIL NOW!
WHIRR

RUMBLE

THWOMP

I'M SO SICK OF PERISTALSIS! WHY DOES IT KICK IN AT THE WORST TIME?!

SEGMENTS (OR PARTS) OF THE SMALL INTESTINE MIX THE FOOD AND DIGESTIVE JUICES TOGETHER.

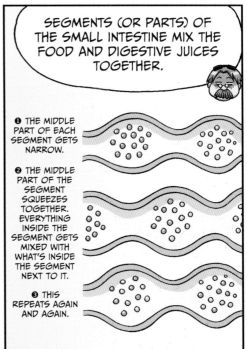

❶ THE MIDDLE PART OF EACH SEGMENT GETS NARROW.

❷ THE MIDDLE PART OF THE SEGMENT SQUEEZES TOGETHER. EVERYTHING INSIDE THE SEGMENT GETS MIXED WITH WHAT'S INSIDE THE SEGMENT NEXT TO IT.

❸ THIS REPEATS AGAIN AND AGAIN.

PERISTALSIS SQUEEZES AND RELAXES THE MUSCLE TO SEND THE FOOD DOWN.

WHAT WE JUST FELT IS *SEGMENTAL* MOVEMENT.

SEGMENTAL?

ISN'T PERISTALSIS ENOUGH? WHY DOES THE SMALL INTESTINE NEED TO MOVE SO MUCH?

RUMBLE

THWAK

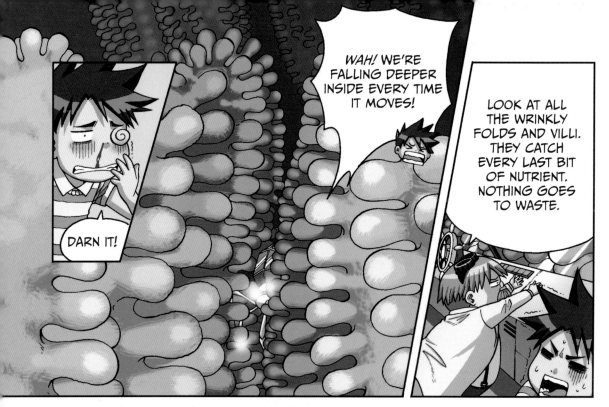

WAH! WE'RE FALLING DEEPER INSIDE EVERY TIME IT MOVES!

LOOK AT ALL THE WRINKLY FOLDS AND VILLI. THEY CATCH EVERY LAST BIT OF NUTRIENT. NOTHING GOES TO WASTE.

DARN IT!

THAT'S WHY WE KEEP ON GETTING SUCKED IN DEEPER.

AUGGHHH!

HUH?

SLURM

DR. BRAIN, WHAT IS *THAT*?

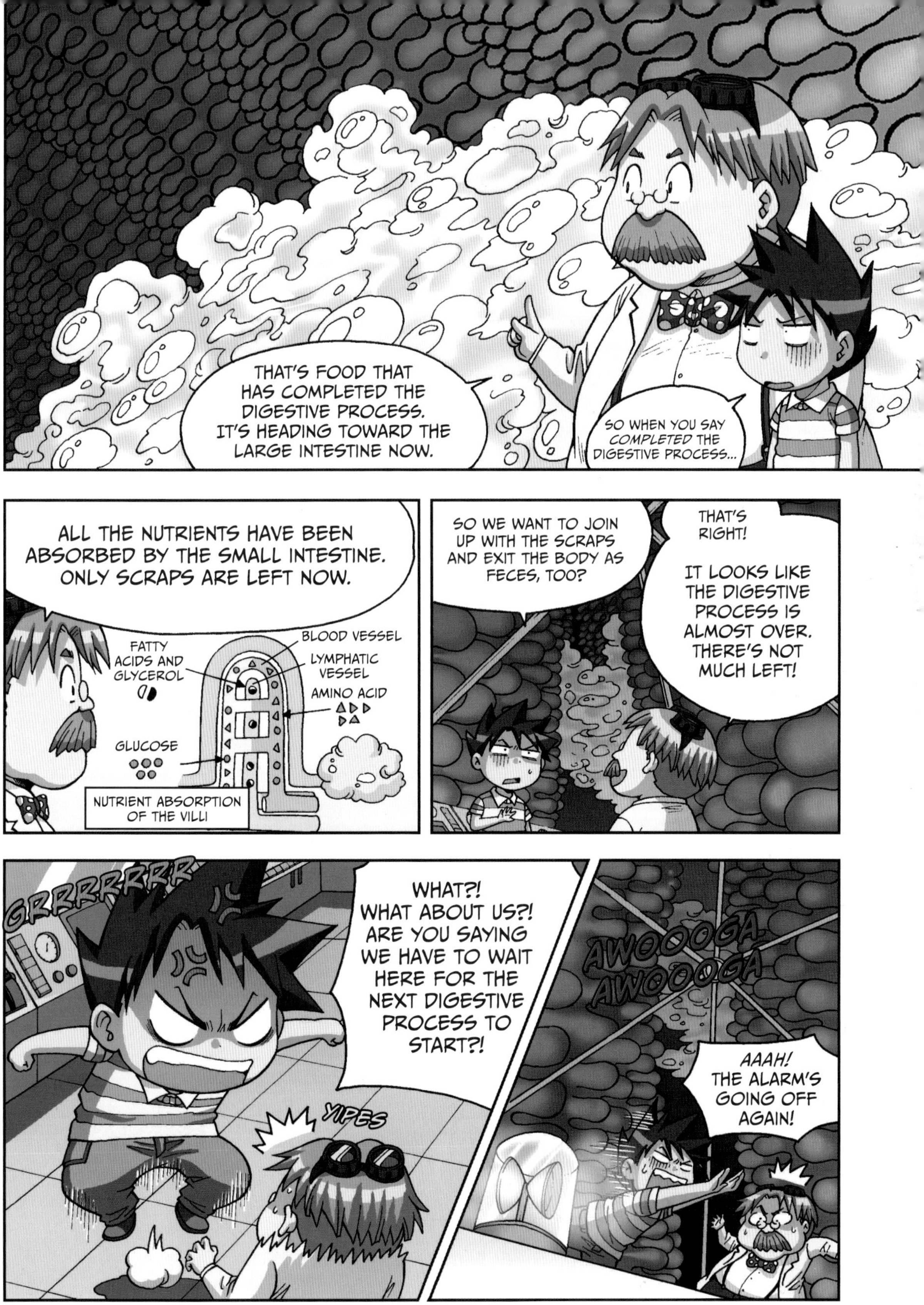
THAT'S FOOD THAT HAS COMPLETED THE DIGESTIVE PROCESS. IT'S HEADING TOWARD THE LARGE INTESTINE NOW.
SO WHEN YOU SAY *COMPLETED* THE DIGESTIVE PROCESS...
ALL THE NUTRIENTS HAVE BEEN ABSORBED BY THE SMALL INTESTINE. ONLY SCRAPS ARE LEFT NOW.
FATTY ACIDS AND GLYCEROL
BLOOD VESSEL
LYMPHATIC VESSEL
AMINO ACID
GLUCOSE
NUTRIENT ABSORPTION OF THE VILLI
SO WE WANT TO JOIN UP WITH THE SCRAPS AND EXIT THE BODY AS FECES, TOO?
THAT'S RIGHT!
IT LOOKS LIKE THE DIGESTIVE PROCESS IS ALMOST OVER. THERE'S NOT MUCH LEFT!
GRRRRRRR
WHAT?! WHAT ABOUT US?! ARE YOU SAYING WE HAVE TO WAIT HERE FOR THE NEXT DIGESTIVE PROCESS TO START?!
YIPES
AWOOOGA AWOOOGA
AAAH! THE ALARM'S GOING OFF AGAIN!

THIS IS REALLY BAD.

NOW WHAT?!

THE *HIPPOCRATES* IS ALMOST ALL OUT OF ENERGY...

DRAG

WHAT?!

HOW ARE WE GOING TO ESCAPE THE VILLI?!

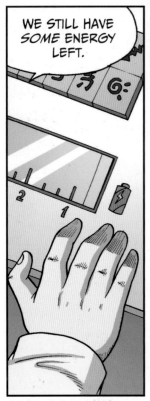

WE STILL HAVE SOME ENERGY LEFT.

HMMMM

WE'VE GOT TO TAKE A CHANCE. WE NEED TO USE ALL THE ENERGY WE HAVE TO ESCAPE THESE FOLDS.

BUT IF WE USE *ALL* THE ENERGY, WHAT ARE WE GOING TO DO NEXT?

DON'T WORRY.

IF WE CAN MAKE IT TO THE LARGE INTESTINE, WE WON'T *NEED* ANY ENERGY. WE CAN JUST FOLLOW ALONG WITH THE SCRAPS. IT'S A SLIPPERY PATH ALL THE WAY TO THE ANUS!

SLIPPERY? HOW CAN THE LARGE INTESTINE BE SLIPPERY? THE SMALL INTESTINE IS CRAZY CURVY. AREN'T THEY BOTH INTESTINES?

HAH— THEY PLAY VERY DIFFERENT ROLES!

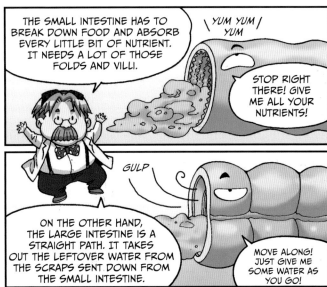

THE SMALL INTESTINE HAS TO BREAK DOWN FOOD AND ABSORB EVERY LITTLE BIT OF NUTRIENT. IT NEEDS A LOT OF THOSE FOLDS AND VILLI.

YUM YUM YUM

STOP RIGHT THERE! GIVE ME ALL YOUR NUTRIENTS!

GULP

ON THE OTHER HAND, THE LARGE INTESTINE IS A STRAIGHT PATH. IT TAKES OUT THE LEFTOVER WATER FROM THE SCRAPS SENT DOWN FROM THE SMALL INTESTINE.

MOVE ALONG! JUST GIVE ME SOME WATER AS YOU GO!

I UNDERSTAND! BUT I'M GOING TO DRIVE THIS TIME!

WHAT?!

SNAG

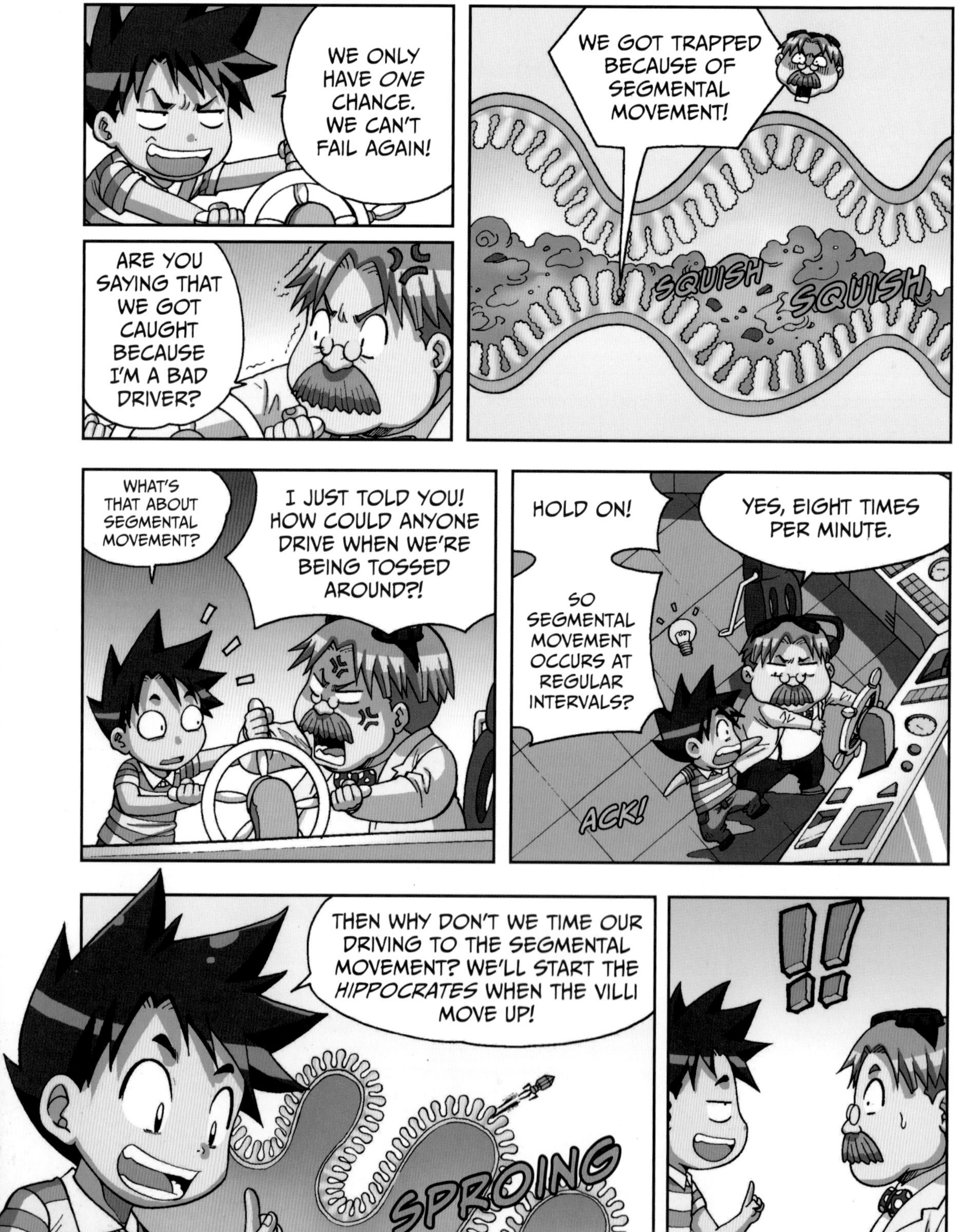

WE ONLY HAVE *ONE* CHANCE. WE CAN'T FAIL AGAIN!
ARE YOU SAYING THAT WE GOT CAUGHT BECAUSE I'M A BAD DRIVER?
WE GOT TRAPPED BECAUSE OF SEGMENTAL MOVEMENT!
SQUISH
SQUISH
WHAT'S THAT ABOUT SEGMENTAL MOVEMENT?
I JUST TOLD YOU! HOW COULD ANYONE DRIVE WHEN WE'RE BEING TOSSED AROUND?!
HOLD ON!
YES, EIGHT TIMES PER MINUTE.
SO SEGMENTAL MOVEMENT OCCURS AT REGULAR INTERVALS?
ACK!
THEN WHY DON'T WE TIME OUR DRIVING TO THE SEGMENTAL MOVEMENT? WE'LL START THE *HIPPOCRATES* WHEN THE VILLI MOVE UP!
SPROING
!!

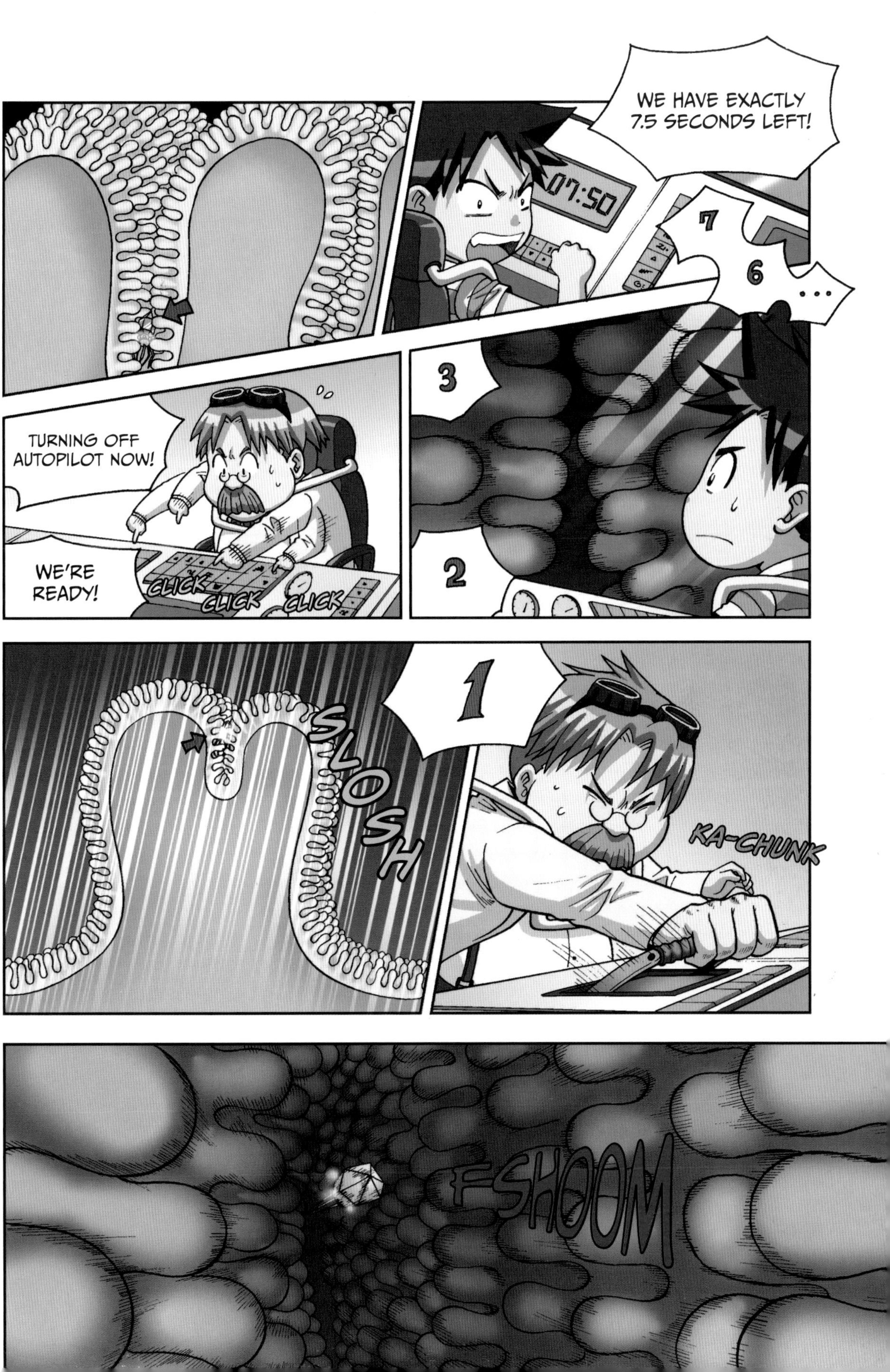
WE HAVE EXACTLY 7.5 SECONDS LEFT!
07:50
7
6
...
TURNING OFF AUTOPILOT NOW!
WE'RE READY!
CLICK CLICK CLICK
3
2
1
SLOSH
KA-CHUNK
FSHOOM

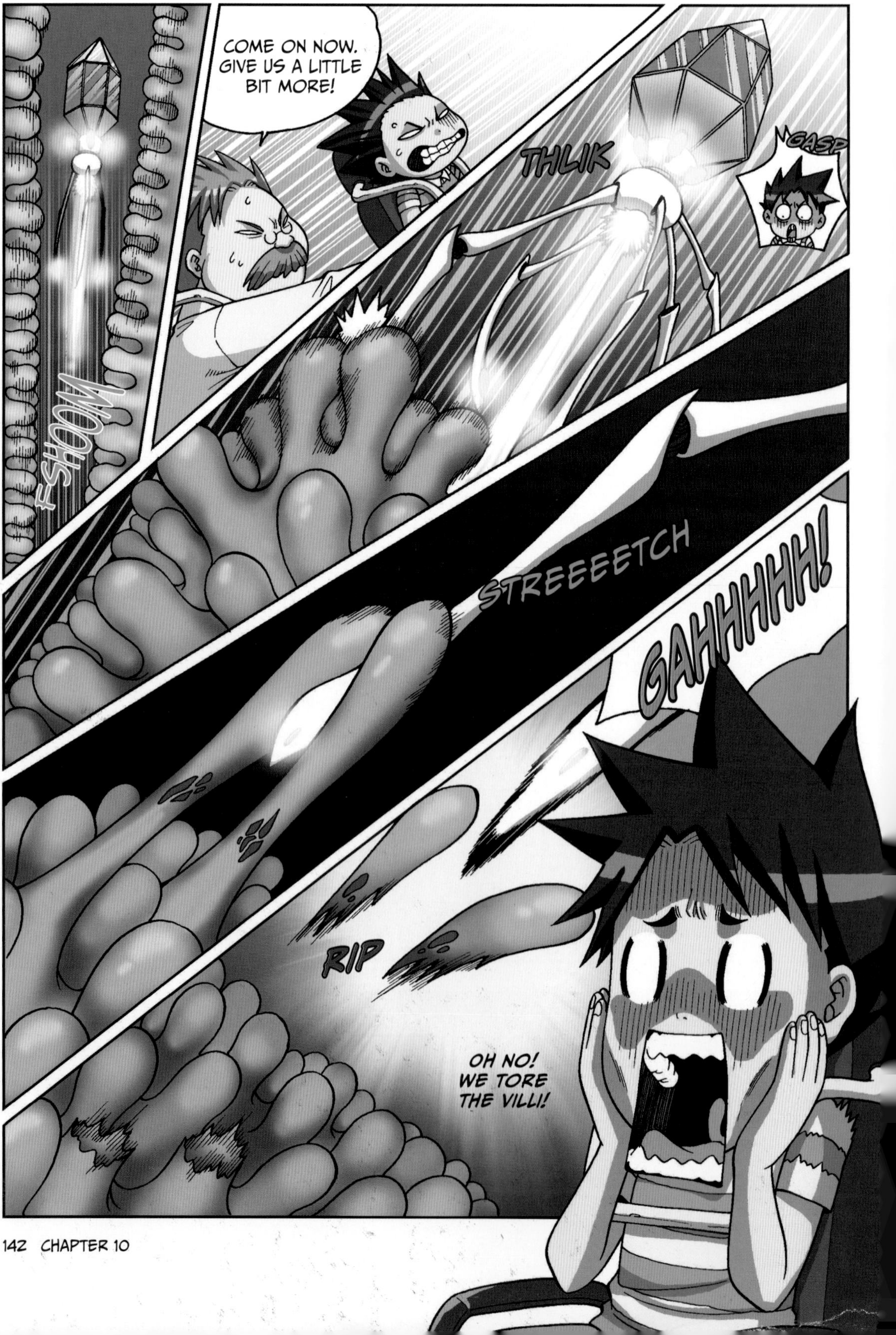
FSHOOM
COME ON NOW. GIVE US A LITTLE BIT MORE!
THLIK
GASP
STREEEEETCH
GAHHHHH!
RIP
OH NO! WE TORE THE VILLI!

FSHOOOOOM

YAY! WE MADE IT!

BUT WE TORE PHOEBE'S VILLI!

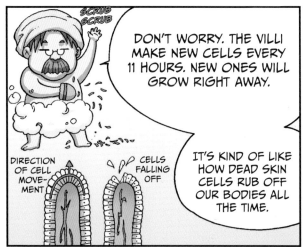

SCRUB SCRUB

DON'T WORRY. THE VILLI MAKE NEW CELLS EVERY 11 HOURS. NEW ONES WILL GROW RIGHT AWAY.

IT'S KIND OF LIKE HOW DEAD SKIN CELLS RUB OFF OUR BODIES ALL THE TIME.

DIRECTION OF CELL MOVE-MENT

CELLS FALLING OFF

WHEW—THAT'S LUCKY.

EH?

HAHAHA

DR. BRAIN! LOOK AHEAD!

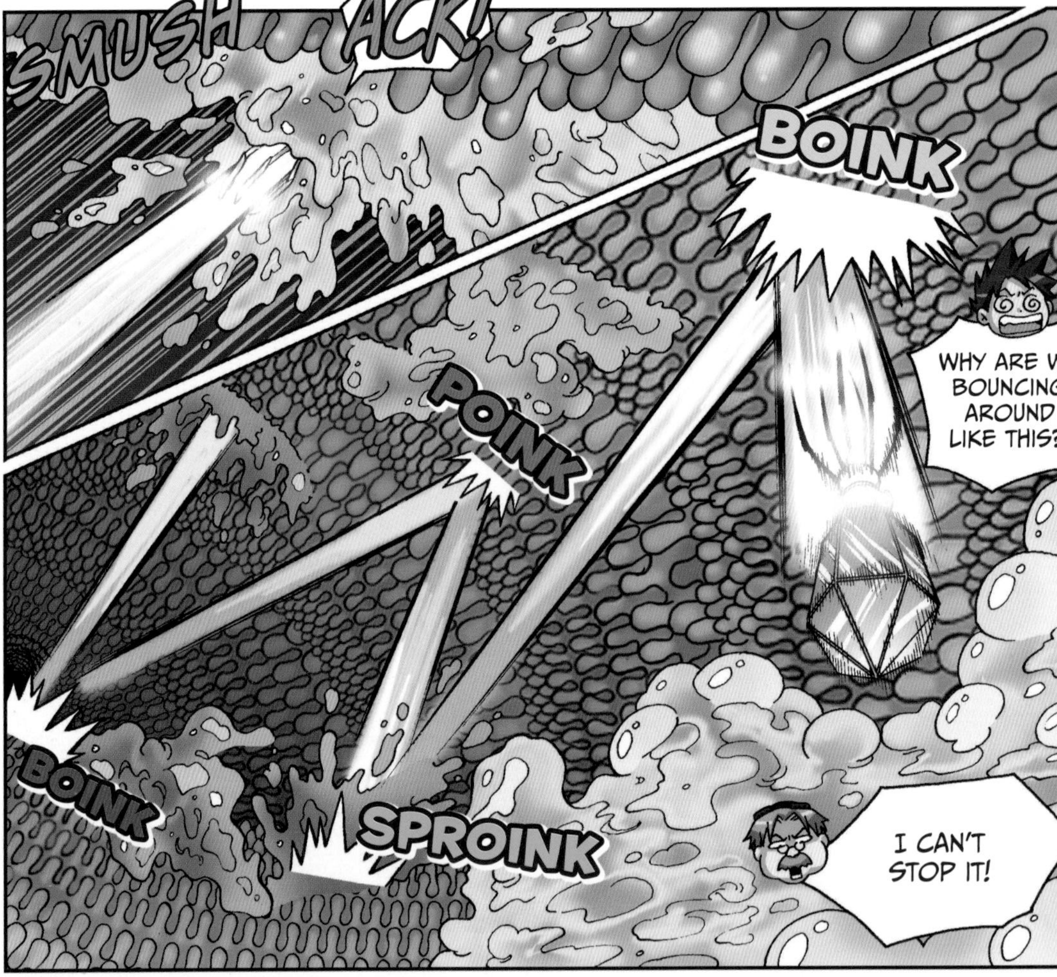
SMUSH
ACK!
BOINK
WHY ARE WE BOUNCING AROUND LIKE THIS?!
POINK
BOINK
SPROINK
I CAN'T STOP IT!

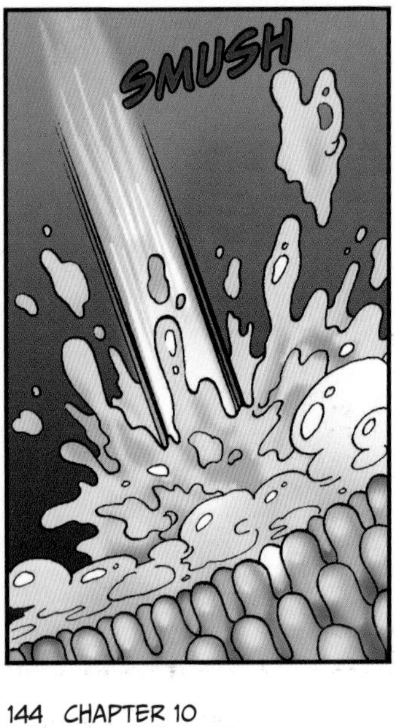
SMUSH

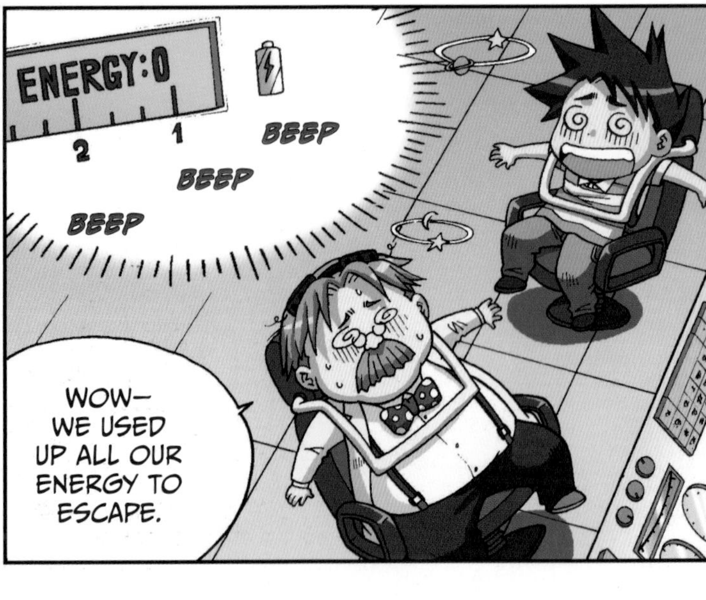
ENERGY:0
2
1
BEEP
BEEP
BEEP
WOW— WE USED UP ALL OUR ENERGY TO ESCAPE.

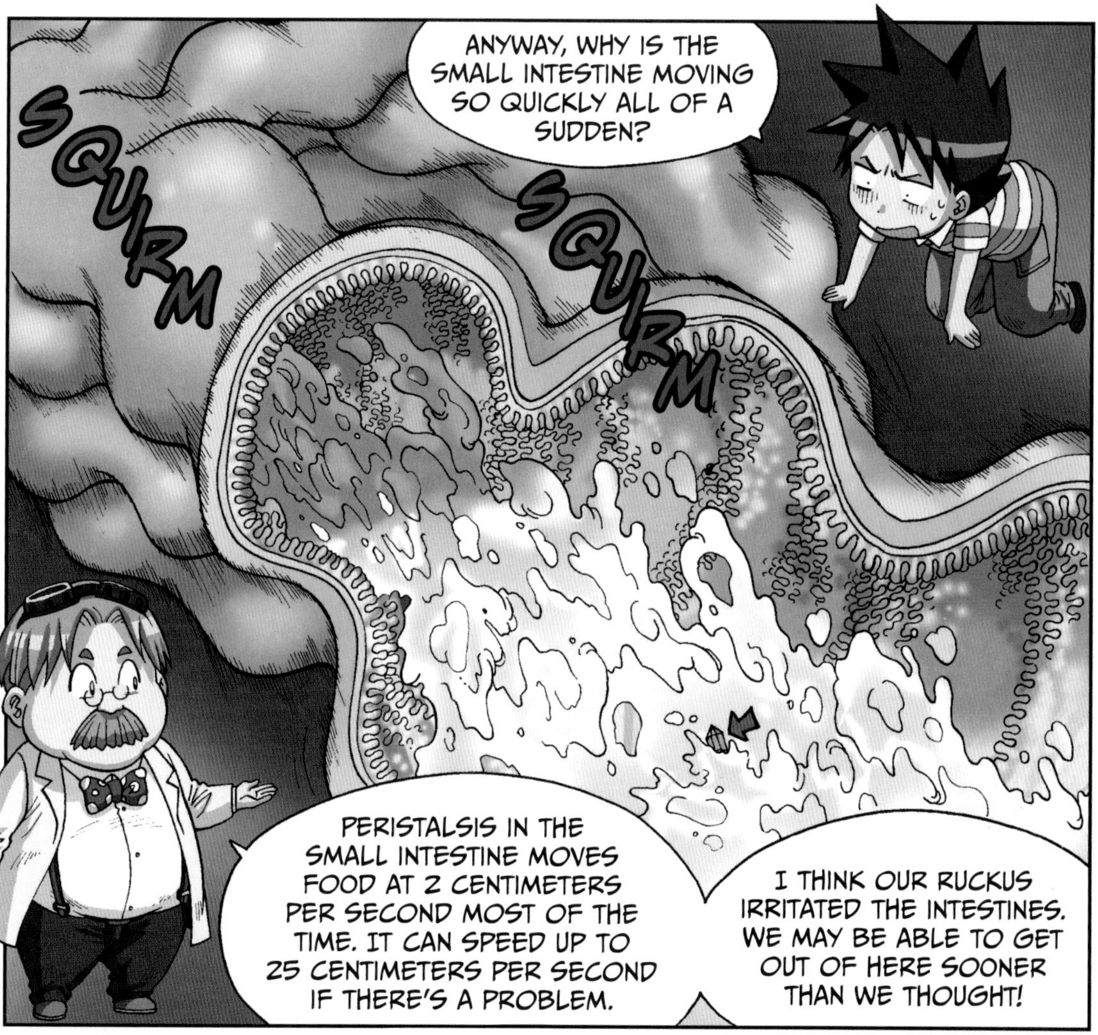
SQUIRM
SQUIRM
ANYWAY, WHY IS THE SMALL INTESTINE MOVING SO QUICKLY ALL OF A SUDDEN?
PERISTALSIS IN THE SMALL INTESTINE MOVES FOOD AT 2 CENTIMETERS PER SECOND MOST OF THE TIME. IT CAN SPEED UP TO 25 CENTIMETERS PER SECOND IF THERE'S A PROBLEM.
I THINK OUR RUCKUS IRRITATED THE INTESTINES. WE MAY BE ABLE TO GET OUT OF HERE SOONER THAN WE THOUGHT!
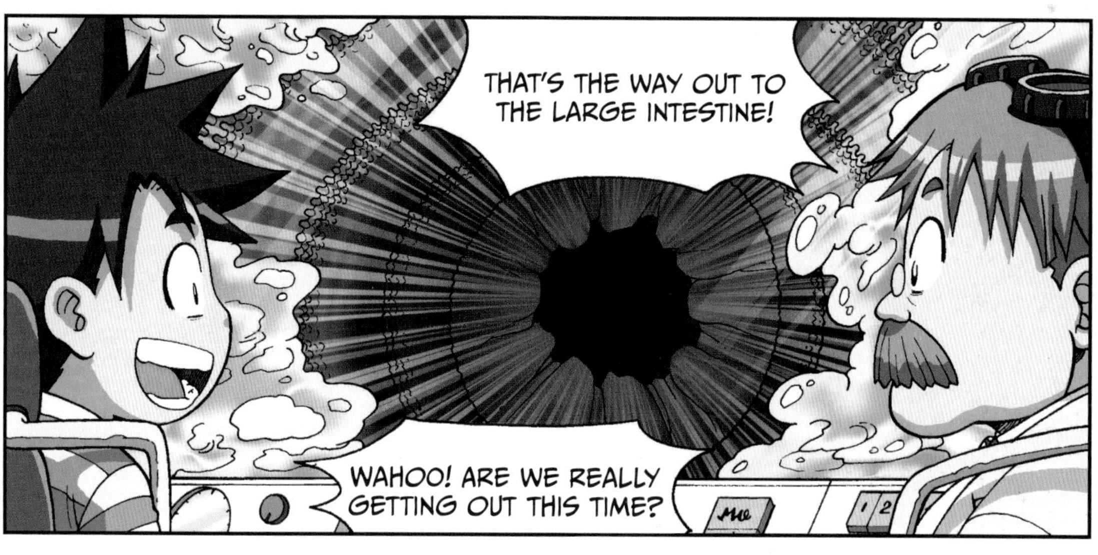
THAT'S THE WAY OUT TO THE LARGE INTESTINE!
WAHOO! ARE WE REALLY GETTING OUT THIS TIME?

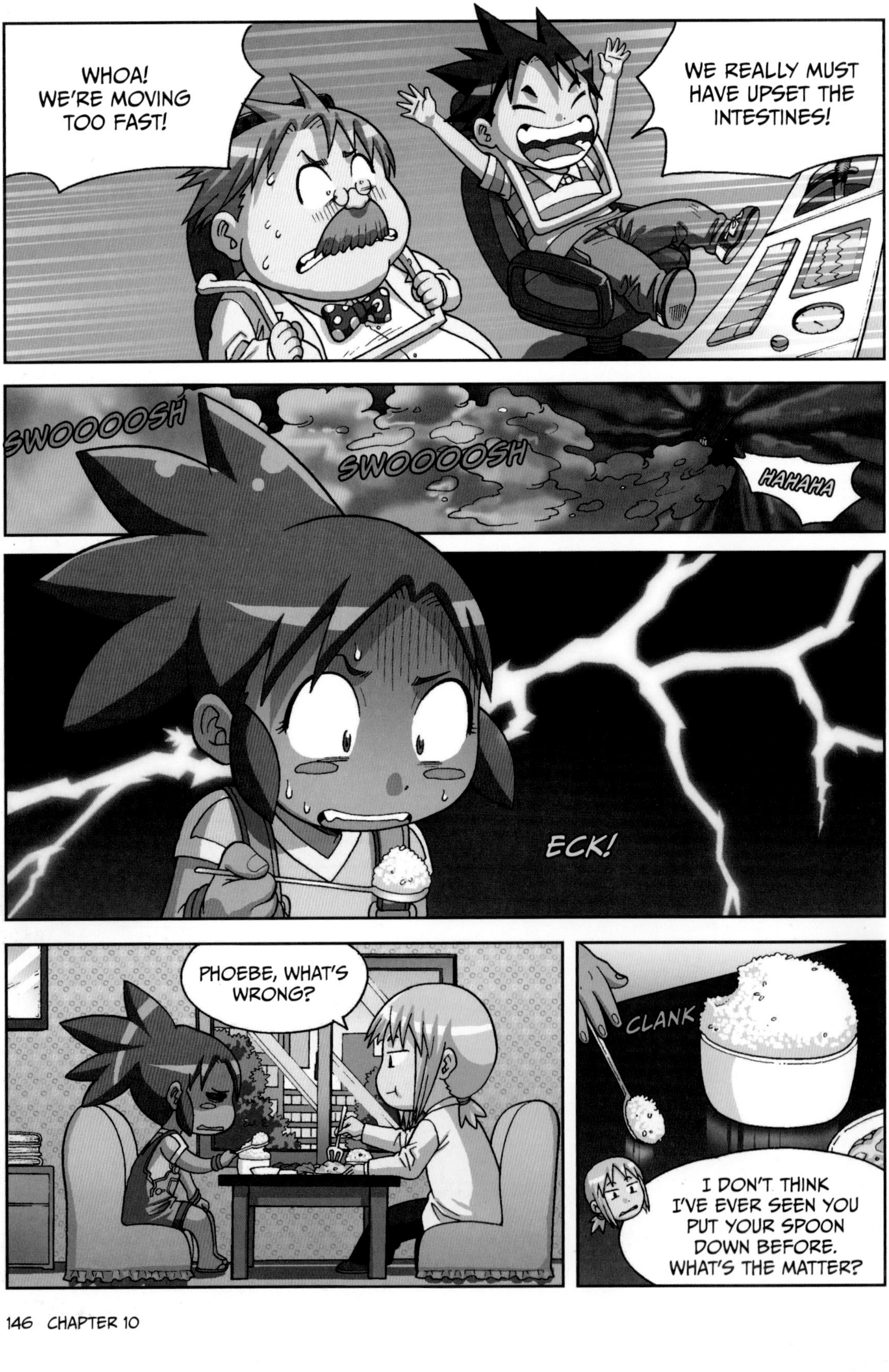
WHOA! WE'RE MOVING TOO FAST!
WE REALLY MUST HAVE UPSET THE INTESTINES!
SWOOOOSH
SWOOOOSH
HAHAHA
ECK!
PHOEBE, WHAT'S WRONG?
CLANK
I DON'T THINK I'VE EVER SEEN YOU PUT YOUR SPOON DOWN BEFORE. WHAT'S THE MATTER?

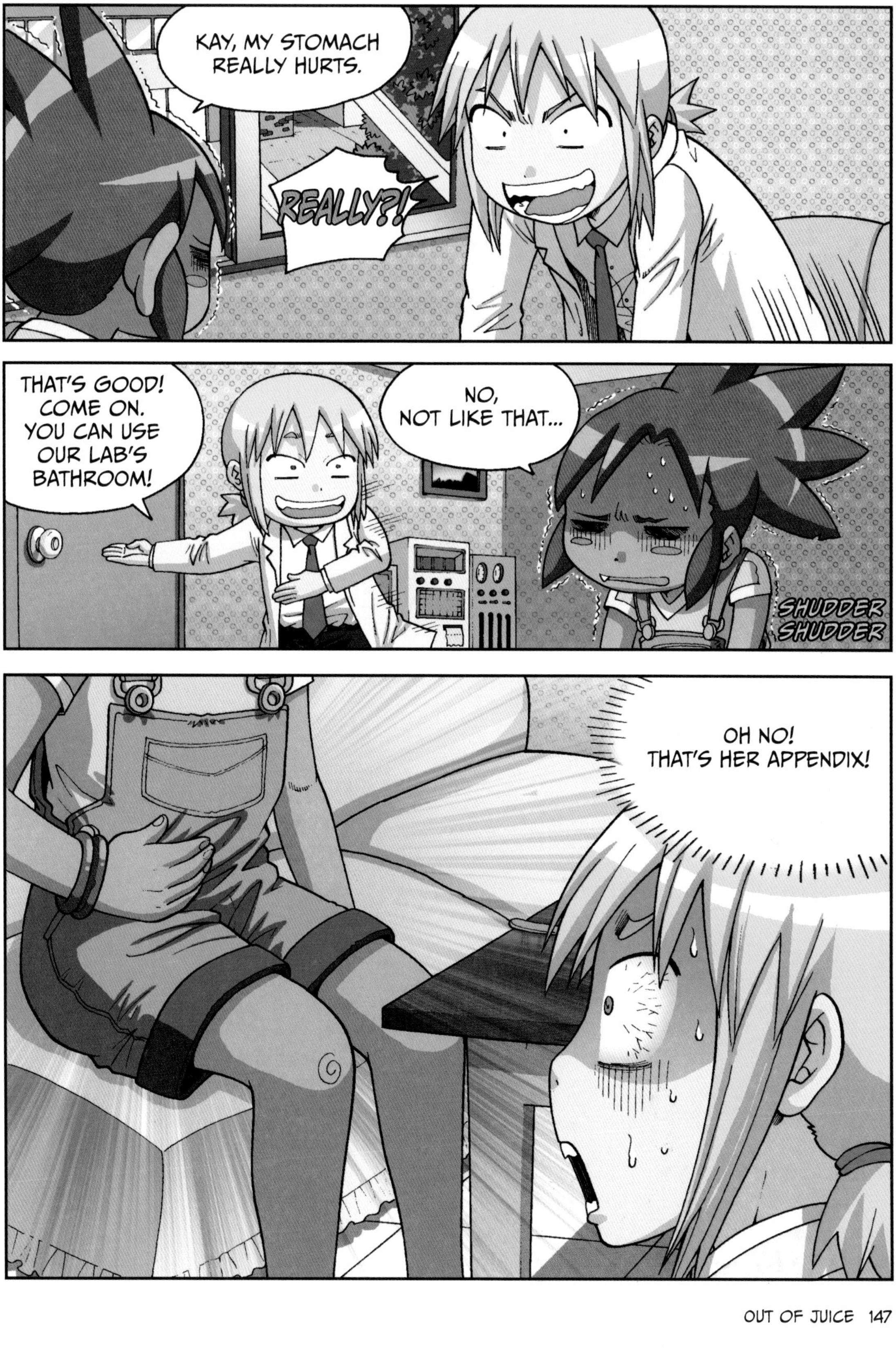
KAY, MY STOMACH REALLY HURTS.
REALLY?!
THAT'S GOOD! COME ON. YOU CAN USE OUR LAB'S BATHROOM!
NO, NOT LIKE THAT...
SHUDDER SHUDDER
OH NO! THAT'S HER APPENDIX!

VILLI AND FOLDS OF THE SMALL INTESTINE

The small intestine is the longest organ in the human body. But it is only 2.5 centimeters (about an inch) wide. How can this organ absorb all the nutrients we need from food? The folds of the jejunum and ileum are packed with villi that absorb the nutrients our bodies need. If you stretched out all the intestine's folds, they would cover a tennis court!

INCREASING SURFACE AREA WITH MICROVILLI

If you use an electron microscope to magnify the villi 2,000 times, you will see that each cell on the outside of the villus has up to 3,000 microvilli on it. These microvilli increase the surface area of each villus, which allows the small intestine to more efficiently absorb nutrients from food. Without the microvilli, the small intestine would have 60 times less surface area.

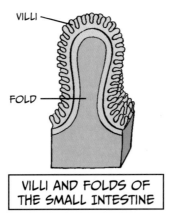

VILLI

FOLD

**VILLI AND FOLDS OF
THE SMALL INTESTINE**

THE BRIEF WONDROUS LIFE OF VILLI

We call the cells in our bodies that can grow new versions of themselves *stem cells*. Thanks to stem cells, our bodies can make new blood and new skin when we're cut or wounded. There are stem cells under the villi of the small intestine, too. New villi cells are made about every 11 hours. The newly created villi cells move upward, and the older cells get pushed until they fall off. This is how the small intestine always has healthy villi to absorb nutrients: They are constantly being replaced. In fact, you have a new lining on your small intestine every four to five days.

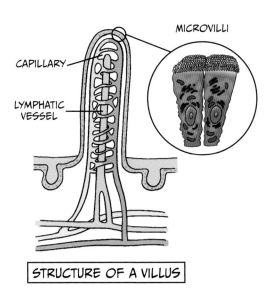

CAPILLARY

MICROVILLI

LYMPHATIC
VESSEL

STRUCTURE OF A VILLUS

SENSORY CELLS IN THE SMALL INTESTINE

There are special cells called *sensory cells* on the inner wall of your small intestine. These cells detect the kinds of food that come into the small intestine. If the food has a lot of protein in it, your body secretes more pancreatic juice to help break it down. If the food has a lot of fat in it, your body makes more bile to help break it down.

THE SMALL INTESTINE AND DIARRHEA

When you eat spoiled food, you may get diarrhea. Bacteria in spoiled food can prevent the small intestine from absorbing as much water as it usually does. Some bacteria can even make the small intestine release extra water, which also causes diarrhea. In mild cases, it's okay to let diarrhea run its course. When it's really bad or lasts more than a day, you should see a doctor. It's important to drink extra water when you have diarrhea or else you can get dehydrated.

INTO THE LARGE INTESTINE!

BURBLE

BURBLE

I CAN'T SEE OUTSIDE WITH ALL THESE FOOD SCRAPS.

DON'T WORRY! AND TAKE A SEAT. WE'RE IN THE LARGE INTESTINE, SO YOU CAN RELAX A BIT NOW.

THERE'S REALLY NOTHING WE CAN DO. WE JUST HAVE TO WAIT AND SEE!

WHEW

ARE YOU SURE? WHAT IF SOMETHING HAPPENS? WE DON'T HAVE ANY ENERGY LEFT...

DON'T WORRY!

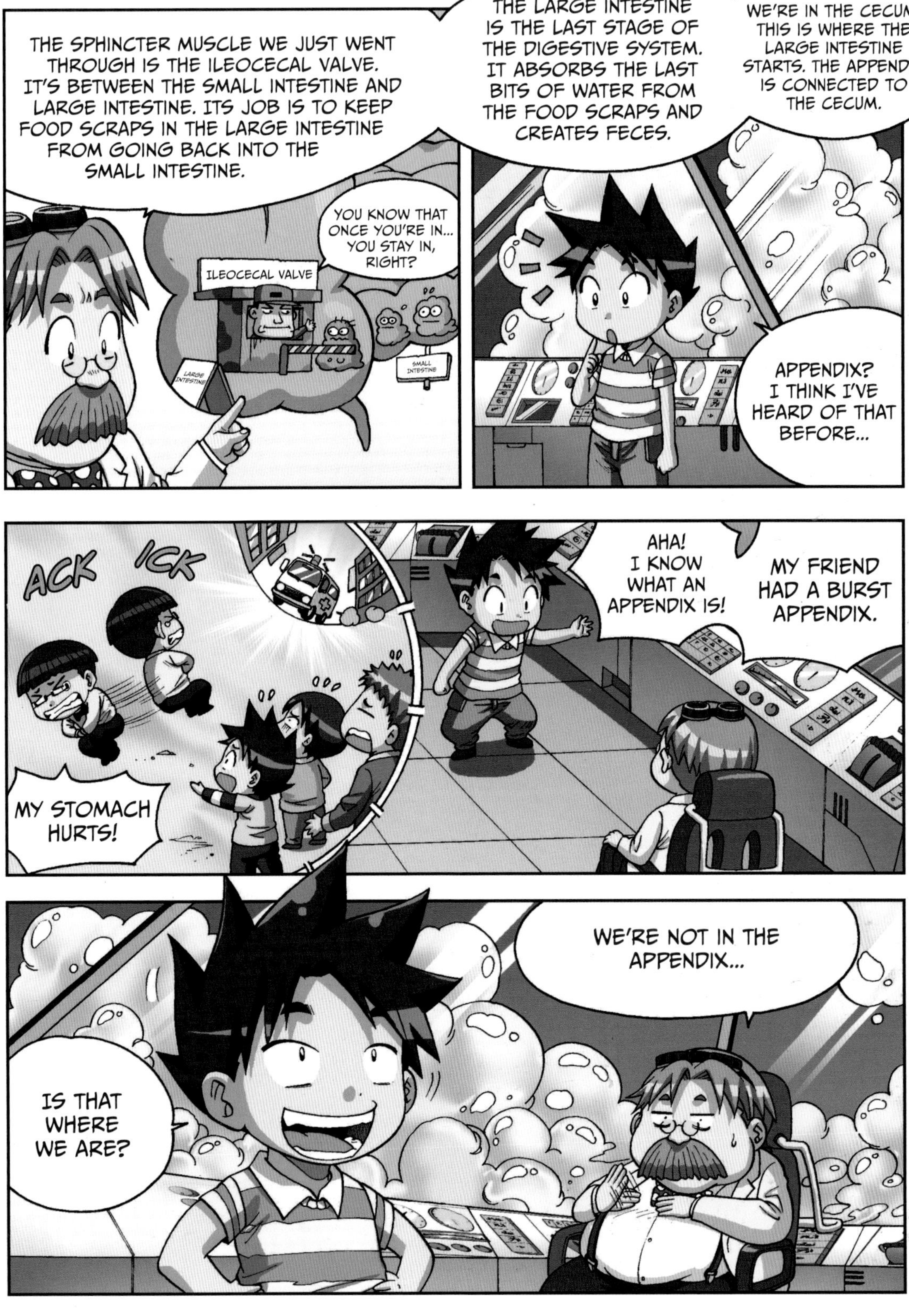
THE SPHINCTER MUSCLE WE JUST WENT THROUGH IS THE ILEOCECAL VALVE. IT'S BETWEEN THE SMALL INTESTINE AND LARGE INTESTINE. ITS JOB IS TO KEEP FOOD SCRAPS IN THE LARGE INTESTINE FROM GOING BACK INTO THE SMALL INTESTINE.
ILEOCECAL VALVE
YOU KNOW THAT ONCE YOU'RE IN... YOU STAY IN, RIGHT?
LARGE INTESTINE
SMALL INTESTINE
THE LARGE INTESTINE IS THE LAST STAGE OF THE DIGESTIVE SYSTEM. IT ABSORBS THE LAST BITS OF WATER FROM THE FOOD SCRAPS AND CREATES FECES.
WE'RE IN THE CECUM. THIS IS WHERE THE LARGE INTESTINE STARTS. THE APPENDIX IS CONNECTED TO THE CECUM.
APPENDIX? I THINK I'VE HEARD OF THAT BEFORE...
AHA! I KNOW WHAT AN APPENDIX IS!
MY FRIEND HAD A BURST APPENDIX.
ACK
ICK
MY STOMACH HURTS!
WE'RE NOT IN THE APPENDIX...
IS THAT WHERE WE ARE?

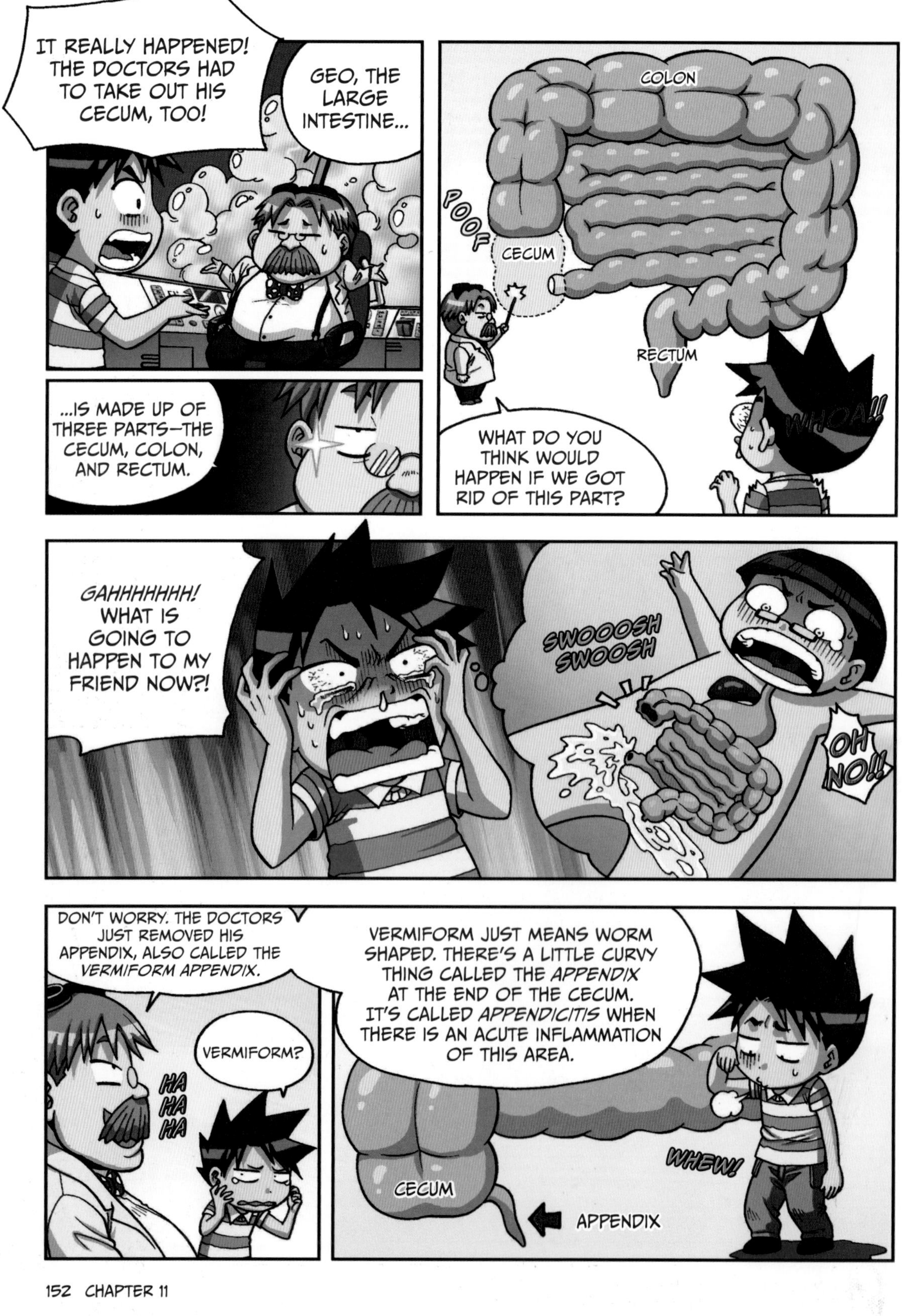
IT REALLY HAPPENED! THE DOCTORS HAD TO TAKE OUT HIS CECUM, TOO!
GEO, THE LARGE INTESTINE...
COLON
POOF
CECUM
RECTUM
...IS MADE UP OF THREE PARTS—THE CECUM, COLON, AND RECTUM.
WHAT DO YOU THINK WOULD HAPPEN IF WE GOT RID OF THIS PART?
WHOA!!
GAHHHHHHH! WHAT IS GOING TO HAPPEN TO MY FRIEND NOW?!
SWOOOSH SWOOSH
OH NO!!
DON'T WORRY. THE DOCTORS JUST REMOVED HIS APPENDIX, ALSO CALLED THE *VERMIFORM APPENDIX*.
VERMIFORM?
HA HA HA
VERMIFORM JUST MEANS WORM SHAPED. THERE'S A LITTLE CURVY THING CALLED THE *APPENDIX* AT THE END OF THE CECUM. IT'S CALLED *APPENDICITIS* WHEN THERE IS AN ACUTE INFLAMMATION OF THIS AREA.
WHEW!
CECUM
APPENDIX

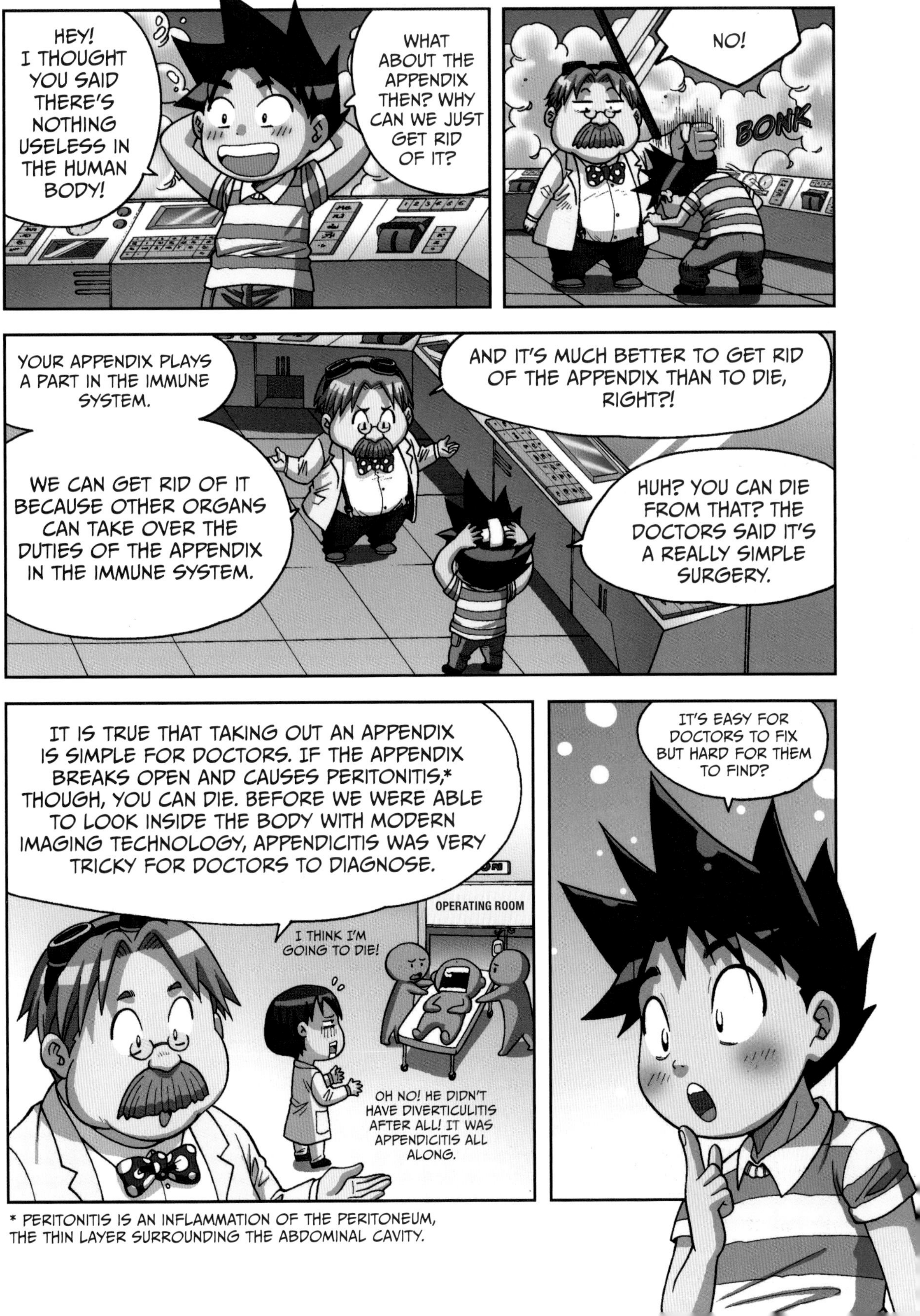
HEY! I THOUGHT YOU SAID THERE'S NOTHING USELESS IN THE HUMAN BODY!
WHAT ABOUT THE APPENDIX THEN? WHY CAN WE JUST GET RID OF IT?
NO!
BONK
YOUR APPENDIX PLAYS A PART IN THE IMMUNE SYSTEM.
WE CAN GET RID OF IT BECAUSE OTHER ORGANS CAN TAKE OVER THE DUTIES OF THE APPENDIX IN THE IMMUNE SYSTEM.
AND IT'S MUCH BETTER TO GET RID OF THE APPENDIX THAN TO DIE, RIGHT?!
HUH? YOU CAN DIE FROM THAT? THE DOCTORS SAID IT'S A REALLY SIMPLE SURGERY.
IT IS TRUE THAT TAKING OUT AN APPENDIX IS SIMPLE FOR DOCTORS. IF THE APPENDIX BREAKS OPEN AND CAUSES PERITONITIS,* THOUGH, YOU CAN DIE. BEFORE WE WERE ABLE TO LOOK INSIDE THE BODY WITH MODERN IMAGING TECHNOLOGY, APPENDICITIS WAS VERY TRICKY FOR DOCTORS TO DIAGNOSE.
OPERATING ROOM
I THINK I'M GOING TO DIE!
OH NO! HE DIDN'T HAVE DIVERTICULITIS AFTER ALL! IT WAS APPENDICITIS ALL ALONG.
IT'S EASY FOR DOCTORS TO FIX BUT HARD FOR THEM TO FIND?

* PERITONITIS IS AN INFLAMMATION OF THE PERITONEUM, THE THIN LAYER SURROUNDING THE ABDOMINAL CAVITY.

EMERGENCY ROOM

APPENDICITIS CAN BE DIFFICULT TO DIAGNOSE...

SOME PEOPLE WITH APPENDICITIS FEEL LIKE THEY HAVE INDIGESTION. EACH PERSON CAN FEEL A LITTLE BIT DIFFERENTLY. IT'S EASY FOR BOTH A PATIENT AND A DOCTOR TO MAKE THE WRONG DECISION AND CHOOSE THE WRONG TREATMENT.

WHERE THE PAIN IS CAN GIVE US CLUES ABOUT WHAT'S GOING WRONG.

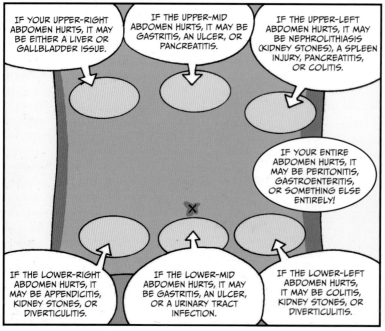

IF YOUR UPPER-RIGHT ABDOMEN HURTS, IT MAY BE EITHER A LIVER OR GALLBLADDER ISSUE.

IF THE UPPER-MID ABDOMEN HURTS, IT MAY BE GASTRITIS, AN ULCER, OR PANCREATITIS.

IF THE UPPER-LEFT ABDOMEN HURTS, IT MAY BE NEPHROLITHIASIS (KIDNEY STONES), A SPLEEN INJURY, PANCREATITIS, OR COLITIS.

IF YOUR ENTIRE ABDOMEN HURTS, IT MAY BE PERITONITIS, GASTROENTERITIS, OR SOMETHING ELSE ENTIRELY!

IF THE LOWER-RIGHT ABDOMEN HURTS, IT MAY BE APPENDICITIS, KIDNEY STONES, OR DIVERTICULITIS.

IF THE LOWER-MID ABDOMEN HURTS, IT MAY BE GASTRITIS, AN ULCER, OR A URINARY TRACT INFECTION.

IF THE LOWER-LEFT ABDOMEN HURTS, IT MAY BE COLITIS, KIDNEY STONES, OR DIVERTICULITIS.

WE ALREADY TOLD YOU HER PAIN IS IN THE LOWER-RIGHT ABDOMEN! IT IS APPENDICITIS!

GASP

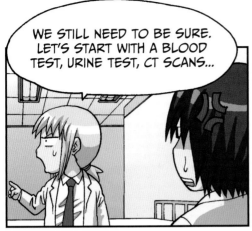

WE STILL NEED TO BE SURE. LET'S START WITH A BLOOD TEST, URINE TEST, CT SCANS...

KAY, I AM THE ATTENDING PHYSICIAN HERE!

YIPES!

DID YOU HAVE ANY BURNING SENSATION IN YOUR BELLY YESTERDAY AFTER EATING?

YES, I TOOK AN ANTACID, TOO.

PFFFFFT

DID YOU HAVE DIARRHEA?

NO, SHE DIDN'T! YOU DON'T ALWAYS HAVE DIARRHEA WHEN YOU HAVE APPENDICITIS!

GRRRR

YOU MIGHT HAVE APPENDICITIS WHEN YOU HAVE INDIGESTION AND FEEL PAIN IN YOUR LOWER-RIGHT ABDOMEN A HALF DAY OR FULL DAY LATER, BUT...

KAY, WHAT IS... APPENDICITIS...?

AN INFECTION OF THE APPENDIX! YOU NEED AN APPENDECTOMY!

APPENDICITIS?! I KNEW IT!

WHAT DO YOU MEAN?

THE APPENDIX IS THE GIZZARD! THAT'S WHERE ALL THE SAND IS KEPT!

AND I ALWAYS SWALLOW WATERMELON SEEDS AND CHEWING GUM. EVERYONE ALWAYS SAID I WAS GOING TO GET APPENDICITIS. *WAHH!*

WHY WOULD YOU HAVE A GIZZARD? YOU'RE NOT A CHICKEN. BESIDES, SEEDS AND GUM ALL COME OUT AS FECES ANYWAY.

REALLY???

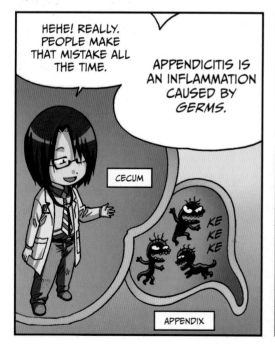

HEHE! REALLY. PEOPLE MAKE THAT MISTAKE ALL THE TIME.

APPENDICITIS IS AN INFLAMMATION CAUSED BY *GERMS.*

CECUM

KE KE KE

APPENDIX

CHANCES ARE THAT YOU HAVE APPENDICITIS IF YOU FEEL PAIN WHEN YOU PRESS ON YOUR LOWER-RIGHT ABDOMEN.

PELVIS -------- NAVEL

TO BE EXACT, IF YOU DREW A LINE FROM YOUR NAVEL TO YOUR PELVIC BONE, IT IS IN THE OUTER THIRD.

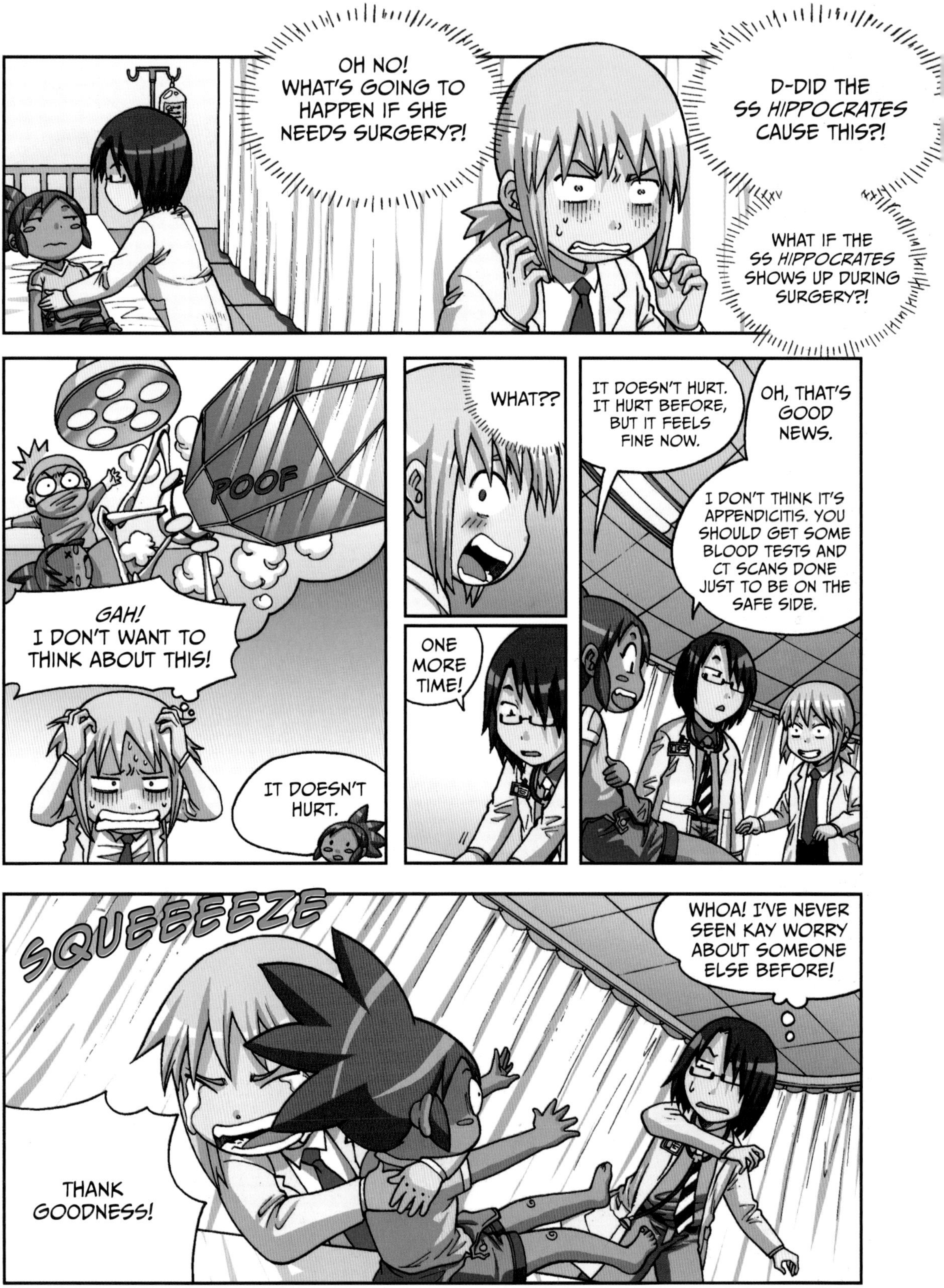

OH NO! WHAT'S GOING TO HAPPEN IF SHE NEEDS SURGERY?!
D-DID THE SS *HIPPOCRATES* CAUSE THIS?!
WHAT IF THE SS *HIPPOCRATES* SHOWS UP DURING SURGERY?!
POOF
GAH! I DON'T WANT TO THINK ABOUT THIS!
IT DOESN'T HURT.
WHAT??
ONE MORE TIME!
IT DOESN'T HURT. IT HURT BEFORE, BUT IT FEELS FINE NOW.
OH, THAT'S GOOD NEWS.
I DON'T THINK IT'S APPENDICITIS. YOU SHOULD GET SOME BLOOD TESTS AND CT SCANS DONE JUST TO BE ON THE SAFE SIDE.
SQUEEEEEEZE
WHOA! I'VE NEVER SEEN KAY WORRY ABOUT SOMEONE ELSE BEFORE!
THANK GOODNESS!

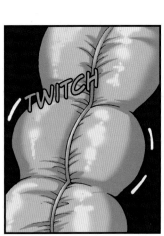

IT'S SHAKING! I DIDN'T KNOW THE LARGE INTESTINE MOVED.

OH!

SURE, THE LARGE INTESTINE HAS SEGMENTAL MOVEMENT AND SLOW PERISTALSIS, TOO.

MOVEMENT IS GOOD! YAY!

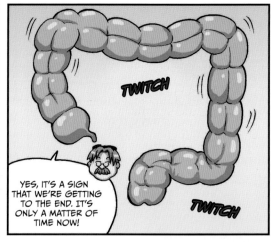

YES, IT'S A SIGN THAT WE'RE GETTING TO THE END. IT'S ONLY A MATTER OF TIME NOW!

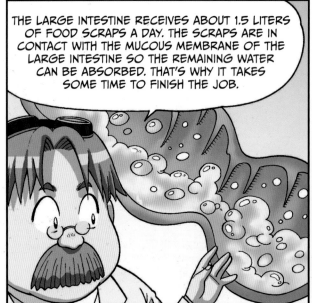

THE LARGE INTESTINE RECEIVES ABOUT 1.5 LITERS OF FOOD SCRAPS A DAY. THE SCRAPS ARE IN CONTACT WITH THE MUCOUS MEMBRANE OF THE LARGE INTESTINE SO THE REMAINING WATER CAN BE ABSORBED. THAT'S WHY IT TAKES SOME TIME TO FINISH THE JOB.

WHAT'S THAT THEN? THAT GAS KEEPS BUBBLING UP.

OH, THAT?

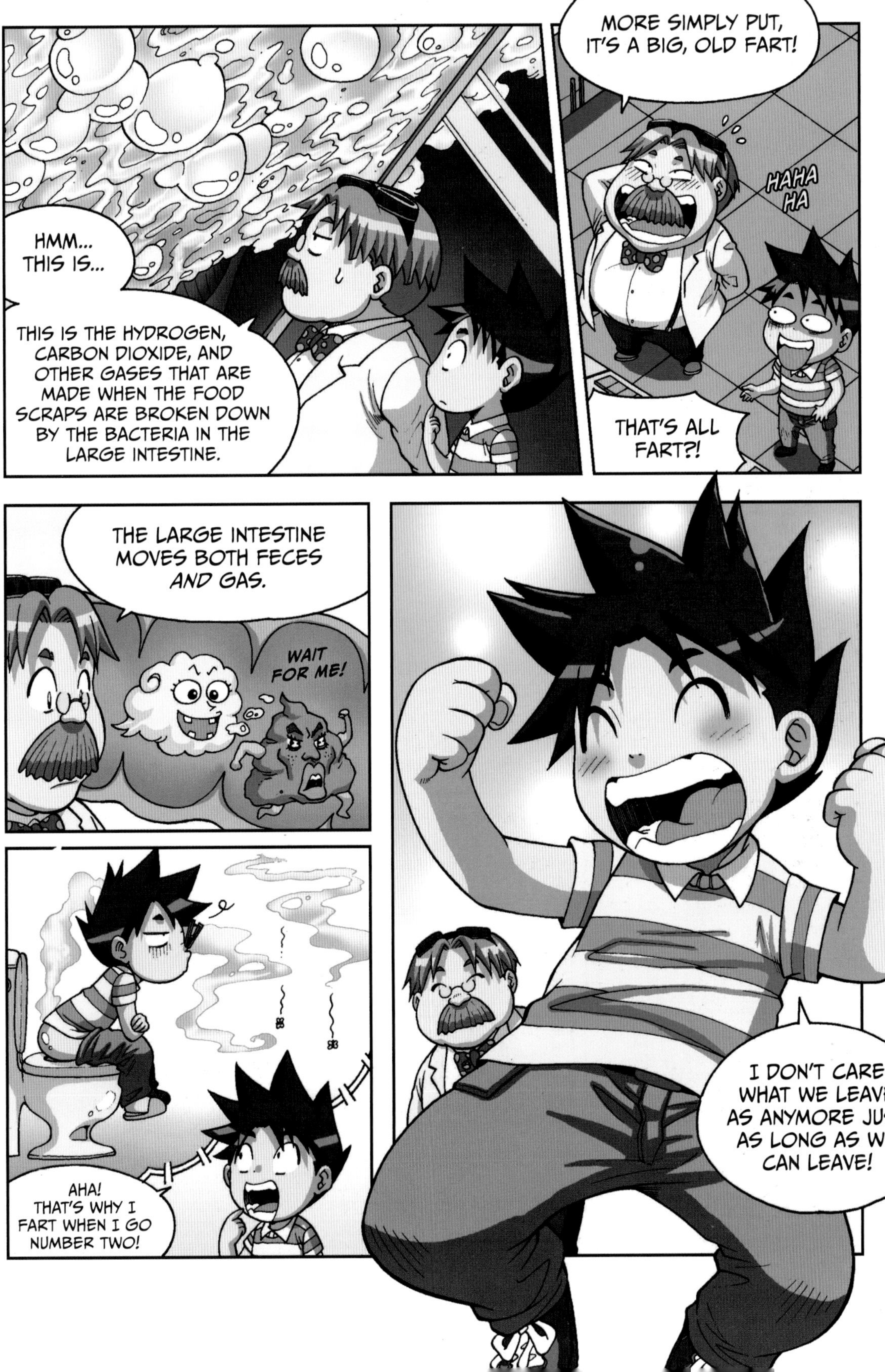
HMM... THIS IS...
THIS IS THE HYDROGEN, CARBON DIOXIDE, AND OTHER GASES THAT ARE MADE WHEN THE FOOD SCRAPS ARE BROKEN DOWN BY THE BACTERIA IN THE LARGE INTESTINE.
MORE SIMPLY PUT, IT'S A BIG, OLD FART!
HAHA HA
THAT'S ALL FART?!
THE LARGE INTESTINE MOVES BOTH FECES AND GAS.
WAIT FOR ME!
AHA! THAT'S WHY I FART WHEN I GO NUMBER TWO!
I DON'T CARE WHAT WE LEAVE AS ANYMORE JUST AS LONG AS WE CAN LEAVE!

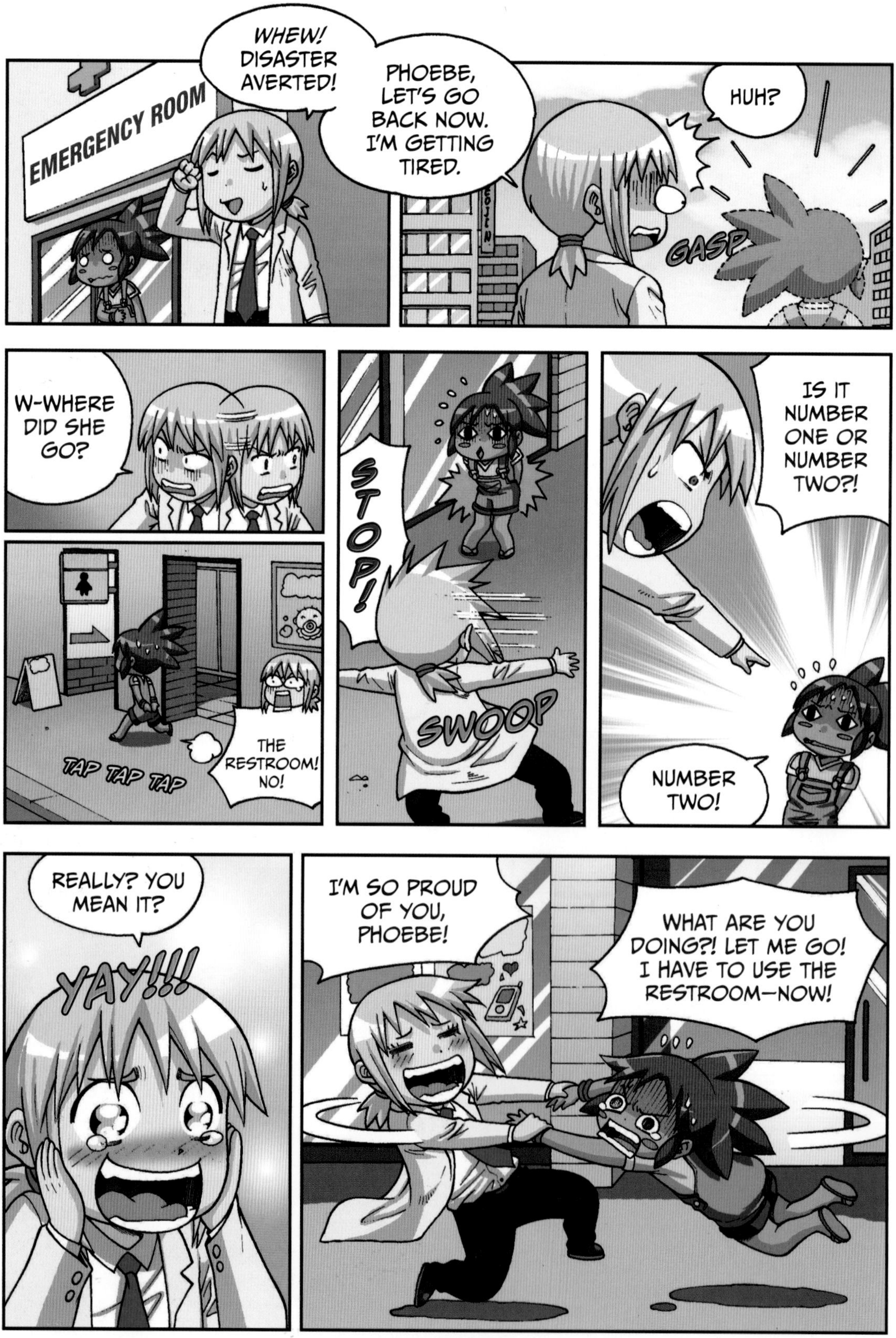
EMERGENCY ROOM
WHEW! DISASTER AVERTED!
PHOEBE, LET'S GO BACK NOW. I'M GETTING TIRED.
HUH?
GASP
W-WHERE DID SHE GO?
TAP TAP TAP
THE RESTROOM! NO!
STOP!
SWOOP
IS IT NUMBER ONE OR NUMBER TWO?!
NUMBER TWO!
REALLY? YOU MEAN IT?
YAY!!!
I'M SO PROUD OF YOU, PHOEBE!
WHAT ARE YOU DOING?! LET ME GO! I HAVE TO USE THE RESTROOM—NOW!

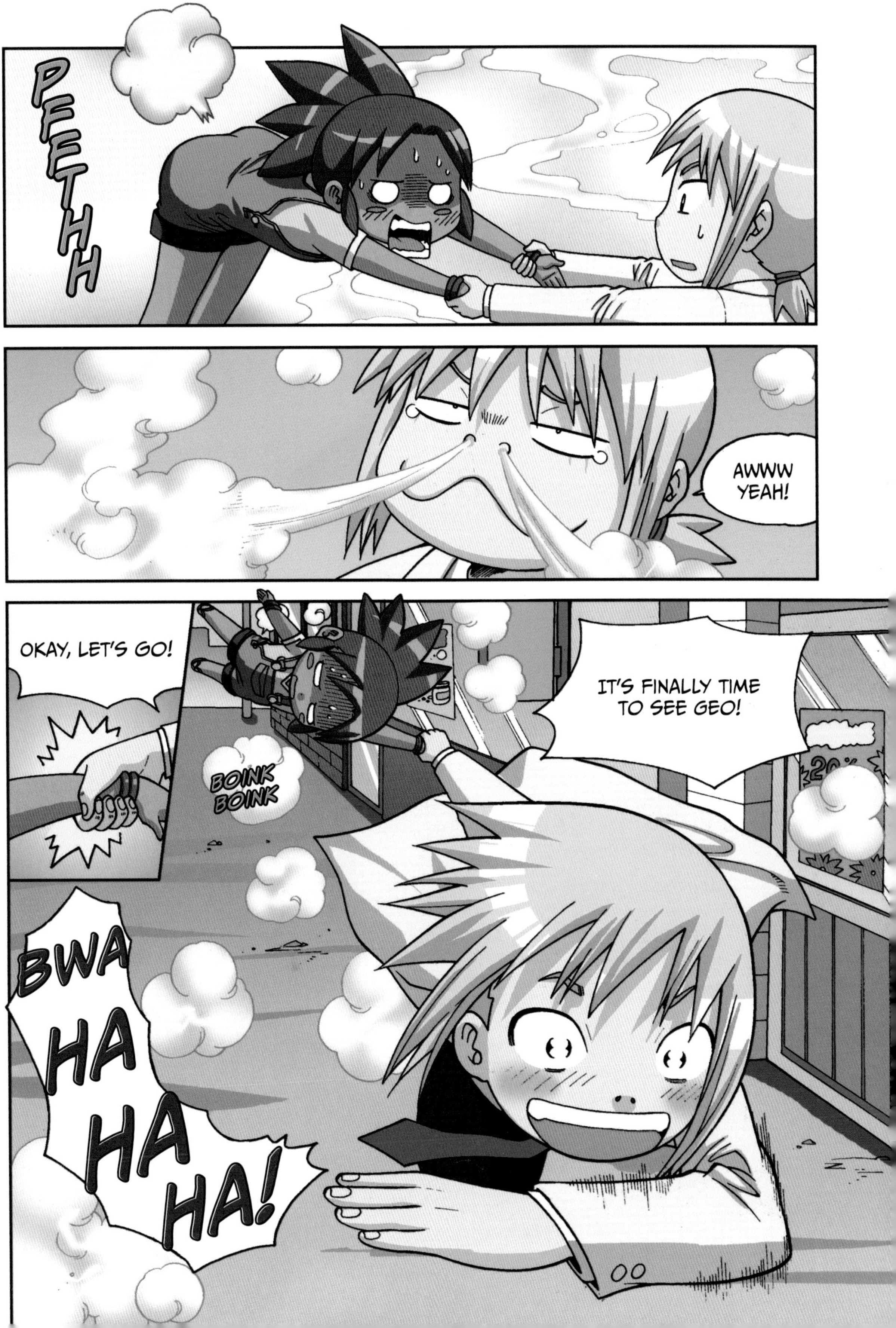
PFFFTHHH
AWWW YEAH!
OKAY, LET'S GO!
IT'S FINALLY TIME TO SEE GEO!
BOINK BOINK
BWA HA HA HA HA!

DIGESTIVE SYSTEM

LAST STOP, THE LARGE INTESTINE

The large intestine absorbs whatever water is left in the food scraps. These food scraps shrink down to about one-fourth of their original size and then exit the body as feces. The large intestine is 1.5 meters (about 5 feet) long and made up of three parts—the cecum, colon, and rectum. Although it's just one-fourth as long as the small intestine, it's called the *large* intestine because it's twice as wide.

ILEOCECAL VALVE

The ileocecal valve is the entrance to your large intestine. It's a sphincter made up of two sides that look like plump lips. It stops food scraps and bacteria from going back into the small intestine, a very important job.

COLON
ILEOCECAL VALVE
CECUM
APPENDIX
RECTUM
ANUS

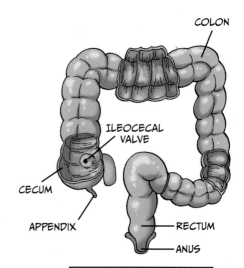

STRUCTURE OF THE LARGE INTESTINE

CECUM

The cecum is the first part of your large intestine, and it is also the widest. The appendix, attached to the lowest part of the cecum, is 6–9 centimeters (2.5–3.5 inches) long. Some doctors believe the appendix helps the immune system.

COLON

The colon makes up most of the large intestine. It absorbs water from the food scraps and stores feces until you go to the bathroom.

RECTUM

The rectum is the last part of the large intestine. It is about 10–15 centimeters (4–6 inches) long and is connected to the anus. You feel the need to use the restroom when the rectum swells up with feces and gas.

COLON BACTERIA AND GUT FLORA

The large intestine is the only place in the internal organs where many microbes are very active. Inside the large intestine's slippery mucus, there are more than 100 trillion microbes of many colors, shapes, and sizes. These microorganisms (a collection of friendly bacteria, fungi, and viruses) are also known as *gut flora*.

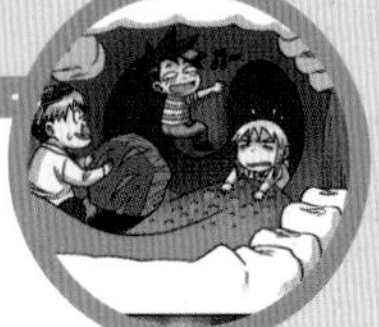

They break down the dietary fibers our bodies can't handle and create nutrients we need, like vitamin K, vitamin B1, and vitamin B2. They also break down proteins and amino acids to make amine and ammonia. These activities all help the large intestine stay strong. Some of the foods you eat have live bacteria in them, like yogurt and kimchi. It might sound scary, but this bacteria is already in your intestines, too, and won't hurt you.

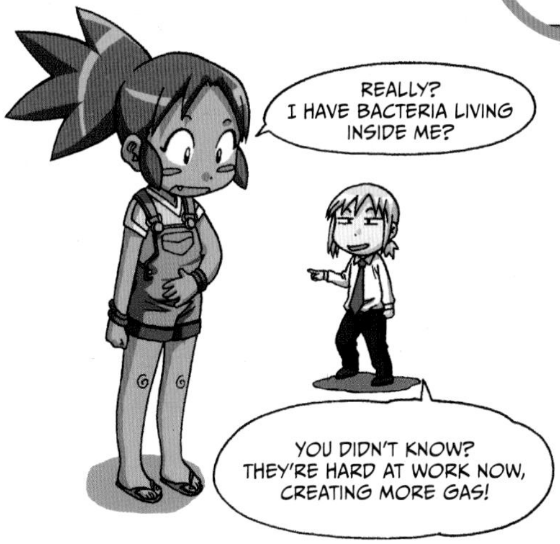
REALLY? I HAVE BACTERIA LIVING INSIDE ME?
YOU DIDN'T KNOW? THEY'RE HARD AT WORK NOW, CREATING MORE GAS!

MEDICAL TECHNOLOGY IMPROVES DIAGNOSES

You saw how appendicitis can be hard for doctors to diagnose. But today when doctors aren't sure if a patient has appendicitis, they use CT scans, a special kind of X-ray. Before they began using CT scans to diagnose appendicitis, doctors at one Boston hospital would find a healthy appendix 20 percent of the time during appendicitis surgery. That means they were wrong for 1 out of every 5 patients! After they began using CT scans, doctors found a healthy appendix only 3 times out of 100. That's a big improvement for patients. Doctors don't always need a CT scan to find appendicitis, though. They can also use ultrasounds to diagnose appendicitis for young children or pregnant women to avoid the risks of using X-rays.

GETTING TO KNOW YOUR HEALTH THROUGH FECES

Feces are lumps of digestive fluid, gut flora, and undigested food scraps. Even though they are solid, they are made of 70 percent water. You make 100–200 grams of feces at a time when you are healthy. Most of the time, they have some yellowish color in them because of the bile in your digestive system. Bile starts out green and breaks down into yellow. If you see your feces in a different color, there can be many causes (such as disease, medication, and even the food you eat). It's best to see a doctor if you're not sure why your feces are a strange color. Red or black stools can mean you are bleeding inside. That is a big problem.

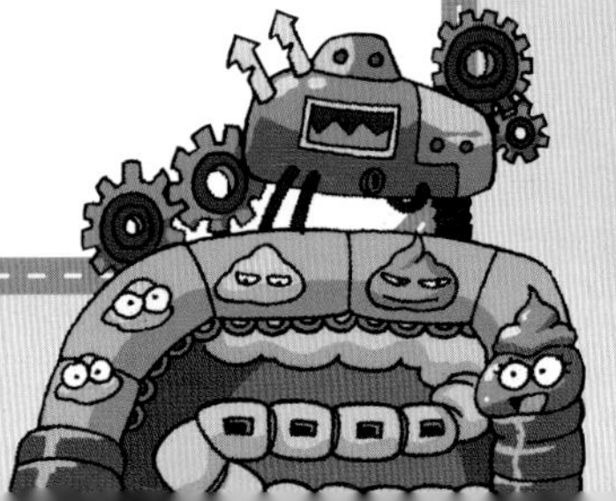

THE END...?

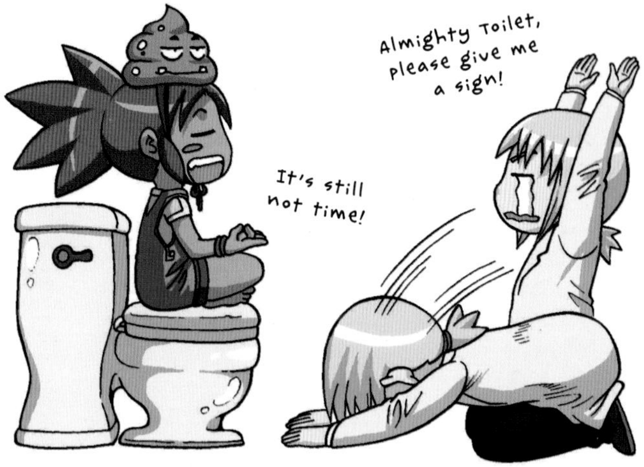
Almighty Toilet, please give me a sign!
It's still not time!

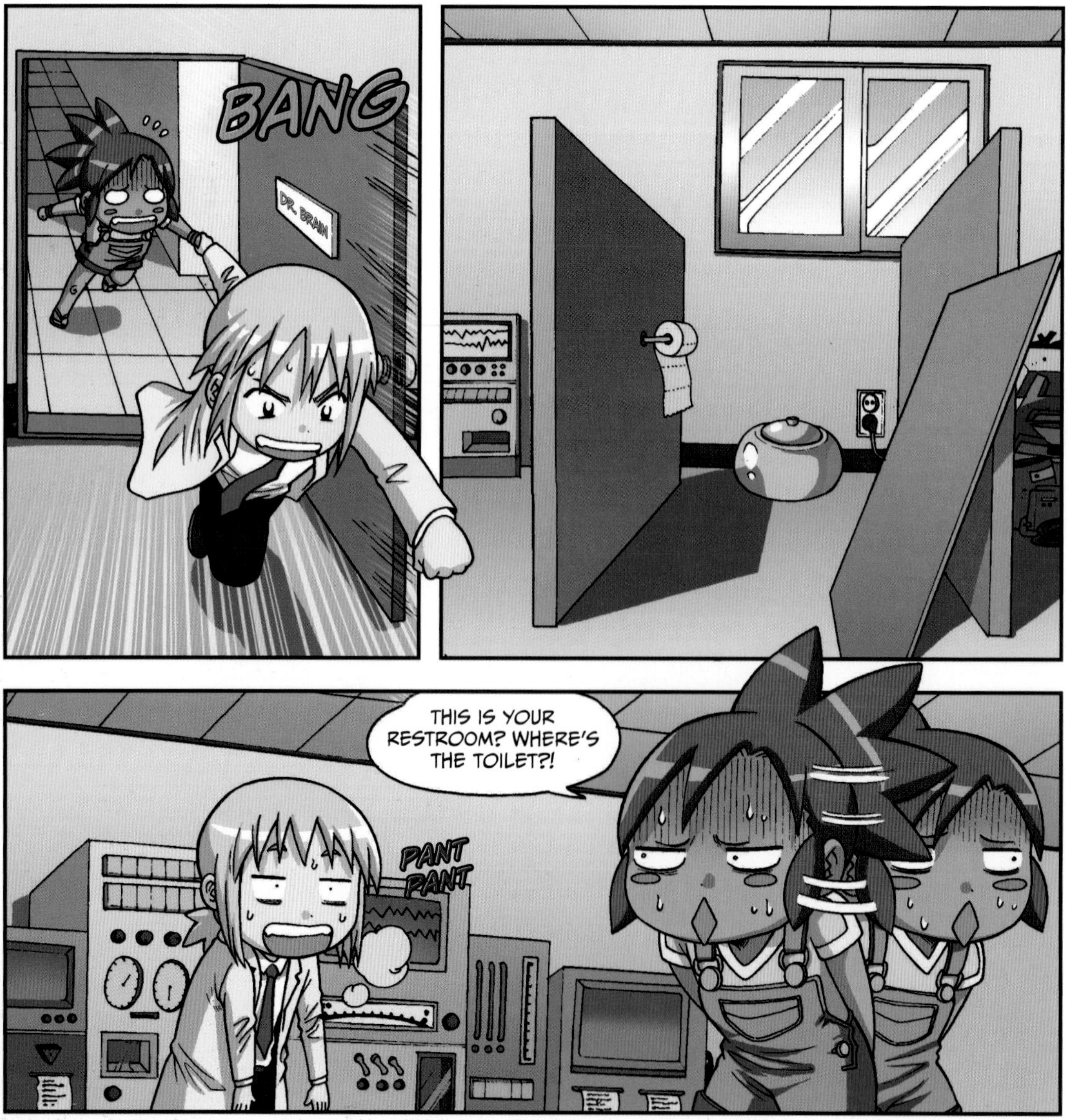
BANG
DR. BRAIN
THIS IS YOUR RESTROOM? WHERE'S THE TOILET?!
PANT PANT

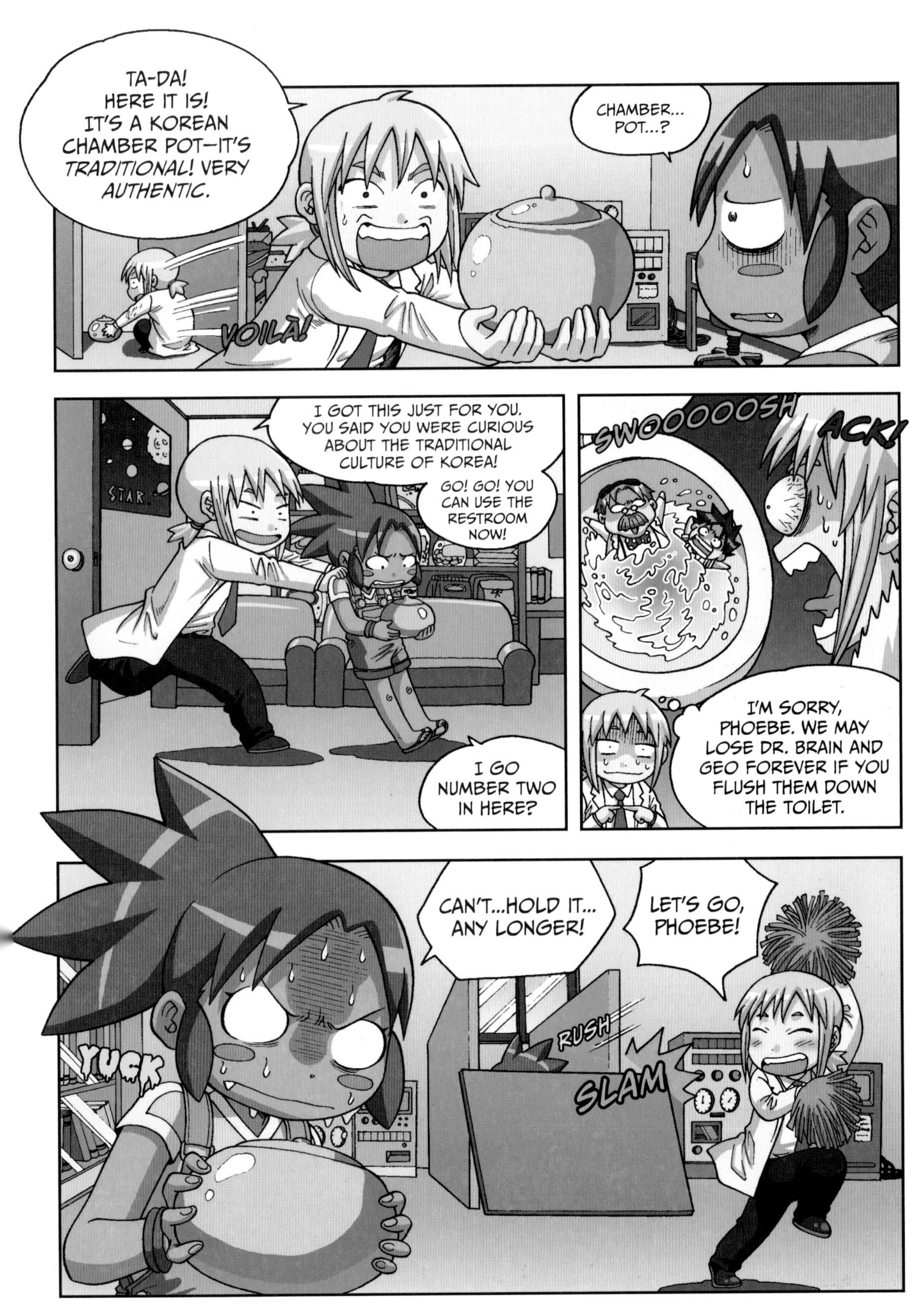
TA-DA! HERE IT IS! IT'S A KOREAN CHAMBER POT—IT'S *TRADITIONAL!* VERY *AUTHENTIC.*
VOILÀ!
CHAMBER... POT...?
I GOT THIS JUST FOR YOU. YOU SAID YOU WERE CURIOUS ABOUT THE TRADITIONAL CULTURE OF KOREA!
GO! GO! YOU CAN USE THE RESTROOM NOW!
STAR
I GO NUMBER TWO IN HERE?
SWOOOOOOSH
ACK!
I'M SORRY, PHOEBE. WE MAY LOSE DR. BRAIN AND GEO FOREVER IF YOU FLUSH THEM DOWN THE TOILET.
CAN'T...HOLD IT... ANY LONGER!
LET'S GO, PHOEBE!
YUCK
RUSH
SLAM

THE END...?

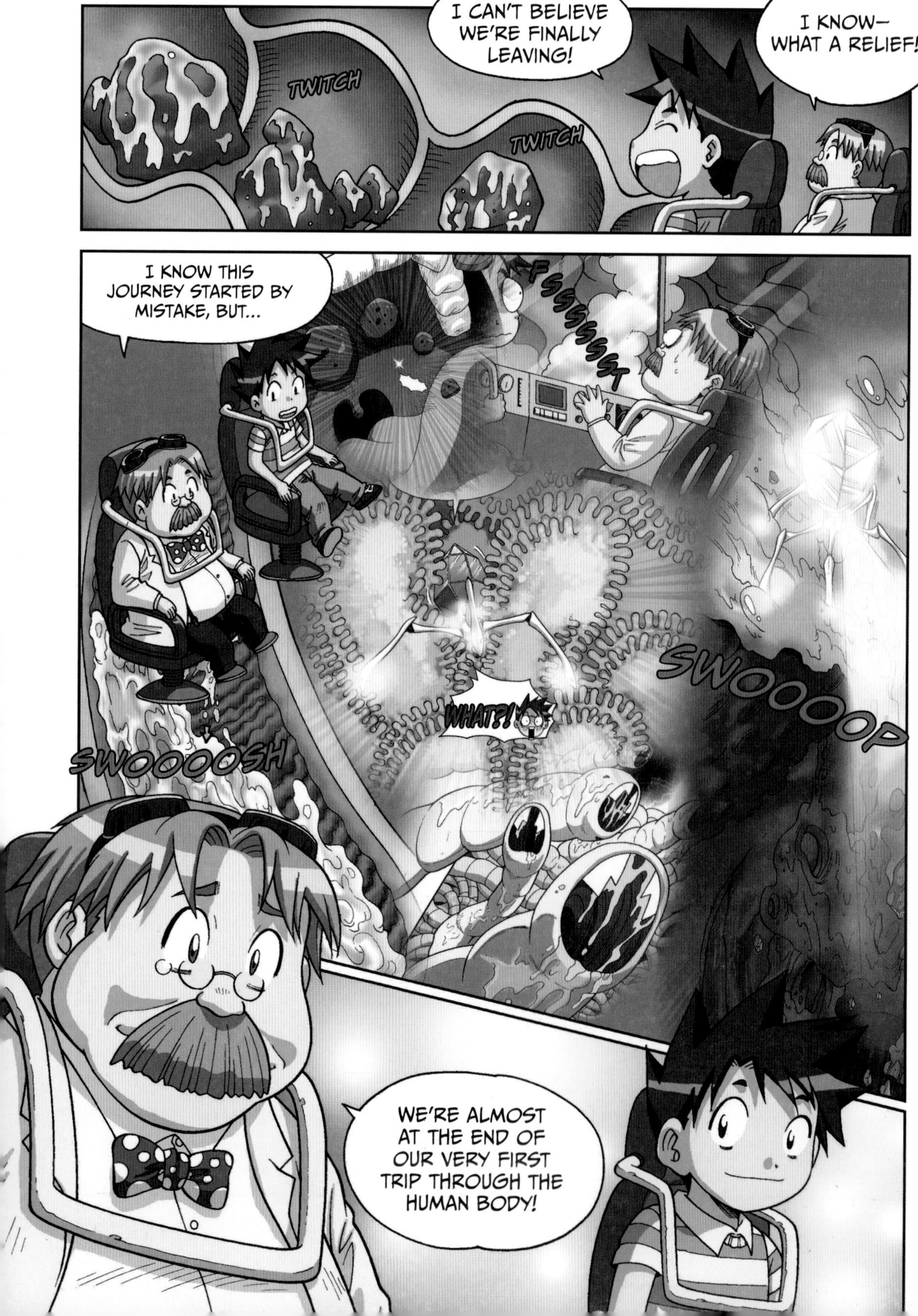
TWITCH
TWITCH
WOW! I CAN'T BELIEVE WE'RE FINALLY LEAVING!
I KNOW— WHAT A RELIEF!
I KNOW THIS JOURNEY STARTED BY MISTAKE, BUT...
FSSSSSSK
SWOOOOSH
WHAT?!
SWOOOOOP
WE'RE ALMOST AT THE END OF OUR VERY FIRST TRIP THROUGH THE HUMAN BODY!

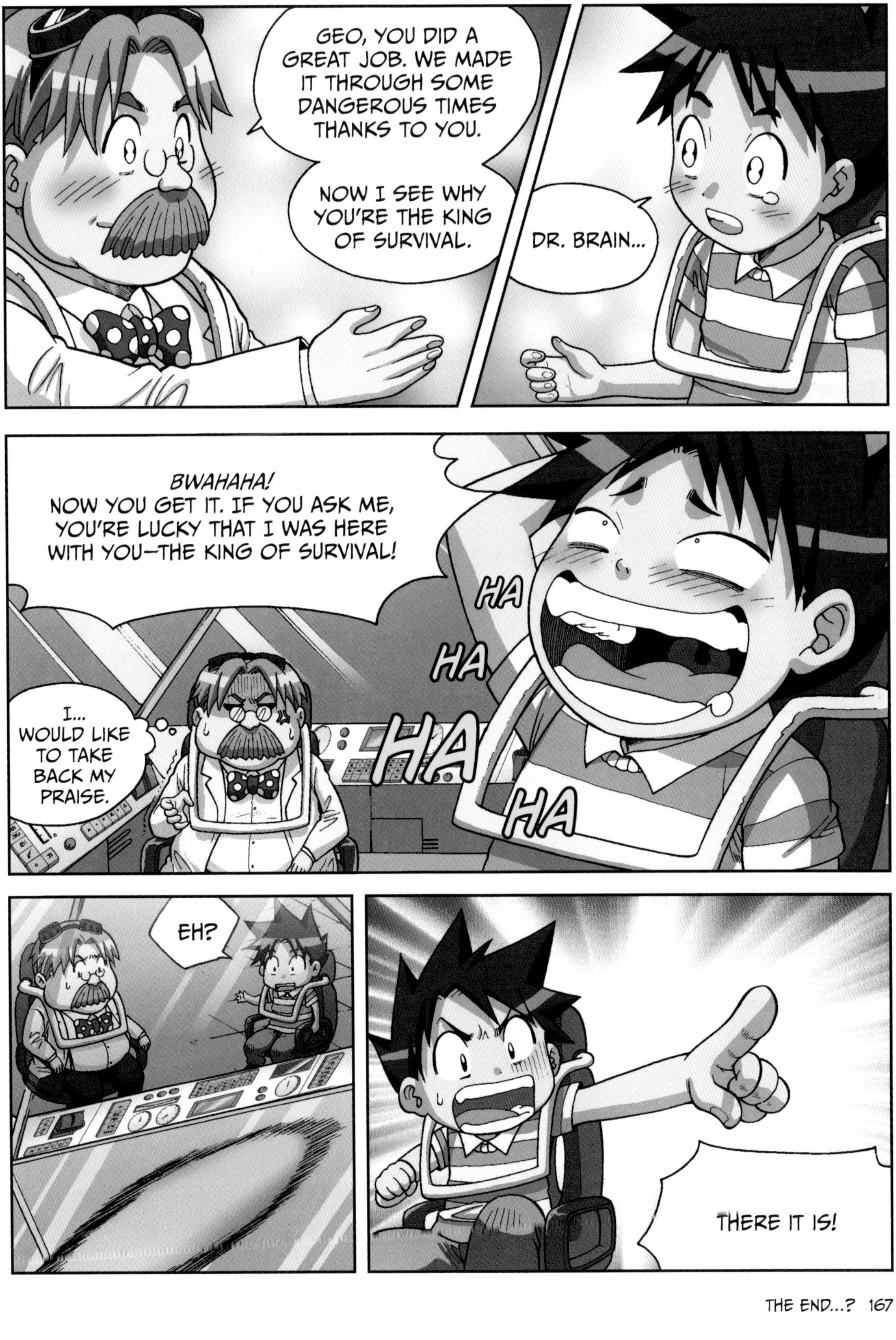
GEO, YOU DID A GREAT JOB. WE MADE IT THROUGH SOME DANGEROUS TIMES THANKS TO YOU.
NOW I SEE WHY YOU'RE THE KING OF SURVIVAL.
DR. BRAIN...
BWAHAHA! NOW YOU GET IT. IF YOU ASK ME, YOU'RE LUCKY THAT I WAS HERE WITH YOU—THE KING OF SURVIVAL!
HA
HA
HA
HA
I... WOULD LIKE TO TAKE BACK MY PRAISE.
EH?
THERE IT IS!

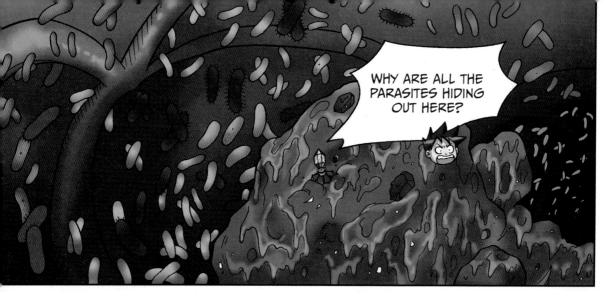

WHY ARE ALL THE PARASITES HIDING OUT HERE?

GEO, THOSE AREN'T PARASITES. THEY'RE COLON BACTERIA.

BACTERIA?

ISN'T THAT WHAT CAUSES DIARRHEA?! WE HAVE TO GET RID OF THEM—NOW!

OH, THAT'S RIGHT. WE'RE OUT OF ENERGY.

GRRRR

I CAN'T BELIEVE WE CAN'T DESTROY THEM BEFORE WE LEAVE!

NOOO

EVEN IF WE HAD THE ENERGY, WE SHOULDN'T DESTROY THE BACTERIA THAT LIVE HERE.

WHAT? WHY NOT?!

THESE BACTERIA AND OTHER MICROORGANISMS ARE SUPPOSED TO LIVE IN THE LARGE INTESTINE. THEY'RE KNOWN AS *GUT FLORA*. THERE ARE HUNDREDS OF TYPES—AND OVER 100 TRILLION IN TOTAL—LIVING INSIDE THE HUMAN BODY!

100,000,000,000,000!!

EACH PLAYS ITS OWN ROLE IN THE LARGE INTESTINE. SOME ARE IN CHARGE OF CLEANING. SOME ARE IN CHARGE OF MOVING FLUIDS AROUND. SOME ARE IN CHARGE OF BREAKING DOWN ANY UNDIGESTED FIBER. THEY ALL DO DIFFERENT JOBS, BUT THEIR GOAL IS THE SAME.

SWEEP SWEEP

SPECIAL DELIVERY!

KA-CHOP

FIBER

THEY KEEP THE INTESTINE CLEAN AND PROTECT IT FROM INTRUDERS!

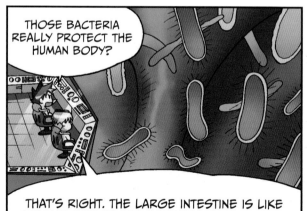

THOSE BACTERIA REALLY PROTECT THE HUMAN BODY?

THAT'S RIGHT. THE LARGE INTESTINE IS LIKE A HOME FOR THOSE BACTERIA, LIKE *E. COLI*. THEY WANT TO PROTECT THEIR HOME FROM HARMFUL BACTERIA. ALSO, THEY MAKE VITAMINS K AND B WHEN THEY BREAK DOWN DIETARY FIBERS. THESE NUTRIENTS AND WATER ARE ABSORBED BY THE LARGE INTESTINE AND GO INTO THE BLOOD.

BUT DON'T WE GET FOOD POISONING AND DIARRHEA FROM *E. COLI*?

Food Poisoning Outbreak

THE END...? 169

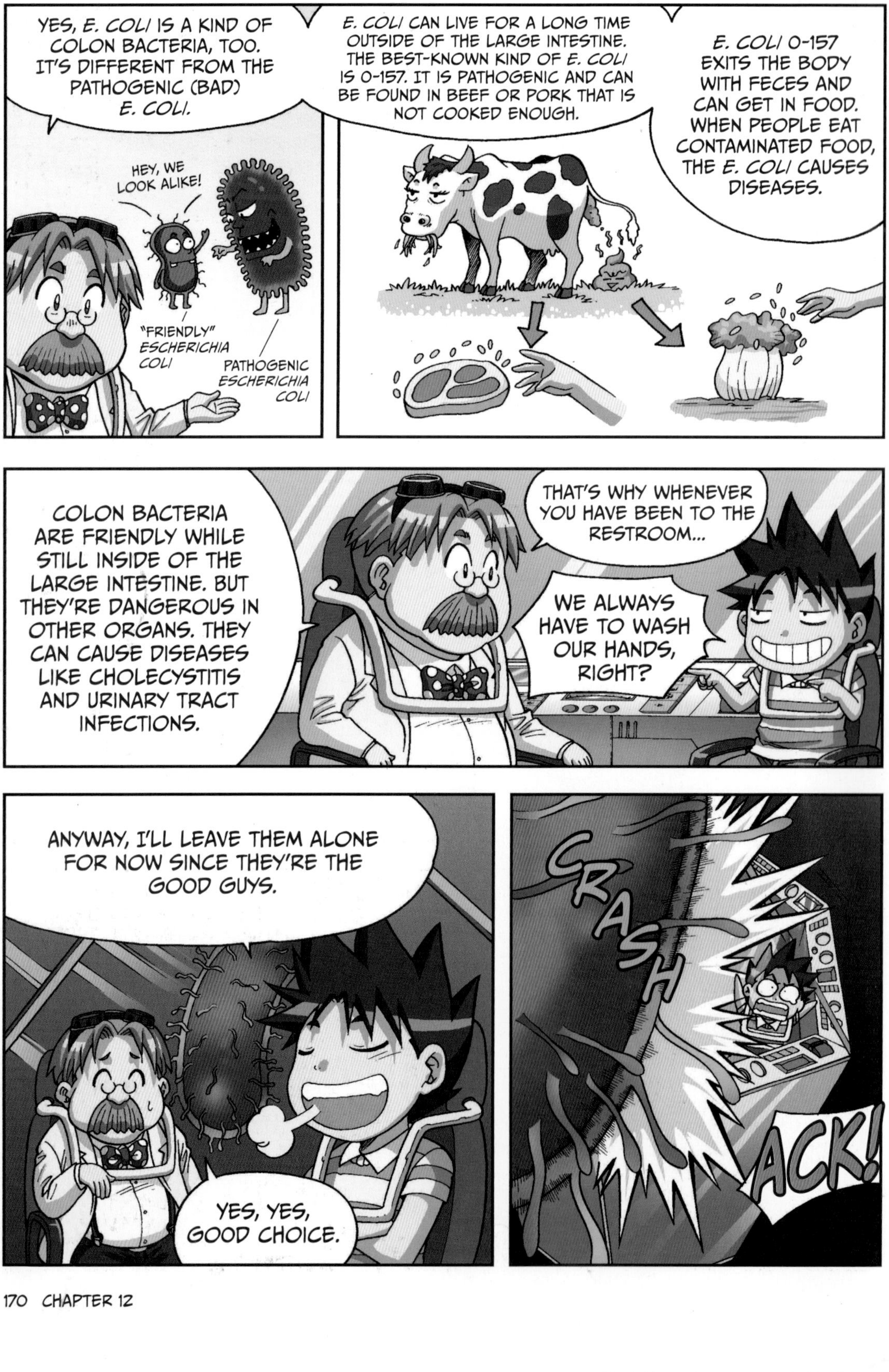
YES, E. COLI IS A KIND OF COLON BACTERIA, TOO. IT'S DIFFERENT FROM THE PATHOGENIC (BAD) E. COLI.
HEY, WE LOOK ALIKE!
"FRIENDLY" ESCHERICHIA COLI
PATHOGENIC ESCHERICHIA COLI
E. COLI CAN LIVE FOR A LONG TIME OUTSIDE OF THE LARGE INTESTINE. THE BEST-KNOWN KIND OF E. COLI IS O-157. IT IS PATHOGENIC AND CAN BE FOUND IN BEEF OR PORK THAT IS NOT COOKED ENOUGH.
E. COLI O-157 EXITS THE BODY WITH FECES AND CAN GET IN FOOD. WHEN PEOPLE EAT CONTAMINATED FOOD, THE E. COLI CAUSES DISEASES.
COLON BACTERIA ARE FRIENDLY WHILE STILL INSIDE OF THE LARGE INTESTINE. BUT THEY'RE DANGEROUS IN OTHER ORGANS. THEY CAN CAUSE DISEASES LIKE CHOLECYSTITIS AND URINARY TRACT INFECTIONS.
THAT'S WHY WHENEVER YOU HAVE BEEN TO THE RESTROOM...
WE ALWAYS HAVE TO WASH OUR HANDS, RIGHT?
ANYWAY, I'LL LEAVE THEM ALONE FOR NOW SINCE THEY'RE THE GOOD GUYS.
YES, YES, GOOD CHOICE.
CRASH
ACK!

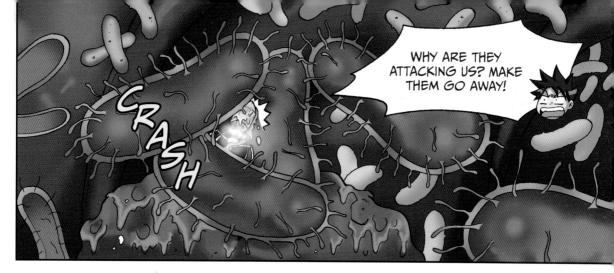

WHY ARE THEY ATTACKING US? MAKE THEM GO AWAY!

CRASH

WHY ARE THE COLON BACTERIA ATTACKING US ALL OF A SUDDEN?

THEY MUST THINK WE'RE INTRUDERS!

INTRUDERS?

REMEMBER WHEN I SAID THE COLON BACTERIA ARE IN CHARGE OF FIGHTING HARMFUL INTRUDERS TO PROTECT THE INTESTINE?

I MADE THE SS HIPPOCRATES TO LOOK LIKE A VIRUS.

IT'S FOOLING THE BACTERIA! I MUST HAVE DONE A GOOD JOB!

HA HA!

HOW IS THAT GOOD FOR US RIGHT NOW?!

DON'T WORRY! THE SS HIPPOCRATES IS MADE SO THAT BACTERIA CAN'T BREAK IT DOWN. WE WILL BE OUT OF HERE SOON. THE LARGE INTESTINE IS ALMOST DONE ABSORBING THE WATER.

SWOOOO

WHAT IS THAT NOISE?!

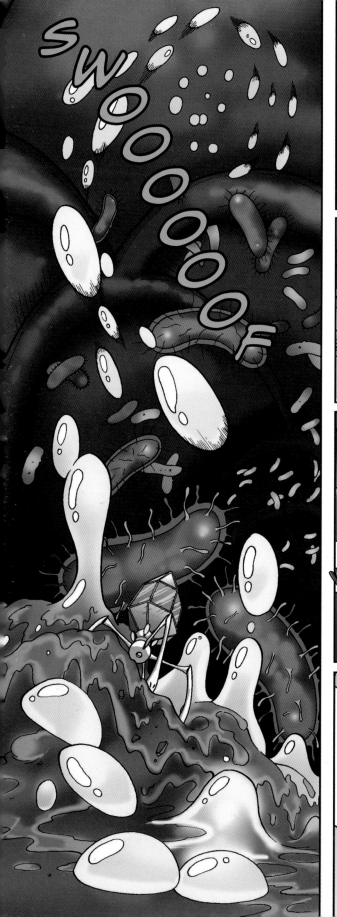

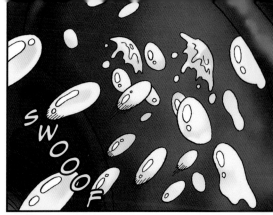

LOOK, IT'S THE LARGE INTESTINE ABSORBING THE WATER.

YAY! WE'LL BE OUT OF HERE IN NO TIME!

MWA HA HA HA!

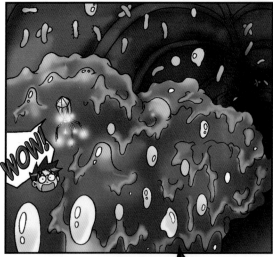

WOW!

THESE FOOD SCRAPS ARE STARTING TO REALLY LOOK LIKE POOP NOW THAT THE WATER IS GONE!

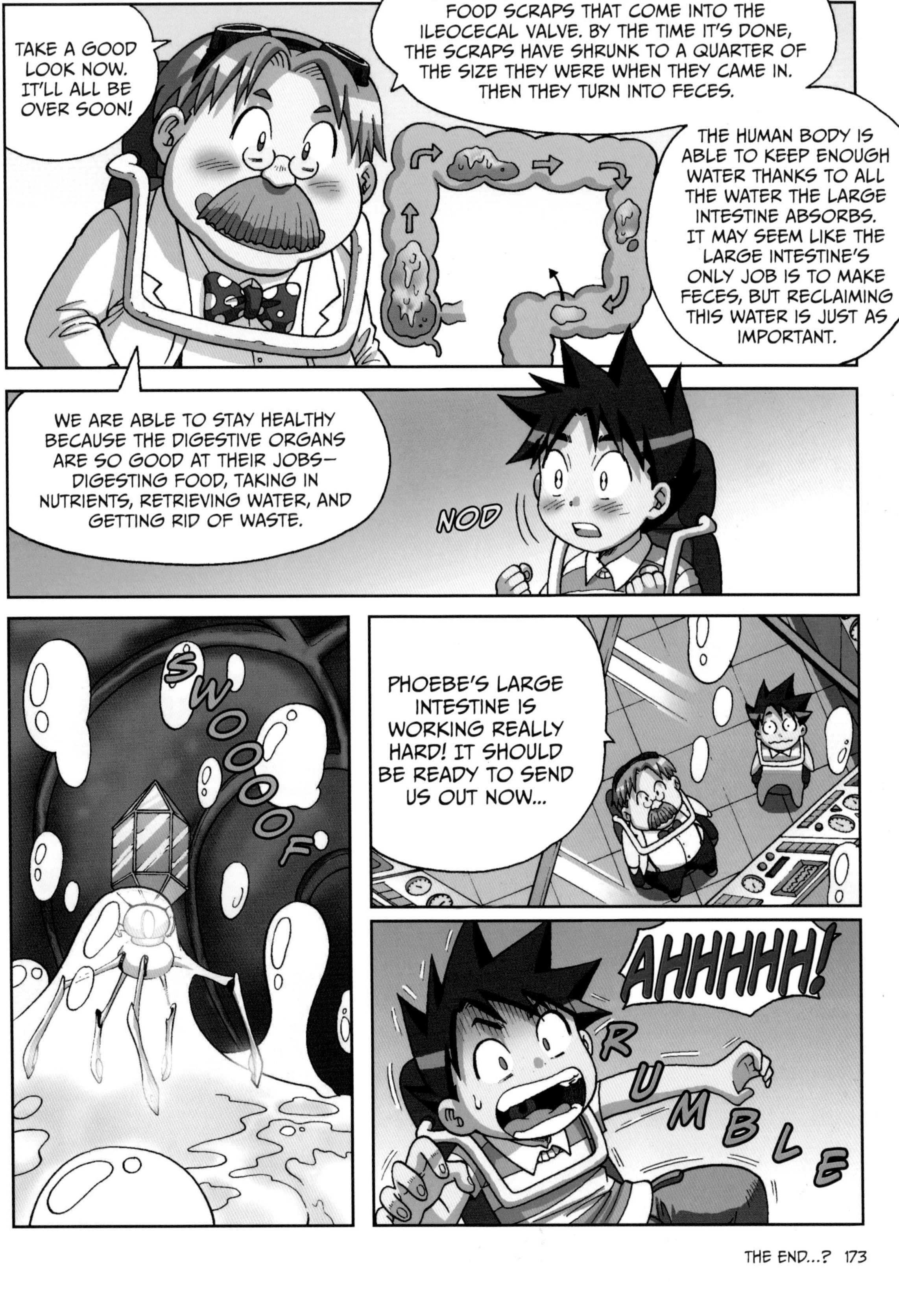
TAKE A GOOD LOOK NOW. IT'LL ALL BE OVER SOON!
THIS IS WHAT THE LARGE INTESTINE DOES. IT SUCKS OUT WATER FROM THE FOOD SCRAPS THAT COME INTO THE ILEOCECAL VALVE. BY THE TIME IT'S DONE, THE SCRAPS HAVE SHRUNK TO A QUARTER OF THE SIZE THEY WERE WHEN THEY CAME IN. THEN THEY TURN INTO FECES.
THE HUMAN BODY IS ABLE TO KEEP ENOUGH WATER THANKS TO ALL THE WATER THE LARGE INTESTINE ABSORBS. IT MAY SEEM LIKE THE LARGE INTESTINE'S ONLY JOB IS TO MAKE FECES, BUT RECLAIMING THIS WATER IS JUST AS IMPORTANT.
WE ARE ABLE TO STAY HEALTHY BECAUSE THE DIGESTIVE ORGANS ARE SO GOOD AT THEIR JOBS—DIGESTING FOOD, TAKING IN NUTRIENTS, RETRIEVING WATER, AND GETTING RID OF WASTE.
NOD
SWOOOOF
PHOEBE'S LARGE INTESTINE IS WORKING REALLY HARD! IT SHOULD BE READY TO SEND US OUT NOW...
AHHHHH!
RUMBLE

THE END...?

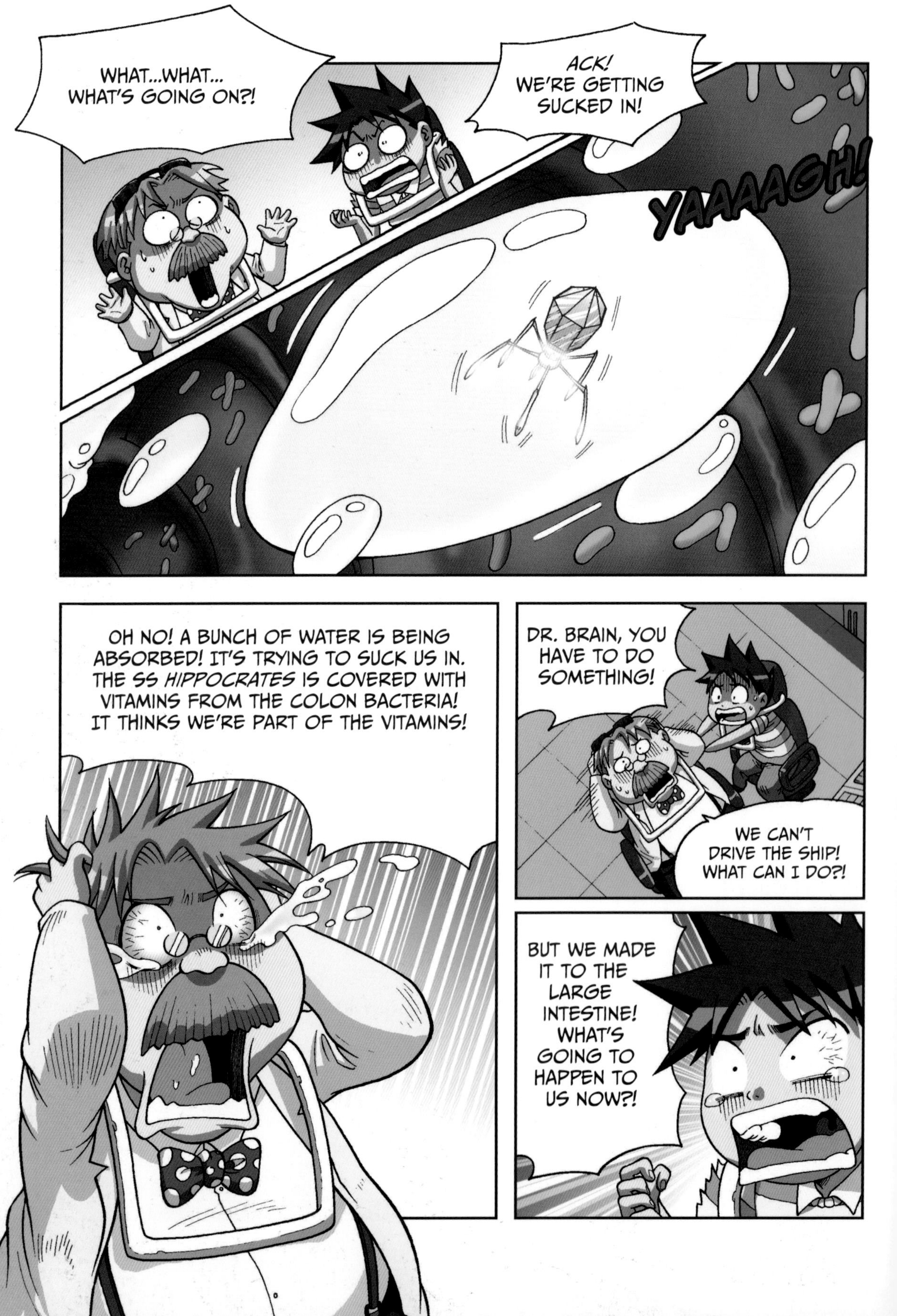

WHAT...WHAT... WHAT'S GOING ON?!
ACK! WE'RE GETTING SUCKED IN!
YAAAAGH!
OH NO! A BUNCH OF WATER IS BEING ABSORBED! IT'S TRYING TO SUCK US IN. THE SS *HIPPOCRATES* IS COVERED WITH VITAMINS FROM THE COLON BACTERIA! IT THINKS WE'RE PART OF THE VITAMINS!
DR. BRAIN, YOU HAVE TO DO SOMETHING!
WE CAN'T DRIVE THE SHIP! WHAT CAN I DO?!
BUT WE MADE IT TO THE LARGE INTESTINE! WHAT'S GOING TO HAPPEN TO US NOW?!

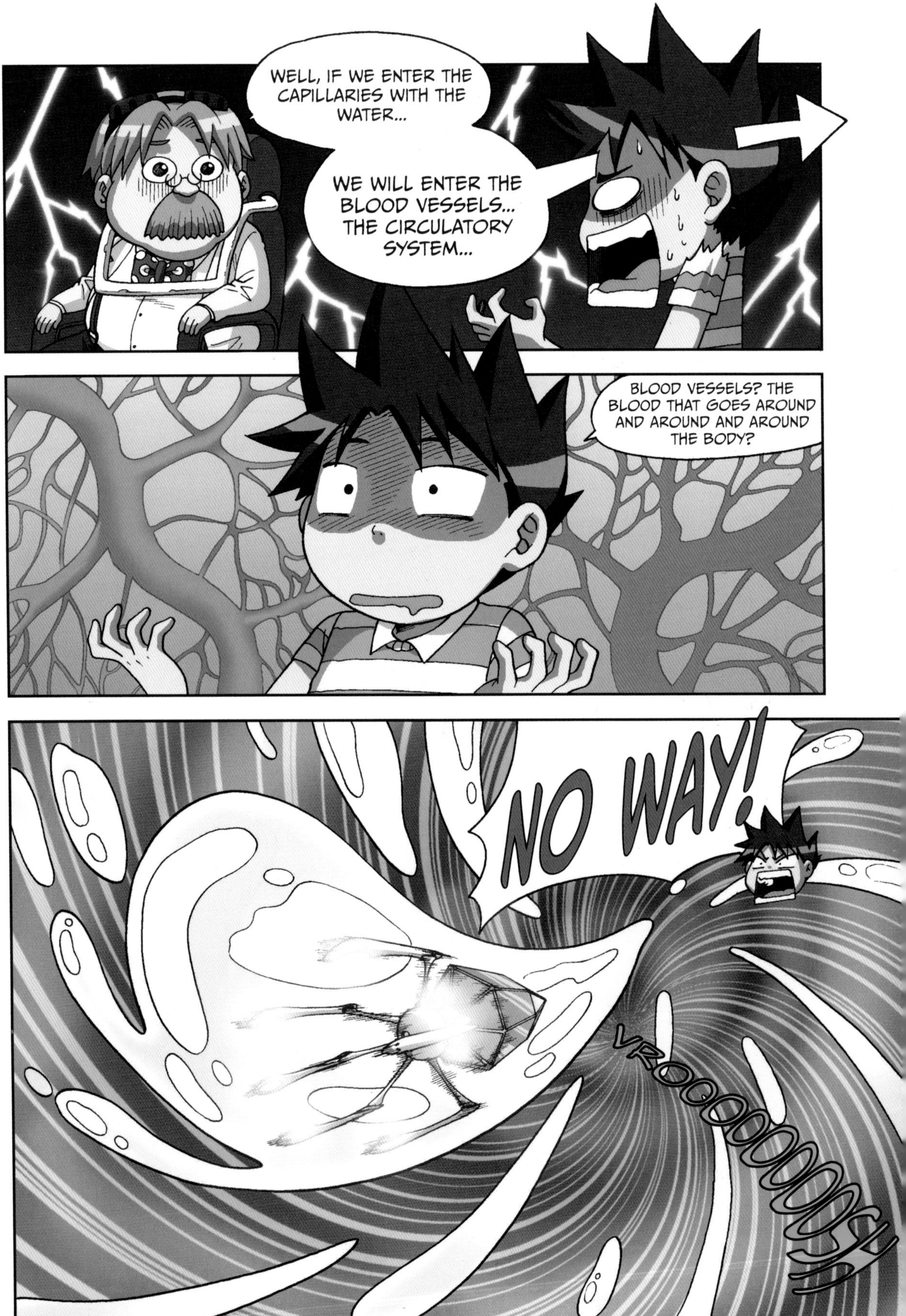
WELL, IF WE ENTER THE CAPILLARIES WITH THE WATER...
WE WILL ENTER THE BLOOD VESSELS... THE CIRCULATORY SYSTEM...
BLOOD VESSELS? THE BLOOD THAT GOES AROUND AND AROUND AND AROUND THE BODY?
NO WAY!
VROOOOOOOOSH

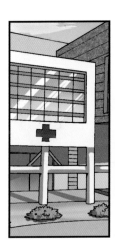

KAY, WHAT ARE YOU LOOKING FOR? YOU'RE BEING KIND OF GROSS.

WHY ISN'T THE SHIP GROWING? IT SHOULD HAVE ENOUGH SUNLIGHT!

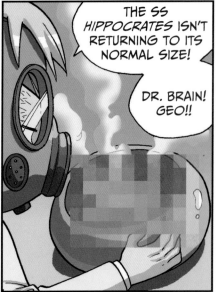

THE SS HIPPOCRATES ISN'T RETURNING TO ITS NORMAL SIZE!

DR. BRAIN! GEO!!

PHOEBE! ARE YOU SURE YOU POOPED EVERYTHING OUT?!

YES! YES! I POOPED EVERYTHING OUT!

I'M SERIOUS!

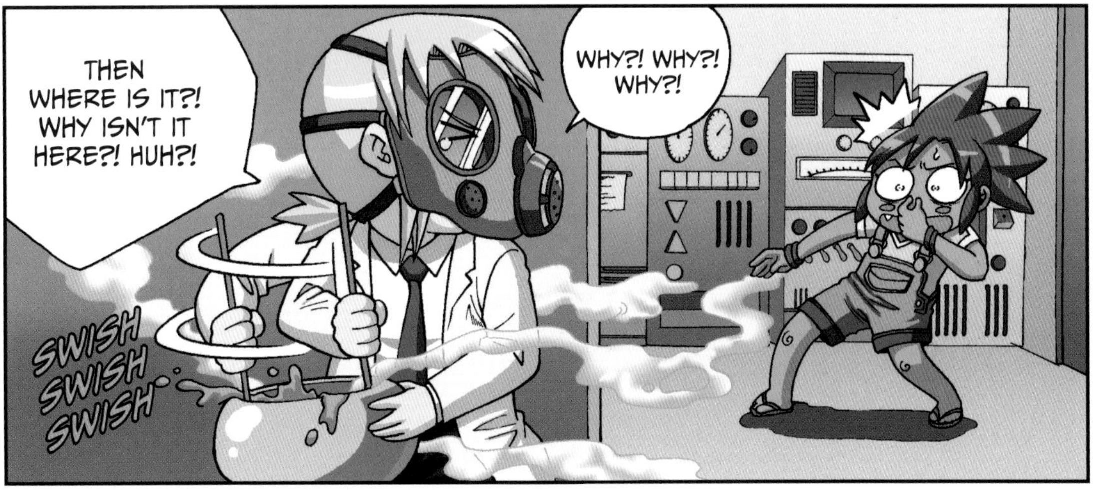
THEN WHERE IS IT?! WHY ISN'T IT HERE?! HUH?!
WHY?! WHY?! WHY?!
SWISH SWISH SWISH

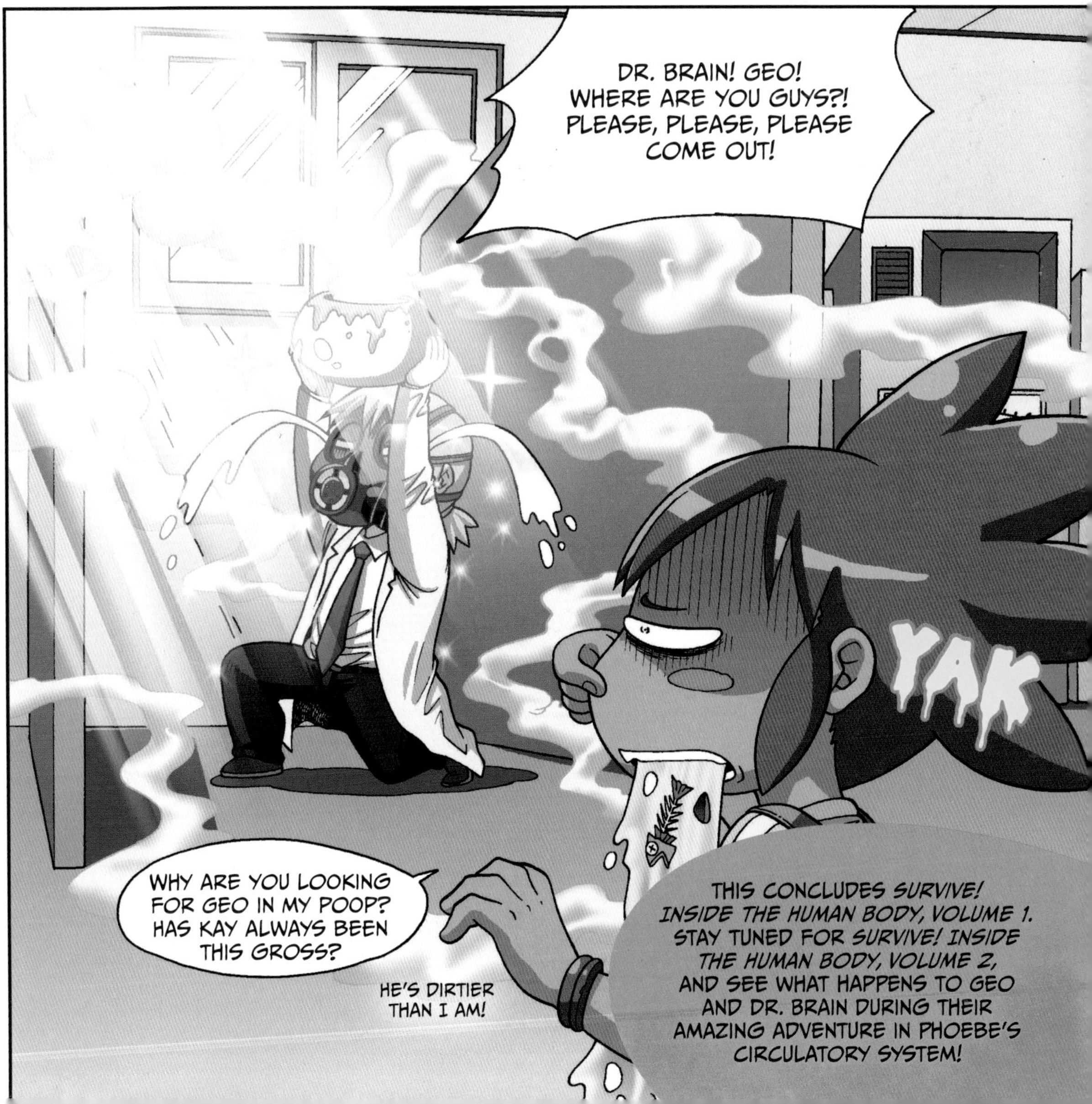
DR. BRAIN! GEO! WHERE ARE YOU GUYS?! PLEASE, PLEASE, PLEASE COME OUT!
YAK
WHY ARE YOU LOOKING FOR GEO IN MY POOP? HAS KAY ALWAYS BEEN THIS GROSS?
HE'S DIRTIER THAN I AM!
THIS CONCLUDES *SURVIVE! INSIDE THE HUMAN BODY, VOLUME 1.* STAY TUNED FOR *SURVIVE! INSIDE THE HUMAN BODY, VOLUME 2,* AND SEE WHAT HAPPENS TO GEO AND DR. BRAIN DURING THEIR AMAZING ADVENTURE IN PHOEBE'S CIRCULATORY SYSTEM!

INDEX

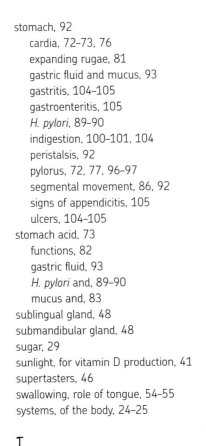

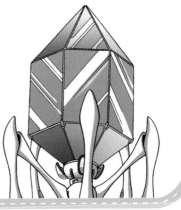

THE SURVIVE! SERIES

ABOUT THESE BOOKS

The *Survive!* series is a translation of a best-selling science comic book series from Mirae N Co., Ltd. of South Korea, with over 20 million copies sold worldwide. These books show kids real science in a fun and approachable way.

The editors at No Starch Press have checked and rewritten the translated text, and two medical doctors have reviewed the content for clarity and accuracy. The result is the book you hold in your hands.

We hope you enjoy *Survive!* Stay tuned for more of Geo's amazing adventures.

ABOUT THE AUTHOR

Gomdori co. is a group of authors, artists, and creative professionals who create fun and educational stories for kids. *Survive! Inside the Human Body* was written by Seok-young Song, an author who has worked on educational comics with Gomdori co. for over 12 years.

ABOUT THE ILLUSTRATOR

Hyun-dong Han studied manhwa (Korean comics) at Kongju National University. His debut series *New Tales of the Nine Tailed Fox* ran for six years, and he's well known for his work on *Ghost Tunes* and the *Survive!* series.

DON'T MISS THE OTHER BOOKS IN THE SERIES!

VOL. 2: THE CIRCULATORY SYSTEM
SURVIVE!
INSIDE THE HUMAN BODY
GOMDORI CO. & HYUN-DONG HAN

VOL. 2: THE CIRCULATORY SYSTEM

A Heart-Pounding Adventure!

After they're sucked inside Phoebe's capillaries, Geo and Dr. Brain are in for a wild ride. Starting from the liver, they make their way around the super-strong heart, crinkly lungs, and other circulatory organs, learning all along the way.

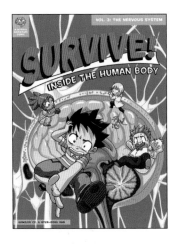

VOL. 3: THE NERVOUS SYSTEM
SURVIVE!
INSIDE THE HUMAN BODY
GOMDORI CO. & HYUN-DONG HAN

VOL. 3: THE NERVOUS SYSTEM

Build Your Brain Power!

When Geo gets stuck in Phoebe's nervous system, things get really weird. You'll learn all about neurons, our magnificent and mysterious brains, and so much more. You'll also learn how medical techniques like EEGs, CT scans, and PET scans really work!

MORE SMART BOOKS FOR CURIOUS KIDS!

PYTHON FOR KIDS

A PLAYFUL INTRODUCTION TO PROGRAMMING

by JASON R. BRIGGS
DEC 2012, 344 PP., $34.95
ISBN 978-1-59327-407-8
full color

SUPER SCRATCH PROGRAMMING ADVENTURE!

LEARN TO PROGRAM BY MAKING COOL GAMES

by THE LEAD PROJECT
AUG 2012, 160 PP., $24.95
ISBN 978-1-59327-409-2
full color

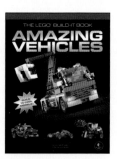

THE LEGO® BUILD-IT BOOK, VOL. 1: AMAZING VEHICLES

by NATHANAËL KUIPERS *and* MATTIA ZAMBONI
JULY 2013, 136 PP., $19.95
ISBN 978-1-59327-503-7
full color

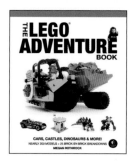

THE LEGO® ADVENTURE BOOK, VOL. 1: CARS, CASTLES, DINOSAURS & MORE!

by MEGAN H. ROTHROCK
NOV 2012, 200 PP., $24.95
ISBN 978-1-59327-442-9
hardcover, full color

THE MANGA GUIDE™ TO PHYSICS

by HIDEO NITTA, KEITA TAKATSU, *and* TREND-PRO CO., LTD.
MAY 2009, 248 PP., $19.95
ISBN 978-1-59327-196-1

WONDERFUL LIFE WITH THE ELEMENTS

THE PERIODIC TABLE PERSONIFIED

by BUNPEI YORIFUJI
SEPT 2012, 208 PP., $17.95
ISBN 978-1-59327-423-8
hardcover with pull-out poster

phone: 800.420.7240 or 415.863.9900 | fax: 415.863.9950
sales@nostarch.com | www.nostarch.com